JOURNAL FOR THE STUDY OF THE NEW TESTAMENT
SUPPLEMENT SERIES

14

Executive Editor, Supplement Series
David Hill

Publishing Editor
David E Orton

JSOT Press
Sheffield

THE
PASSION
ACCORDING TO
LUKE

The Special Material of Luke 22

Marion L. Soards

Journal for the Study of the New Testament
Supplement Series 14

For
Martha, David, and Grace

Copyright © 1987 Sheffield Academic Press

Published by JSOT Press
JSOT Press is an imprint of
Sheffield Academic Press
The University of Sheffield
343 Fulwood Road
Sheffield S10 3BP
England

Typeset by Sheffield Academic Press
and
printed in Great Britain
by Billing & Sons Ltd
Worcester

British Library Cataloguing in Publication Data

Soards, Marion L.
    The Passion according to Luke : the special
    material of Luke 22.—(Journal for the
    study of the New Testament. Supplement
    series, ISSN 0143-5108; 14).
    1. Bible, N.T. Luke—Commentaries
    I. Title   II. Series
    226'.406   BS2595.3

    ISBN 1-85075-036-X
    ISBN 1-85075-037-8 Pbk

CONTENTS

PREFACE

This monograph is a revision of my doctoral dissertation presented at Union Theological Seminary, New York in 1984. The work focuses on Luke 22, a portion of Luke's Passion Narrative that, in comparison with Luke 23, has gone without attention in recent scholarship. This study introduces the reader to the questions concerning the text that have been raised by previous scholarship, delineates a fresh method for assessing the text, and attempts to meet three ends: (1) it defines what material in Luke 22 is *special Lukan material*, i.e. not found in Mark; (2) it assesses the special Lukan material with regard to its probable origin; and (3) it comments on Luke's apparent purpose(s) in including this material in his version of the portion of the account of Jesus' Passion narrated in Luke 22. The work moves away from earlier studies that focused primarily on word-statistical analysis and deals with the lines of thought that run through Luke 22, relating this chapter to the Gospel according to Luke as a whole.

Chapter 1 introduces some problems in the study of Luke's Passion Narrative, namely, the differences between the Passion accounts in Luke and Mark. This chapter describes the need for a careful definition and analysis of the special Lukan Passion Narrative material. It outlines a method employed in Chapters 2 and 4 for defining what portions of Luke 22 are special Lukan material; it describes the steps taken in Chapters 3 and 5 toward determining the origin of the special material and suggests that after defining the material and its origin one may gain new or clearer insights into Luke's purpose in this section of his Gospel.

Chapters 2 and 4 practice a fivefold method to isolate the special Lukan Passion Narrative material in Luke 22.1-38 (Chapter 2) and 22.39-71 (Chapter 4). These chapters identify the portions of Luke 22 that (1) are entirely without parallel in Mark, (2) represent an agreement of Luke with Matthew or John against Mark, (3) form a story sequence different from that of Mark, (4) have a low level of verbal correspondence between Luke and Mark, and (5) contain so-called telltale Lukan language. Analysis of these five types of material defines the scope of the special Lukan Passion Narrative material.

Chapters 3 and 5 analyze the special Lukan Passion Narrative material in Luke 22.1-38 (Chapter 3) and Luke 22.39-71 (Chapter 5). They seek to deem the most probable origin of the non-Markan portions of Luke 22. In light of the scope and origin of the special Lukan material in Luke 22 these chapters comment on Luke's purpose in this part of his version of the Passion Narrative.

Chapter 6 summarizes the work done in Chapters 2 through 5 and states the conclusion of the study, namely that Luke worked in a variety of ways using materials of diverse origins to produce ch. 22. *Negatively*, this study demonstrates that Luke did not employ a single, coherent source in addition to Mark for composing ch. 22. *Positively*, it demonstrates that Luke 22 is theologically consistent with the remainder of the Gospel, and indeed it argues that in writing Luke has carefully developed his own christological, eschato-logical, and ecclesiological tendencies. In terms of christology, Jesus is shown to be in charge of the events of the Passion and is portrayed as the one in whom the plan of God is realized. The eschatological significance of the Last Supper and the ensuing episodes of ch. 22 are heightened so that Luke's readers understand that Jesus' Passion inaugurated the penultimate eschatological era of the Last Days. With regard to ecclesiology, Luke recounts Jesus' interaction with his disciples in such a manner that the readers receive instruction concerning their own role(s) in the working out of God's plan.

The Passion Narratives are vital areas for ongoing scholarly research. I regret that the works by J.A. Fitzmyer (*The Gospel according to Luke X-XXIV* [AB 28A; Garden City, NY: Doubleday, 1985]), R.J. Karris (*Luke: Artist and Theologian—Luke's Passion Account as Literature* [Theological Inquiries; New York: Paulist, 1985]), J. Neyrey (*The Passion according to Luke: A Redactional Study of Luke's Soteriology* [Theological Inquiries; New York: Paulist, 1985]) and F.J. Matera, (*Passion Narratives and Gospel Theologies: Interpreting the Synoptics through their Passion Stories* [Theological Inquiries; New York: Paulist, 1986]) appeared after completion of the present study. I am encouraged, however, to see how often Fitzmyer and I have independently drawn similar conclusions about the origin of Luke's material.

Many people helped with this project. I wish to acknowledge the guidance and support given me by Professors Raymond E. Brown, J. Louis Martyn, and Thomas L. Robinson. Dr Joel Marcus, now of Princeton Theological Seminary, was a selfless conversation partner throughout the course of this investigation. Finally I want to thank both my wife, Martha, for her devotion, patience, and love and my son, David, who in the first two years of his life provided immeasurable inspiration and joy for this work. I dedicate this book to Martha, David, and my new-born daughter Grace with pleasure.

ABBREVIATIONS

The abbreviations used in the notes and bibliography conform to the standard abbreviations of the *Journal of Biblical Literature* and the *Catholic Biblical Quarterly*.

THE PASSION ACCORDING TO LUKE

The Special Material of Luke 22

Chapter 1

INTRODUCTION

The Passion Narrative of the Gospel according to Luke (chs. 22–23) presents a series of problems. Scholars focus on two characteristics of the Lukan Passion Narrative in articulating their interpretative positions: (1) pericope order and (2) content.

Pericope Order
Luke does not generally disturb the order of what is widely taken to be the major source for his work, the Gospel according to Mark.[1] In the Passion Narrative, however, Luke's ordering of pericopes does not so carefully match Markan order as it does throughout the rest of his Gospel.[2] For example, Mark 14.53-72 gives the order (a) interrogation of Jesus, (b) mistreatment of Jesus, and (c) denial by Peter; whereas Luke 22.54-71 is ordered (a) denial by Peter, (b) mistreatment of Jesus, and (c) interrogation of Jesus.

Content
The differences in content of Luke's Passion Narrative and Mark's Passion Narrative may be described in three ways. First, there are noticeable differences in *detail* between Luke and Mark in certain of their common traditions.[3] *Luke and Mark seem to relate the same incident but in remarkably different ways.* For example, in Mark (14.32) Jesus goes to *Gethsemane* and in Luke (22.39) he goes to *the Mount of Olives*.[4] While in 'the garden' Mark has Jesus go away from and return to his disciples three times; Luke's account of the story describes Jesus making only one departure and return.[5]

Second, many elements of the Markan Passion Narrative are absent from Luke's Passion Narrative. These include both whole scenes and individual lines. For example, Luke does not include in his account of Jesus' Passion the following details found in Mark's Passion Narrative:[6]

the story of the anointing of Jesus at Bethany (14.3-9);

Jesus' quotation of Zech 13.7 and his prophecies that accompany the scripture (14.27-28);

the claim by Peter and the other disciples that they will not abandon Jesus (14.31);

Jesus' taking Peter, James, and John with him in Gethsemane when he was 'greatly distressed and troubled' (14.33-34);

Jesus' going away from and returning to Peter, James, and John and his statements to them (14.38b-42);

the notice that 'the betrayer' had given a sign to the crowd that came from the Jewish authorities (14.44);

the statement that the crowd laid hands on Jesus prior to the disciple striking with the sword (14.46);

Jesus' call for the scriptures to be fulfilled and the subsequent flight of the disciples and the young man who slipped out of his *sindon* (14.49b-52);

the fruitless appearance at the 'hearing' conducted by the council of the false witnesses who testified that Jesus claimed he would destroy the temple (14.55-59);

the call by the high priest for an answer from Jesus to the false witnesses and the statement that Jesus was silent (14.60-61a);

the question of the high priest, 'Why do we still need witnesses?' (14.63a);

the statement by the high priest that Jesus had committed blasphemy, the call for a decision from the council, and the unanimous verdict that Jesus was deserving of death (14.64);

Peter's invoking a curse on himself and swearing (14.71a);

the accusations against Jesus by the chief priests before Pilate, Pilate's call for Jesus to answer the charges, and the statement that Jesus was silent before Pilate (15.3-6);

the coming of the crowd to Pilate and the call for him to release a prisoner, Pilate's offer of 'the King of the Jews' for release because he perceived the leaders' envy of Jesus, and the chief priests' stirring up the crowd to call for Barabbas (15.8-11);

the mocking of Jesus by Roman soldiers (15.16-20a);

the offer of wine mingled with myrrh and Jesus' refusal of it (15.23);

the notice that it was the third hour when Jesus was crucified (15.25);

the deriding by passers-by of Jesus with the repetition of the temple charge and the challenge to come down from the cross (15.29-30);

the unqualified statement that 'those who were crucified with him also reviled him' (15.32b);

the notice of the ninth hour, the Psalm cry by Jesus, and the crowd's subsequent misunderstanding in relation to Elijah (15.34-35, 36b);

the names of the women at the crucifixion (15.40b);

the notice of Pilate's wonder at Jesus' quick death, his inquiry, and the statement that he granted the body to Joseph (15.44-45);

the names of the women who saw where Jesus was buried (15.47a).

Third, in addition to the material found in the Markan Passion Narrative there is what will be referred to as *special Lukan material*. Included are individual lines (e.g. 22.3a, 19e-f, 15-16) and entire scenes (e.g. 22.35-38; 23.6-12, 13-16(?), 27-31, 39b-43).

Scholars differ over what is *special Lukan material*: J.C. Hawkins[7] identifies 22.15, 27-32, 35-38, 51, 53b; 23.7-12, 17-31, 39-43, 46. A.M. Perry[8] distinguishes three categories of such material. First, material in Luke entirely without parallels in the Markan Passion Narrative: 22.15-16, 27ab, 28-32, 35-38, (43-44), 48-49, 51, 53c, 61a, 67b-68; 23.4-16, 22bc, 27-31, (34a), 35a, 39-43, 46b, 48-49a, 51a, 53c, 56b. Second, material in Luke with remote parallel (i.e. less than fifty percent of the same language in discourse, or less than forty percent in narrative) in Mark: 22.3-4, 8, 14, 17, 21, 23, 24-26, 27c, 33, 39-41, 45, 47b, 52a, 55-56, 58-60a, 62, 63-65, 70; 23.1-2, 18-19, 23-25, 32, 33b, 35b-37, 50, 54-56a. Third, material closely paralleled in Mark but with close connection to non-Markan material: 22.18-19a, 47a, 50, 66a; 23.20-21, 33a, (38), 46ac, (47), (51b- 53b). If one eliminates the verses that V. Taylor[9] considers to be insertions of Markan material, special Lukan material remains, namely 22.14-21, 23-33, 35-46a, 47-50a, 51-52a, 53b-54a, 62-71; 23.1-2, 4-24, 27-34a, 35-37, 39-43, 46-48, 55-56. J. Ernst also suggests that Luke worked Mark into a special Lukan source.[10] He lists 22.15-17, 24-30, 31-33, 35-38, 43-44; 23.6-12, 13-16, 27-31, 39b-43 as Lukan material that goes beyond Mark. G. Schneider[11] lists 22.15-18, 24-30, 31-32, 35-38, 43-

44; 23.6-12, 13-16, 27-31, 39b-43. J.A. Fitzmyer[12] lists 22.15-18, 19c-20, 27-33, 35-38, 63-71(?); 23.6-16, 27-32, 35a, 36-37, 39b-43, 46, 47b-49, 56. E. Schweizer[13] lists 22.15-17, 24-38, 39-53, (54-65), 66-71; 23.2, 4-16, 22f., 27-32, 33b, 34a, 35-37, 39-43, 46b, (47), 48, 55f.

Three observations follow from comparison of these lists. First, little of Luke 22–23 is not thought by someone to be special Lukan material. Second, a need exists for determining what portions of Luke 22-23 do go beyond Mark. Third, the origin of this material is highly debated. Some scholars understand this *special Lukan material* to be *free Lukan composition*.[14] Others see Luke incorporating *disparate traditions*, usually from oral tradition into the framework of the Markan Passion Narrative.[15] Still other scholars judge that Luke had available to him an integrated special source that was a *more extensive version or form of the Passion story*. It is even argued that this source formed the basis of the Lukan Passion Narrative and that Luke redacted the Markan material into this other narrative.[16]

Looking back at the three differences between Luke and Mark discussed above, and assuming that Luke used Mark as a source, one must ask how such differences came about. In terms of omissions, did Luke omit because he did not find material in Mark useful or satisfactory? And if so, was he doing that solely because of his own preferences or was he giving priority to another non-Markan source or tradition that did not have that material? In terms of additions, did Luke create the added material himself out of his own reflections? Did he copy it out of another non-Markan written source? Did he draw on oral tradition(s) and reshape them into his own compositions?

Proposal

Further study of the Lukan Passion Narrative should focus on the phenomena described above, especially the last, namely, the material that Luke offers beyond the tradition(s) found in the Markan Passion Narrative. Two facts suggest the need for this study. (1) There is no generally accepted definition of what parts of the Lukan Passion Narrative are material beyond that found in Mark. (2) No consensus exists with regard to the origin of this special Lukan material,[17] however it is defined. By working to meet the needs for a definition of *what* material in the Lukan Passion Narrative goes beyond Mark and for a clear understanding of the *origin* of that material, it may even be possible to provide insight into the *purpose* of Luke's Passion Narrative.[18]

The usual approach to the text of Luke's Passion Narrative is to ask, 'Could Luke have derived this verse from Mark?' This approach is taken by most, if not all, of the scholars mentioned above. For example, Taylor states that his goal is to 'try to distinguish the Markan and non-Markan elements in the Lukan story of the Passion and resurrection'.[19] Taylor seeks to 'inquire how far Luke has made use of Mark, and whether he has employed it as his main source'.[20] He employs the *numerical* or *statistical* method in comparing parallel Markan and Lukan passages in order to determine the degree of verbal correspondence.

By comparing sections of Luke and Mark, Taylor works out the percentages of common words between the two. Typically a *very* high level of verbal correspondence leads Taylor to conclude that Luke is wholly dependent on Mark. For instance a 62.5 percentage of common words leads him to conclude that Luke 22.1-2 is wholly dependent upon Mark 14.1-2.[21]

When common words are lower than 50% Taylor employs a *literary* or *stylistic* method, concerned with the relationships between Mark and Luke in respect to their grammar, vocabulary, and style. At times in such cases he concludes that Luke used Mark, but that Luke also reflects other interests or influences. For example, in comparing Luke 22.3-6 and Mark 14.10-11 Taylor finds the percentage of common words to be 45.4. Taylor argues that Luke 'accepts Mark's tradition' but that he 'appears to reflect Johannine tradition (Jn xiii.2)' and may 'attempt to reconcile two different views'.[22]

At other times when similar percentages of common words appear (i.e. less than 50%), Taylor draws very different conclusions. In comparing Luke 22.21-23 and Mark 14.18-21, Taylor finds the percentage of common words to be 39.1. He argues that 'the narrative is non-Markan and that probably verse 22 is a Markan insertion' into Luke's *other* source.[23]

The outcome of Taylor's work is that he claims Luke used *a single non-Markan written source* that was most likely part of a larger work.[24] This larger work is the Proto-Luke that Taylor posited in his earlier work, *Behind the Third Gospel*.[25] Taylor does modify his earlier view of Proto-Luke by suggesting that Luke himself did not compile Proto-Luke.

At least three objections may be registered against this type of approach. First, the 'Markan elements' that Taylor identifies may not represent Luke's total dependence on Mark. For example, concerning Luke 23.6-16, Taylor says, 'It has nothing characteristic of Mark except *hoi grammateis* in verse 10'.[26] Yet, in the story of Jesus before Herod Antipas, one can argue that Luke reflects thoughts from Mark's Passion Narrative in (a) the idea of Jesus' silence before Herod (Luke 23.9b—see Mark 14.60-61 and 15.4-5), (b) the idea that Jesus was mocked (Luke 23.11a—see Mark 15.16-20), (c) the idea that Jesus was dressed (Luke 23.11b—see Mark 15.17), and perhaps even (d) the idea that Herod *questioned* Jesus (Luke 23.9a—see Mark 14.60-61 and 15.3-4). If such suggestions prove true and there is more of the Markan Passion Narrative in Luke's account than Taylor allows, one is left with something less than the *continuous* account that Taylor claims exists when Markan elements are removed from Luke's Passion Narrative, and the Proto-Luke hypothesis is weakened.

Second, Taylor's basic method seems reductionistic. He compares Luke with Mark exclusively, asking *only* whether Luke could have derived a verse from Mark. The method sets up a situation that produces an artificial either/or: *Either* Luke must be using Mark *or* he must depend on another source. Taylor is overly hasty in taking recourse to a source theory in order to explain the contents of the Lukan Passion Narrative. Had Taylor not subscribed to the Proto-Luke hypothesis before he began his work, he might have approached his study in a different manner.

Third, Taylor portrays an odd image of the author's mind. What would motivate Luke to 'insert' 22.46b ('pray that you won't come into temptation') or 22.50b ('and cut off his right ear') into his work? Are these really insertions from a source or are they signs of Luke's free use of Mark? The compositional technique that Taylor attributes to Luke inevitably reflects a method that is oriented toward word statistics; the statistics relate to a comparison of sections of Mark and Luke that are determined by Taylor, not by the authors of the Gospels. A careful reading and consideration of Luke's story in itself could lead to another outcome.

A fresh study of the Lukan Passion Narrative might ask, 'How is one to imagine that Luke got his information?' This question opens a wider range of possibilities than the results derived from comparing Luke exclusively to Mark. The present study will focus on the material in Luke's Passion Narrative that is *additional* to information found in Mark precisely because such material does not allow a simple comparison of the accounts of Luke and Mark. Such an approach enables us to view Luke in the broad context of pertinent literature of his time—'pertinent' in terms of style, vocabulary, thought, theology, history, politics, and especially, in some instances, as treatments of Jesus' Passion. A cautious delimitation of this literature would be the Septuagint, the Dead Sea Scrolls, Mark, Matthew, John, the Pauline literature, Philo, Josephus, and the *Gospel of Peter*. Of course, attention should be given to other literature when necessary, but the primary focus of study will attend to the documents listed above.[27]

The question 'How is one to imagine that Luke got his information, especially his "additional" material?' will be posed primarily in relation to the *thought* and *content* of the Lukan Passion Narrative. This study will focus on word statistics and stylistic matters only in a secondary fashion. There are at least two reasons for this approach. First, language and style are weak criteria because of the questionable results they can produce when employed as primary methods.[28] Second, in the present state of biblical studies those engaged in strictly statistical and stylistic criticism have argued one another into a stalemate.[29] Moreover, in dealing with a complex piece of ancient literature like Luke's Gospel it is surely a mistake to focus narrowly on the *words* that comprise the larger narrative. Rather than merely analyze words, one should think in relation to the *ideas* that make up the story.

To summarize, the study proposed here will move from two cautious presuppositions. First, the text of Luke's Gospel is to be attributed to the hand of the author until demonstrated otherwise. Second, in composing his Gospel, Luke used Mark as *a* major source for his work. From these two presuppositions, this study attempts to perform two tasks: (1) to determine exactly what material in Luke's Passion Narrative goes beyond Mark, and (2) to analyze that material in order to describe the author's compositional and redactional technique.

Method

To fulfill these tasks it is necessary to devise methods that are appropriate for the completion of the work. First, to determine *what* lines in the Lukan Passion Narrative are special Lukan material, five types of sentences will be considered:

1. sentences that are entirely without parallel in Mark;

2. sentences that represent an agreement of Luke with Matthew or John against Mark;

3. sentences forming a story sequence different from that of Mark;

4. sentences with a low level of verbal correspondence between Luke and Mark; and

5. sentences that contain so-called telltale Lukan language.

While each of these criteria has been used alone or in conjunction with one or more of the other criteria by scholars who have studied the Lukan Passion Narrative,[30] the proposed study is distinctive in that all these criteria will be used with an emphasis on the *thought* and *content* of the narrative.

Those sentences that fit categories 1 and 2 will automatically be designated *special Lukan material*. The sentences that fit categories 3, 4, and 5, however, must be considered individually. The strongest case for designating special Lukan material will arise when sentences meet more than one of these criteria (i.e. 3, 4, and 5). Yet every line must be considered carefully in relation to both its immediate context and the context of pertinent literature of Luke's time.

After identifying the lines to be studied, the next task is to analyze the *origin* of the material. As we have seen, modern analysis of Luke's compositional and redactional technique has typically been based upon word statistics and stylistic observations with the goal of identifying sources that Luke is believed to have used in writing the Passion Narrative.[31] A different analysis, focusing on the *thought-content* of the Passion Narrative rather than the *linguistic content*, will proceed in this way:[32] (1) The special Lukan material will be viewed in meaningful narrative contexts. That is, attention will be given to whole scenes in the Passion Narrative rather than to individual lines or parts of lines.[33] (2) When parallel Markan and Lukan episodes exist and special Lukan material occurs in the Lukan form of the episode, comparison will be made between Mark and Luke (since we believe that Luke used Mark as a major source for his work) to identify the material in the Lukan episode that may come from Mark.[34] (3) Narrative seams will be identified.[35] (4) Parallels between Luke and the pertinent literature of his time will be recognized. Such parallels include (a) material or thoughts that are found in another context in Mark, and (b) information in other canonical and non-canonical literature.[36] (5) Unparalleled material will be identified.[37]

This type of analytical work is a necessary step in coming to terms with the *purpose* of the special Lukan Passion Narrative material. There will, however, be also an inherent *synthetical* dimension to the study, the necessity for which has become apparent in critical biblical study during the past decade. A spate of scholarly literature has reminded the members of the biblical guild that the authors of the books of the Bible were authors of whole volumes and that the task of scholarship is more than dissection of such wholes.[38] Thus, in the present study the analysis of the special Lukan Passion Narrative material will be considered in relation to a reading of the text of Luke–Acts as a unified narrative. By viewing the results of the analysis in this broader arena we should be able to discern more accurately the concerns that motivated Luke to produce the form of the Passion Narrative that he gave to his reader(s).

Chapter 2

SPECIAL LUKAN MATERIAL:
THE PRELIMINARY EVENTS (22.1-38)

This chapter focuses on the events surrounding Luke's account of the last supper that Jesus took with his disciples prior to his Passion.[1] We will locate the special Lukan material in this portion of the Passion Narrative by considering the five types of sentences or lines discussed above (pp. 19-20). Then Chapter 3 provides analysis of that special Lukan material in terms of (1) Luke's compositional technique and (2) his purposes.

The study will begin with a translation of 22.1-38,[2] in which subdivisions of verses are marked by letters of the alphabet. All subsequent references to chapter, verse, and letter (e.g. 22.1a) will refer to these subdivisions. The translation necessarily reflects exegetical matters dealt with later in this study.

Translation of Luke 22.1-38

1a Now the Festival of Unleavened Bread drew near,
 b which is called Passover.

2a And the chief priests and the scribes were looking for a way
        to put him to death,
 b because they were afraid of the people.

3a Then Satan entered Judas,
 b the one called Iscariot,
 c who belonged to the number of the twelve;

4a and he went out and conferred with the chief priests and the
        officers
 b how he might hand him over to them.

5a Now they were delighted,
 b and they agreed to pay him.

6a   So he agreed
b   and he sought an opportunity to hand him over to them
c   apart from a crowd.

7a   The Day of Unleavened Bread came
b   on which the paschal lamb had to be sacrificed.

8a   So he [Jesus] sent Peter and John, saying,
b   'Go prepare the Passover for us
c   so that we may eat it'.

9a   And they said to him,
b   'Where do you want us to prepare it?'.

10a   And he said to them
b   'Look! when you have entered the city, a man carrying a clay
        water jar will meet you.

11a   And you shall say to the master of the house,
b   "The Teacher says to you,
c   Where is the guest room
d   where I may eat the Passover with my disciples?"

12a   And he will show you a large upstairs room that has been
        furnished.
b   Prepare it there'.

13a   They went and found it exactly as he had told them;
b   and they prepared the Passover.

14a   When the hour came
b   he reclined at table,
c   and the apostles with him.

15a   He said to them,
b   'I have eagerly yearned to eat this Passover with you before I
        suffer;

16a   for I say to you
b   that I will surely not eat it
c   until it is fulfilled in the kingdom of God'.

17a   And when he had taken a cup and given thanks
b   he said, 'Take this and divide it among yourselves;

18a   for I say to you
b   that from now on I will surely not drink from the fruit of
        vine
c   until the knigdom of God comes'.

19a   And when he had taken bread and given thanks

b	he broke it
c	and gave it to them saying,
d	'This is my body
e	which is given in behalf of you.
f	Do this in remembrance of me'.

20a	And in the same way the cup after the dinner, saying,
b	'This cup is a new covenant by my blood
c	which is poured out in behalf of you.

21	But look! the hand of the one betraying me is with me on the table.

22a	Now the Son of Man goes as it has been appointed;
b	but woe to that man through whom he is betrayed'.

23a	And they began to discuss among themselves
b	who from among them intended to do this thing.

24a	And indeed contentiousness arose among them
b	which of them was to be thought of as the greatest.

25a	So he [Jesus] said to them,
b	'The Kings of the Gentiles lord it over one another,
c	and the ones of them who wield authority call themselves benefactors;

26a	but you shall not be that way.
b	Rather let the greatest among you become like the youngest.
c	Indeed the one who has authority must be like the one who serves.

27a	For who is greater,
b	the one reclining at table or the one serving?
c	Is it not the one who reclines?
d	Yet in your midst I am like the one who serves.

28	Now you are the ones who have remained with me in my trials.

29	So I allot to you, as my Father allotted to me, a kingdom;

30a	so that you may eat and drink at my table in my kingdom,
b	and you will sit on thrones
c	judging the twelve tribes of Israel.

31a	Simon, Simon, look!
b	Satan demanded to sift you all like wheat.

32a	But I begged concerning you
b	that your faith might not fail,

c   and when you yourself turn around
d   strengthen your brothers'.

33a   But he [Simon] said to him,
b   'Lord, I am ready to go with you both to prison and to death'.

34a   Then he [Jesus] said,
b   'I tell you, Peter,
c   the cock will not crow today
d   until three times you deny that you know me'.

35a   And he said to them,
b   'When I sent you without a purse, bag, or sandals,
c   did you lack anything?'
d   And they said,
e   'Nothing'.

36a   Then he said to them,
b   'But now, let the one who has a purse carry it
c   and likewise a bag;
d   and whoever does not have one,
e   let him sell his mantle
f   and buy a sword.

37a   For I tell you
b   that this scripture must be realized in me
c   "Indeed he was reckoned among the lawless"
d   for in fact that which is about me has its fulfillment'.

38a   Then they said,
b   'Lord, look, here are two swords'.
c   But he said to them,
d   'That's enough'.

Identification of Material

Following the five-type pattern on p. 20 above, we begin with

1. *Material Entirely without Parallel in Mark*

As obvious as this category seems, one finds that it is not always a simple matter to decide whether or not a line in Luke's Passion Narrative is *entirely* without a Markan parallel. The following fit this category unless I indicate clearly the verse is debatable.

Luke 22.3a. There is no mention of *Satan* in Mark's account of the collusion between the Jewish leaders and Judas.[3]

Luke 22.14a-c. The relation of this verse to Mark 14.17 is debatable.[4] Both verses supply narrative transition from the preparation of the Passover to the meal itself. Comparison of 14a-c with Mark 14.17 shows that both have three elements:

First, a temporal reference:

Mark: 'And when it was evening';
Luke: 'When the hour came'.

Second, Jesus attends (or commences) the banquet:

Mark: 'he came';
Luke: 'he reclined at table'.

Third, Jesus' companions:

Mark: 'with the twelve';
Luke: 'and the apostles were with him'.

Although the verses are not similar in vocabulary, there is a striking similarity between the thought patterns of the verses. Thus, it is safe to say that 14a-c has a parallel in Mark's Passion Narrative.

Luke 22.15a-16c. There is no statement in Mark that even approximates the words of Jesus in 15a-b.[5] Verse 16(a-c) is also without a patent parallel in Mark's story.[6] True, the idea of Jesus abstaining from eating the Passover is similar to Jesus' statement in Mark 14.25 that he will not 'drink again of the fruit of the vine until that day when [he drinks] it new in the kingdom of God'. It is, however, impossible to see 16a-c as the parallel to Mark 14.25, since Luke seems to offer a closer match to that part of Mark in 18a-c. At most, one might suggest that 16a-c is a Lukan peculiarity modelled on Luke 22.18a-c, which may be a rough parallel to Mark 14.25. Therefore, it is best to designate 16a-c as material entirely without parallel in Mark.

Luke 22.17a-18c. It is difficult to decide whether 17a-18c should be designated as Lukan material without parallel in Mark. There is a vague similarity between 17a-b and Mark 14.23, but since the strongest case for a parallel to Mark can be made with reference to v. 18, we will focus on 18a-c as the key to determining whether or not vv. 17-18 are special Lukan material.

Verse 18a-c may form a rough parallel to Mark 14.25. Taylor points out that 14 of the 21 words in 18a-c are found in Mark 14.25.[7]

Similarly Perry[8] observes that 66% of Luke's wording in v. 18 has a parallel in Mark.[9] Nevertheless, both scholars argue that 18a-c is material from a special Lukan source other than Mark. Taylor[10] and Perry form their arguments using observations related to the structure of the larger unit 22.15-18. Perry contends that even though 66% of Luke's words have a parallel in Mark, 48% of 18a-c matches Luke 22.16. He attributes such parallelism to Luke's other source.

One should notice that 18a-c is *not* loosely appended to vv. 15-17 as the rough parallel in Mark 14.25 is to its preceding verses in 14.22-24. Rather 18a-c is an integral part of a balanced structure. Verses 15-16 and 17-18 have four instances of parallellism: *legō gar hymin* in 16a and 18a; the emphatic construction *ou mē* + subjunctive in 16b and 18b; *heōs hotou* in 16c and *heōs hou* in 18c; and also the mention of *basileia tou theou* in 16c and 18c. Such parallelisms are not frequent in Luke[11] and suggest that vv. 15-18 are a polished unit. *As a whole*, this unit is not derived from Mark. Yet, granted the complex nature of 15a-18c, it seems best to say that the unit *as a whole* is without an exact match in Mark; but it is necessary to recognize that within the unit, 17a-18c have rough parallels in Mark 14.23, 25.

Luke 22.19a-20c. The relationship of these two verses to Mark 14.22-23 is a point of contention, since it is possible that there is some connection between 19a-20c and 1 Cor 11.23-25 or a source that was available to both Luke and Paul. In order to understand the complexity of the possible relationship of 19a-20c to Mark and Paul (or a tradition like that in 1 Corinthians), it may be helpful to create a three-column chart of the contents of the verses, comparing Luke with Mark 14.22-23 and 1 Cor 11.23-25. By reading down the page (all columns) the text of Luke appears in Luke's order. Words found in Mark and Luke are in normal type under *Mark*. Words found in 1 Corinthians and Luke are under *Paul*. When a word or words in Luke's text occurs in Mark, 1 Corinthians, and Luke, the text appears under *both/[neither]*. When a word in Luke's text is not matched in either Mark or 1 Corinthians, the word is placed within brackets under *both/[neither]*. Any necessary explanations are offered below the word to which they pertain and are placed within parentheses.

Mark	Luke in Agreement with Both/[Neither]	Paul
kai		
labōn		
(Paul=*elaben*)		
	arton	
		eucharistēsas
	eklasen	
	kai	
edōken		
autois		
	[*legōn*]	
	(Mark and Paul=*eipen*)	
	touto	
	estin to sōma mou	
	(This order is Markan; *mou* precedes *estin* in Paul.)	
		to
		hyper
		hymōn
	[*didomenon*]	
		touto
		poieite
		eis
		tēn
		emēn
		anamnēsin
	kai	
	(Markan order)	
		to
	potērion	
		hōsautōs
		meta
		to deipnēsai
		legōn
		(Mark=*eipen*)
	touto	
		to potērion
		hē kainē
	diathēkē	
	(Mark=*diathēkēs*)	

                                                    en
                        tō haimati
                        (Mark=*to haima*
                        in a different
                        order and sense)

                        [*mou*]
                        (Paul=*emō* and *emō*
                        precedes *haimati*)
        to
        hyper
                        [*hymōn*]
                        (Mark=*pollōn*)
        ekchynnonenon
        (not Markan order)

From this chart one is able to see that there is an excellent case for the argument that in 19a-20c Luke is following, or is at least being influenced by, a non-Markan tradition.[12] Indeed, a strong case may be made that Luke is not dependent upon Paul, but rather that both Paul and Luke have a common liturgical source that influenced them.[13] (It is not necessary to think of Luke's *source* as written, since the eucharistic words could have been fixed and preserved in the oral life of the early Church.) One can see, however, that Luke does not merely abandon Mark in favor of the source similar to Paul's; and so 19a-20c is not *entirely* without parallel in Mark (only 19e-f is that). The complicated relationship of these verses to both Mark and the tradition reflected in 1 Corinthians will cause us to consider this material further below.

Luke 22.24a-27d. There is nothing in Mark's Passion Narrative that matches 24a-27d. Yet it may be that these lines are not entirely without parallel in Mark's Gospel (cf., for instance, Mark 10.41-45).[14] Comparison of 24a-27d and Mark 10.41-45 shows, however, that all the elements in 24a-27d do not have exact matches in Mark. One may divide Luke 22.24a-27d in three parts. First, 24a-b provides a transition from the situation in 22.21-23b and introduces the subsequent dispute. Then, Jesus speaks in 25a-26c, taking the behavior of Gentile kings as an example and saying that the apostles are to have different aspirations. Finally, Jesus continues to speak in 27a-d. He poses a riddle, answers it, and gives a christological teaching.

In Mark 10.41-45, there are also three distinct parts. First, v. 41 provides a transition from the previous material and introduces a situation quite different from that in Luke. Then, in Mark 10.42-44, Jesus speaks, taking the behavior of 'those who are supposed to rule over the Gentiles' as an example and teaching the twelve that the way to greatness is through service. Finally, in 10.45, Jesus continues to speak. The verse, loosely appended to the material that goes before it, is a christological teaching focusing on the Son of Man.

One may compare the structure of the sections as follows:

Mark		Luke
10.41	Introduction	22.24
10.42-44	Example and Teaching	22.25-26
10.45	Christological Conclusion	22.27

While the structure of these passages is remarkably similar, the same cannot be said for the contents. The introductions (Mark 10.41 and Luke 22.24) are not at all alike. The christological conclusions to the passages are alike only in the thought that Jesus (Mark's Son of Man) serves.[15] Only the central portions of the passages are comparable.[16] Thus, it is best to understand 24a-b and 27a-d as Lukan material that is not matched in Mark. But one must recognize that 24a-27d form a unified whole; so we will consider these verses in relation to Luke's redactional and compositional technique.

Luke 22.28-30c. Jesus continues to speak in these verses. There is nothing similar to 28-30c in Mark.

Luke 22.31a-32d. As Jesus continues to speak, he now addresses Simon Peter[17] directly. These two verses are also without parallel in Mark.

Luke 22.35a-38d. Still further lines are without parallel in Mark. It is true that Jesus is speaking to the apostles and that the earlier admonition to this group, at Luke 9.1-6, is matched at Mark 6.7-13. The specific portion of 35a-38d that might be related to the sending out of the twelve is 35b. Yet even this line is not a parallel to the Markan material. It is much closer to Luke 10.4 (the instructions given to the seventy[-two] prior to their being sent out by Jesus), a verse not matched in Mark.

Conclusions. This survey of Luke 22.1-38 identified verses that are *entirely* without parallel in Mark's Gospel: 22.3a, 15a-16c, 19e-f, 24a-b, 27a-d, 28-30c, 31a-32d, 35a-38d.[18] It also recognized the complex nature of 22.17a-18c, 19a-20c, 24a-27d.

2. Material Representing an Agreement of Luke with Matthew or John against Mark

We will be concerned with both similar thought patterns and exact verbal parallels in this section.[19]

Luke 22.3a. Both Luke and John mention Satan in connection with the betrayal by Judas. John 13.2 says that at the time of the supper the devil (*diabolos*) had already put it into Judas' heart to betray Jesus. Indeed, one finds an even closer verbal parallel in John 13.27, where John says that after Judas ate the crust of bread that Jesus gave to him Satan entered into him (*eisēlthen eis ekeinon ho satanas*).

We noticed that 3a is without parallel in Mark. When the special Lukan material in this section of the Passion Narrative is analyzed, we will consider the significance of this agreement between Luke and John.

Luke 22.3b. Two phenomena need attention in this line. First, Matthew (26.14) and Luke agree in saying at this point in their Passion Narratives that Judas was *called* by a certain name. Matthew says that one of the twelve 'who was called Judas Iscariot' (*ho legomenos Ioudas Iskariōtēs*) went to the chief priests. Luke says that Satan entered 'Judas, the one called Iscariot' (*Ioudan ton kaloumenon Iskariōtēn*), who belonged to the twelve and who went out and conferred with the chief priests and the officers.[20] The differences in vocabulary (Matthew: *legein* and Luke: *kalein*) and in the ways that Matthew and Luke use 'called' (Matthew: 'called Judas Iscariot' and Luke: 'Judas, the one called Iscariot') do not suggest this so-called agreement of Matthew and Luke has significance.[21]

Second, both Matthew and Luke have *Iskariōtēs* whereas Mark 14.10 reads *Iskariōth*.[22] But a study of the pattern of employment of these forms of Iscariot by the Synoptic evangelists does not show this agreement to be any more significant than the first. Mark uses both forms of the name. *Iskariōth* occurs at Mark 3.19 and 14.10, while

Iskariōtēs appears at 14.43. Matthew (10.4; 26.14) always uses *Iskariōtēs*. Luke uses *Iskariōt(h)* twice, and he, like Mark, knows both forms of the name. At 6.16 Luke uses *Iskariōth*, agreeing with Mark against Matthew; but in 22.3b he happens to agree with Matthew. Such variation shows that the second agreement of Luke with Matthew in 22.3b is also likely a matter of chance.

Luke 22.6b. The word *eukarian*, translated 'opportunity', is cited as an agreement of Matthew and Luke against Mark's *eukairōs* (14.11).[23] The Markan sentence, 'And he looked for a way that he might opportunely betray him' (*kai ezētei pōs auton eukairōs paradoi*) is awkward and Matthew and Luke sought to improve it by supplying the verb *ezētei* with a simple substantive object—an improvement that easily could have occurred to each author independently.[24]

Luke 22.14a. I. Buse suggests that the mention of the 'hour' in 14a reminds one of John 13.1, the introduction to the Book of Glory (John 13.1–20.31).[25] The word 'hour' (*hōra*) is the Johannine technical term for the Passion, death, resurrection, and ascension of Jesus.[26] An analysis of Luke's usage does not show 'hour' to be a technical term. *Hōra* appears in Luke's Gospel seventeen times. The word can impart a sense of immediacy (2.38; 7.21; 10.21; 12.12; 13.31; 20.19; 24.33), imply suddenness (12.39, 40, 46), or function as a general or specific time reference (22.59; 23.44 twice). 'Hour' can also *designate an appointed time* (1.10; 14.17; 22.53—eschatological time?), and this sense best fits 22.14a. But this connotation is not as comprehensive as the Johannine sense.

Luke 22.15-18(20). Scholars, working independently, argue that these verses are similar to John's account of the Last Supper. E. Osty suggests that Luke and John are similar to one another in the solemnity and majesty that they ascribe to the words and actions of Jesus at the meal.[27] F. Rehkopf states that the structure of Luke 22.15-18(20) is like that of John 13.4–11 in which majestic proceedings precede the prediction of the betrayal.[28] Finally, Buse cites the work of Taylor to argue that Luke, like John, does not understand the Last Supper to be a Passover.[29]

In response, observations about matters such as *majesty* and *solemnity* are so general that they are not helpful. Indeed, Jesus is a majestic figure throughout the Gospels of both Luke and John, but he is no less majestic in Matthew's Gospel and, in its own way, in Mark's Gospel. Further, in light of what is said in Luke 22.1-20, it is difficult to see how Buse can maintain that Luke does not understand the Last Supper to have been a Paschal meal.

Luke 22.18b. Several scholars suggest that Luke 22.18b and Matt 26.29 are in minor agreement here against Mark.[30] Both evangelists add a temporal qualifier, 'from now on', to the thought in Mark 14.25 (Matthew: *ap' arti*; Luke: *apo tou nyn*).

It was argued earlier that v. 18 should be taken as a part of the unified whole formed by Luke 22.15a-18c. Now one sees that Luke *makes sense* of Mark 14.25 not only by incorporating the thought of abstinence from the cup into a new unit (vv. 15-18) but also by adding a definite temporal qualifier. Matthew, like Luke (with different vocabulary), adds a definite temporal qualifier to Mark's nebulous thought, but he takes over Mark's material without substantive change. The 'minor agreement' in this instance between Luke and Matthew is much less striking than the almost exact verbal agreement between Mark and Matthew.

Luke 22.20b. Some scholars[31] claim that in this verse, Luke's text is in agreement with Matthew against Mark. Luke describes the covenant as 'new'. Some ancient versions of Matt 26.28 also modify *diathēkēs* with *kainēs*. Yet, the reading of Matt 26.28 that is text-critically preferable does not include *kainēs*. If the word *new* had been present originally in Matthew, there is no good reason why any scribe would have deleted it. It is best to understand the presence of *kainēs* in Matthew as a scribal harmonization to Luke 22.20b.[32] Therefore, no significant agreement exists here.

Luke 22.21. Matthew and Luke agree against Mark at this point in their Passion Narratives by mentioning *the hand* of the betrayer. In Luke, the hand of the betrayer is the subject of the sentence, 'But behold! the hand of the one betraying me is with me on the table'. This sentence in Luke's account is the first announcement by Jesus of the approaching betrayal. In Mark Jesus has already announced that he will be betrayed (14.18).[33] Then the disciples 'say to him one after another, "Is it I?"' (14.19). Matching the Lukan Jesus' announcement of the forthcoming treachery is the Markan Jesus' ambiguous answer to the queries of the disciples, 'It is one of the twelve, one who is dipping bread into the dish with me' (14.20). Matt 26.23 is somewhere between Mark's account and Luke's. Like Mark, Matthew has already had Jesus announce the betrayal, and the disciples have questioned Jesus. Then Jesus speaks: 'The one who dipped his hand in the dish with me, this one will betray me'. Given the almost exact match between Mark and Matthew (except in the use of 'hand'), it is probably best to see this minor agreement on 'hand' between Luke and Matthew as evidence of the continued existence and influence of oral tradition alongside the written Gospel.[34]

Luke 22.21-23. Scholars suggest at least three points of agreement between Luke and John in these verses. First, both evangelists offer the same order of events by announcing the betrayal after the meal (see John 13.1-30).[35] Second, as P. Parker observes, Luke 22.22 and John 14.2-3 use the verb *poreuesthai* as a metaphor for the death of Jesus, whereas Mark and Matthew prefer *hypagein*.[36] Third, Luke and John portray an interaction among the disciples after Jesus' announcement.[37]

The significance of the first agreement in narrative order will inform the discussion of Luke's redactional and compositional technique in this part of his Passion Narrative. Therefore, we will delay consideration of this phenomenon until later.

It is difficult to respond to the second observation, since at 7.33, John also uses *hypagein* as a metaphor for Jesus' death. This metaphor is misunderstood by 'the Jews' who wonder where Jesus is *going*. The Jews use *poreuesthai*, and there is no metaphorical value to their words. Further, Luke generally avoids the verb *hypagein* and uses the verb *poreuesthai*. Thus, there may not be much significance in the agreement of Luke and John in employing the same, common verb as a metaphor for Jesus' death.

Finally, the reaction of the disciples to Jesus' announcement of his being betrayed is not alike in Luke and John. In Luke the disciples discuss among themselves to whom Jesus is referring. In John (13.22) the disciples merely look at one another—a good dramatic narrative device to heighten their reaction—before they ask Jesus directly who the betrayer is.

Luke 22.24-38. Both Luke and John have 'last discourses' by Jesus following the Last Supper. This 'similarity' between Luke and John is extremely general in nature. When we consider the purposes that seem to have motivated Luke in this section, we will, however, give detailed attention to the presence of a so-called farewell discourse by Jesus in Luke's account.

Luke 22.24-30. Osty argues that in two regards these verses are similar to John 13.12-17: (1) Jesus claims in both Luke and John that true greatness is in service, and (2) Jesus gives himself as an example.[38] Osty is correct that Jesus gives himself as an example in both Luke and John. Yet the same is true in Mark 10.45; and so nothing is particularly significant about this agreement.

Concerning Osty's other suggested similarity, it is difficult to see that either Luke or John says that true greatness is in service. As noted above,[39] Luke admonishes 'the great' to do service. John, on the other hand, issues a call to genuine humility. The sections of Luke and John that Osty compares are, in fact, at least as different as are Luke and Mark.

Luke 22.24a-27d. Buse makes a creative suggestion concerning the interpretation of 24a-27d and John 13.1-20, proposing that the two passages form a commentary on one another. He argues that Luke needs to have Jesus serving somehow—John does; and John needs to have the disciples arguing about who is the greatest—Luke does.[40] That both Luke and John were content with their narratives the way we read them in their separate works does not offer much support for this alleged point of contact between the two Gospels.

Luke 22.27a-d. Another kind of relationship between Luke and John is proposed by H. Klein. He argues that the Lukan logion found at 27a-d is developed into a scene in John 13.4-5, 12-17. Klein does not suggest that John depended directly upon Luke; rather both were heirs to a common tradition. Study of John 13.1-20 does not seem to support Klein's argument at this point.[41]

Luke 22.28 and 30b-c. Verse 28 is compared to both Matt 19.28[42] and John 14.9,[43] where there is mention of Jesus' earthly sojourn. Matthew has Jesus refer to 'you who have followed me'; in John Jesus asks, 'Have I been with you so long . . . ?' The nearly exact verbal agreement between 30b-c and the parallel portion of Matt 19.28 suggests that 'the ones who have remained with me in my trials' in 22.28 is probably related to Matthew rather than John.

Luke 22.31-34. The placement of Jesus' prediction of denial by the disciples, especially by Peter, is a further agreement in narrative order between Luke and John. Both evangelists have Jesus' statement in the context of the Supper, whereas Mark and Matthew record the prediction as made on the road to the Mount of Olives.

Luke 22.31-32. Several scholars suggest that an oral tradition lies behind these verses and John 21.15-18.[44] The argument is that both evangelists speak of (a) Peter's restoration and (b) a charge given to him by Jesus. In both Gospels, Jesus also addresses Simon Peter simply as Simon.

Luke does not, however, portray a restoration but a penitent return. The charge given to Simon, 'Strengthen your brothers', is a charge to bolster the band of apostles in the crisis that will follow the arrest and execution of Jesus. In John 21 there is a conversation between Jesus and Peter that grieves Peter. In the exchange Jesus continually admonishes Simon to care for his (Jesus') flock. The *flock* apparently refers to the Church at large. At the conclusion of the triple exchange between Jesus and Simon Peter, Jesus offers a prophecy concerning Peter's death. It is difficult to see these portions of Luke and John as depending on one another. Moreover, as early as John 13.36, one learned that Peter would return.[45]

Luke 22.33b. As noticed above, Luke and John agree in placing Jesus' prediction of Peter's denial at the Supper. A further agreement between Luke and John demands attention here. In both Luke and John (13.37), Peter calls Jesus 'Lord' (*kyrie*). Peter's statement in Luke reads, 'Lord, I am ready to go with you both to prison and to death'. In John, Peter asks, 'Lord, why am I not able to follow you now?' This agreement is not significant and should be attributed to chance.[46]

Luke 22.34c. The single cock-crow is also found in Matt 26.34 and John 13.38. It is better to regard the Markan version as an anomaly than to see the agreement of Matthew, Luke, and John as an oddity. This agreement is probably another example of the continued existence and influence of oral tradition alongside the written Gospel.[47]

Conclusions. This survey identified certain lines in Luke 22.1-38 as material representing an agreement of Luke with Matthew and/or

John against Mark. These are 22.3a, (18b?), (21?), 28, 30b-c, 34c.
Also recognized were agreements between Luke and John in
narrative order concerning the predictions of betrayal (22.21-23b)
and denial (22.31a-34d). There is also the general agreement of Luke
(22.21-38) and John (13.12-16.33) in the presence of a farewell
discourse after the Last Supper.

3. *Material Forming a Story Sequence Different from That of Mark*
This third type of material is often referred to as *transposed* Markan
material, though, as we will see, other interpretations of the
differences in order between Luke and Mark are possible. We will be
concerned primarily with thought patterns in this section.

Luke 22.8a-9b. In Luke's account of the preparation of the Last
Supper Jesus tells Peter and John to prepare the paschal meal. In
response to his directions, they ask him, 'Where do you want us to
prepare it' (9b). Jesus then gives specific instructions (10a-c). In
Mark's story the disciples (all?) ask Jesus where they should prepare
the Passover (14.12). Jesus responds to their inquiry by sending two
unnamed disciples to the city with directions for finding the right
place (14.13). Luke's order of events in vv. 8a-9b differs in that Jesus
sends Peter and John to prepare the Passover *before* they ask him
where to prepare it.[48]

Luke 22.17a-18c. Jesus' issuing of a cup and his statement, 'From
now on I shall not drink from the fruit of the vine until the Kingdom
of God shall come' are frequently described as a transposition of
Markan material (14.23, 25).[49] This judgment rests upon the
assessment of 17a-18c as parallels to Markan material. Above we
argued that it is best to understand the larger unit of 15a-18c as
Lukan material without a patent parallel in Mark, although
reservation was made as to 17a-18c, which have rough parallels to
Mark 14.23, 25. These 'parallels' suggest that the passages are
somehow related. Yet, at most, 17a-18c may be a thorough reworking
of Markan material, not a true transposition. Therefore, one should
not emphasize the difference between Luke and Mark in their *order*
here.

Luke 22.21-23b. In Mark (14.18-21) the betrayal is announced
before the Last Supper. In 21-23b, the announcement *follows* the
meal.[50]

Further, in Mark's story, the saying about the Son of Man and the woe over the betrayer appears *after* the questioning by the disciples.[51] Luke's telling of the incident has the Son of Man saying and the woe (22a-b) *before* the questioning by the disciples. Thus, there is a double difference in the order of 21-23b from Mark's sequence.

Luke 22.24-27. The teaching of Jesus in these verses is frequently thought to be Luke's version of Mark 10.41-45.[52] Above we argued that 24a-b and 27a-d are not matched in Mark's Gospel, but 25a-26c may be compared to Mark 10.42-44.[53]

Luke 22.33a-34d. The boast by Peter concerning his readiness to die with Jesus and Jesus' prediction of Peter's denial occur in 33a-34d *before* Jesus and the apostles depart from the upstairs room. In Mark's account, however, Jesus predicts Peter's denial and Peter claims unswerving loyalty to Jesus *after* the group leaves the banquet room and goes to the Mount of Olives.[54]

Further comparison of 33a-34d and Mark 14.29-31 reveals a second internal difference in the order in which the stories are told. In 33b Peter's statement of readiness occurs *before* the logion about the threefold denial and the (single) cockcrow. In Mark 14.31, Peter states that he is ready to die with Jesus *after* Jesus' prediction of triple denial and the (double) cockcrow. The complex nature of 33a-34d[55] and their obvious relationship to 31a-32d will make it necessary for us to consider these verses again in terms of Luke's redactional and compositional technique.

Conclusions. From this survey we have identified certain sentences and lines in Luke 22.1-38 as forming a story sequence different from that of Mark: namely, 22.8a- 9b, 21-23b (double difference), 25a-26c, 33a-34d (double difference). We noted once more the complicated nature of 17a-18c.[56]

4. *Material with a Low Level of Verbal Correspondence between Luke and Mark*

This fourth category is similar to the one Perry calls 'material in Luke's Passion-narrative with remote parallel in Mark'. Perry defined this type of material by saying, 'Remote agreement is reckoned as agreement in less than 50 per cent of the language in discourse materials, or less than 40 per cent in narrative'.[57]

As stated at the outset of this study, the primary concern of this study is with the *thought* and *content* of the Lukan Passion Narrative. Word statistics function here in a secondary fashion. This approach does not deny the usefulness of statistical observations, provided that they function only in a supportive role to other lines of inquiry.[58]

Luke 22.3a-4b. 3a is without parallel in Mark's account. But the idea of Judas going to the Jewish authorities (3b-4b) in order to arrange with them to betray Jesus is present in Mark 14.10.

Line	Number of Words	Markan Matches
3a	5	1
3b	3	1
3c	6	2
4a	7	3
4b	5	3

10 of Luke's 26 words, or 38%, are matched by words in Mark. The presence of unparalleled material in these lines lowers the level of agreement between Luke and Mark. Yet, even without 3a the degree of verbal correspondence is only 43%.

Luke 22.8a-9b. The exchange between Jesus and the disciples represents a change in order in the larger unit 7a-13b. Taylor demonstrates that the degree of agreement between 7a-13b and the Markan parallel (14.12-16) is 65%.[59] Yet, as we can see, this statistic does not hold for 8a-9b.

Line	Number of Words	Markan Matches
8a	6	2
8b	5	2
8c	2	2
9a	4	1
9b	3	3

10 of Luke's 20 words, or 50%, are matched by words in Mark. The different order of Luke's account from that of Mark seems to be matched by a similar difference in verbal correspondence between the two narratives.

Luke 22.14a-c. This sentence provides the transition from the preparation of the meal to the meal itself. In thought patterns it resembles Mark 14.17, but the vocabulary is different:

Line	Number of Words	Markan Matches
14a	5	2
14b	1	0
14c	5	0

2 of Luke's 11 words, or 18%, are matched by words in Mark. The vocabulary of 14a-c is not similar to Mark 14.17, but the thought patterns are the same. Since the verses that follow 14a-c are without parallel in Mark, we should ask about the relationship of this sentence to Mark 14.17.

Luke 22.17a-18c. We noticed above the complex nature of these verses. On the one hand, they form an integral part of the unit, 15a-18c. On the other hand, there seems to be some relationship between these verses and Mark 14.23, 25.

Line	Number of Words	Markan Matches
17a	4	2
17b	7	3
18a	3	2
18b	12	8
18c	7	5

20 of Luke's 33 words, or 61%, are matched by words in Mark.

Luke 22.19a-20c. As we saw, these lines are probably part of a mixed text. They seem to be a combination of Mark 14.22-24 and a tradition similar to 1 Cor 11.23-25.

Line	Number of Words	Markan Matches
19a	4	3
19b	1	1
19c	4	3
19d	5	5
19e	4	0
19	6	0
20a	8	2
20b	10	6
20c	4	3

23 of Luke's 46 words, or 50%, are matched by words in Mark.

Luke 22.21-23b. These verses are in a different position from the similar portion of Mark's account (14.18-21).

Line	Number of Words	Markan Matches
21	12	4
22a	10	6
22b	8	7
23a	6	1
23b	10	0

18 of Luke's 46 words, or 39%, are matched by words in Mark. Again the differences in order between Luke and Mark are accompanied by the differences in the words employed by the two evangelists.

Luke 22.25a-26c. We saw that these verses form the central portion of a larger section, 24a-27d, that has three parts. The first and third parts (24a-b and 27a-d) of 24a-27d are without parallel in Mark; yet the central, second part (25a-26c) is related to Mark 10.42-44.

Line	Number of Words	Markan Matches
25a	4	1
25b	6	5
25c	6	4
26a	4	4
26b	9	5
26c	6	1

20 of Luke's 35 words, or 57%, are matched by words in Mark—a high percentage granted that what immediately precedes and follows has no Markan parallel.

Luke 22.33a-34d. We saw that there is a double difference between 33a-34d and Mark 14.29-31. First, the historical order is different in Luke and Mark. Second, there is an internal difference in the way the evangelists narrate the parallel incidents.

Line	Number of Words	Markan Matches
33a	4	4
33b	12	3
34a	3	3
34b	3	2
34c	4	2
34d	5	3

17 of Luke's 31 words, or 55%, are matched by words in Mark. Of the three sections of Luke's Passion Narrative that appear in a different order from their parallels in Mark, these lines have the highest percentage of verbal correspondence.

Summary

Luke	Mark	Level of Agreement
22.3a-4b	14.10	38%
22.8a-9b	14.12-16	50%
22.14a-c	14.17	18%
22.17a-18c	14.23, 25	61%
22.19a-20c	14.22-24	50%
22.21-23b	14.18-21	39%
22.25a-26c	10.42-44	57%
22.33a-34d	14.29-31	55%

Conclusions. The results of this survey confirm our insistence that word statistics can function only in a secondary manner. The lowest incidence of Markan vocabulary parallels was for 14a-c: only 18%. Working only with word statistics one would conclude that the passages in this instance were probably not related. Yet the thought patterns behind 14a-c and Mark 14.17 are exactly the same, so that indeed 14a-c and Mark 14.17 are to be recognized as parallels.

The highest rate of vocabulary matches was for 17a-18c. In every section of this study we have recognized the complicated nature of these verses. It was argued above that 17a-18c are, at most, a thorough reworking of Markan material which maintains a striking similarity to the Markan vocabulary. Using only word statistics one would probably assume that 17a-18c were from Mark and would perhaps not recognize the intricate character of the lines which are an integral part of the unit 15a-18c.

In the later portions of this study, we will return to certain of the findings of this survey. We will see that study of vocabulary matches, carefully assessed in the context of other findings, assists in the assessment of Luke's redactional and compositional technique.

5. *Material Containing So-Called Telltale Lukan Language*
Here this study draws upon but also moves beyond earlier works that focus on the language of Luke–Acts,[60] suggesting that certain words are typical of Luke.

Luke 22.2a, 4b, 23b, 24b—'*to*' *to introduce indirect questions*. Seldom outside of Luke-Acts are indirect questions substantivized by *to*.[61] In 22.1-38, however, this phenomenon occurs four times.

Luke 22.3a—'*Satan*'. T. Schramm contends that *satanas* is non-Lukan vocabulary.[62] F. Neirynck takes exception to Schramm's claim. For instance, at 8.12 (par Mark 4.15) Luke replaces *satanas* with *diabolos*; but the same substitution is made by Luke at 4.2 (par Mark 1.13). Luke 4.2 is matched by Matt 4.1 which also replaces Mark's *satanas* with *diabolos*. Thus, Neirynck argues that Luke's substitution of 'the devil' for 'Satan' may be the result of Luke's being influenced by the source he held in common with Matthew. Further, Luke independently employs *satanas* three times in Gospel passages that are without parallel (10.18; 13.16; 22.31) and twice in Acts (5.3; 26.18),[63] so that the mention of Satan entering into Judas at 3a *could be* the result of Luke's redactional tendencies.[64] We will give further attention to the occurrence of *satanas* in this line below.

Luke 22.3b—'*the one called*'. J. Finegan contends that *ton kaloumenon* is Lukan and calls attention to similar expressions in Acts 1.23; 15.22.[65]

Luke 22.4a—'*the chief priests and the officers*'. The 'chief priests' appear regularly in all four Gospels, but only in Luke are they linked with the 'officers' (see also 22.52 and Acts 4.1; 5.24).[66]

Luke 22.14b—'*reclined at table*'. Among the Gospels Luke uses the verb *anapiptein* distinctively. Mark (6.40) and John (6.10) use the verb of the people taking their places at the feeding of the five thousand. Luke does not have the verb in his parallel account (9.14-15). Mark (8.6) and Matthew (15.35) both use *anapiptein* in their stories of the feeding of the four thousand. Luke does not include this second miraculous feeding in his Gospel. John uses the verb to describe the posture of both Jesus and the beloved disciple at the Last Supper. Luke employs the verb *anapiptein* four times but *only* to indicate taking a place at a table (11.37; 14.10; 17.7; 22.14b).[67]

Luke 22.14c—'*the apostles*'. Though Luke does know and use 'the twelve' elsewhere, Finegan demonstrates that Luke commonly substitutes 'the apostles' for Mark's designation, 'the twelve' (see Luke 6.13; 17.5; 22.14; 24.10).[68]

Luke 22.15b—'yearned'. Luke uses the word translated 'yearned' (*epithymein*) four times in the Gospel and once in Acts (20.33). None of the Gospel occurrences has a parallel.[69] At 15.16, the prodigal *yearns* to eat the pods fed to the pigs. At 16.21, Lazarus *yearns* to eat the crumbs from the rich man's table. At 17.22, Jesus tells the disciples that the days are coming when they will *yearn* to see one of the days of the Son of Man, yet they will not see it. Prior to the Passion Narrative, Luke seems to employ the verb to mean deep, frustrated longing. That same depth of emotion is implied in 22.15b.[70]

Luke 22.15b—'before I suffer'. R. Pesch describes *pro tou me pathein* as a 'Lukanism'. The absolute use of *pathein* appears, by comparison with Mark and Matthew,[71] to be preferred Lukan vocabulary. *Pro tou* is also typical of Luke and is a 'Septuagintalism'.[72]

Luke 22.17a—'given thanks'. Luke employs *eucharistein* four times.[73] At 17.16, the Samaritan healed of leprosy *thanks* Jesus for healing him. At 18.11, in a parable, Jesus says the proud Pharisee *thanks* God that he is not like other men. At 22.17 and 19, Jesus *gives thanks* for the cup and the bread. Mark (14.22) and Matthew (26.26) use *eulogein* at this point in their accounts of the Last Supper, but Paul (1 Cor 11.24) also uses *eucharistein* in connection with the bread. This survey does not suggest that *eucharistein* has a technical meaning for Luke. It probably simply means *to give thanks*.

Luke 22.18b—'from now on'. This temporal reference seems to be one of which Luke is particularly fond (1.48; 5.10; 12.52; 22.18b, 69; and Acts 18.6).[74] The phrase acknowledges a turning point in the story and orients the reader toward the ensuing narrative events.

Luke 22.20b—'new'. Luke is unique among the evangelists in describing the covenant as *new*. His understanding of this modifier may be seen in the parable of the wineskin patches (5.36-39), where *kainos* seems to indicate that there is a power in the 'new' that must be recognized and dealt with. But the implication is also that for those accustomed to the 'old' there is a disconcerting quality to the 'new'.

Luke 22.23a—'to discuss among themselves'. The verb *synzētein* will also be used at 24.15 for the activity of the disciples on the road to Emmaus, and twice in Acts (6.9; 9.29) seemingly implying debate. If the notion of debate is present in the verb at 22.23a, we may better understand the transition from 23a-b to 24a, 'indeed contentiousness arose among them . . . .'[75]

Luke 22.26c and 27b—'the one who serves'. It was argued that 25a-26c is Luke's version of Mark 10.42-44, but 27a-d is Lukan material without a match in Mark's Gospel. Yet there is a verbal coherence between the second and third elements of the tripartite unit, 24a-27d, in the circumstantial participial phrase *ho diakonōn*. Luke's special interest in the idea of service, especially table service, is evident from a study of 12.37; 17.7; and Acts 6.1-6.

Luke 22.28—'trials'. Luke employs *peirasmos* six times in the Gospel and once in Acts.[76] At 4.13, *peirasmos* is the devil's action toward Jesus in the temptations. At 8.13, Jesus explains one kind of seed in the parable of the sower as those who 'believe for a while and in time of *trial* fall away'. At 11.4 (par Matt 6.13), the Lord prays in his model prayer, 'Lead us not into *temptation*'. *Peirasmos* also occurs in Luke's twin parallels to Mark 14.38, 'Pray not to enter into temptation!' (22.40, 46). Finally, at Acts 20.19, in his farewell speech to the Ephesian elders at Miletus, Paul says that in *serving* the Lord he has experienced 'trials . . . through the plots of the Jews'.

Two items should be recognized: First, in the Gospel there is an eschatological dimension to *peirasmos*, as a struggle against the evil one. Second, Luke has both Jesus and Paul describe their ministries in their 'farewell' speeches using *peirasmos*.

Luke 22.32a—'begged'. The verb *deisthai* occurs throughout Luke–Acts (fifteen times). On the one hand, the verb means 'to beseech, to plead', with no implication that the activity is 'prayerful', i.e., it is not directed toward God (see 5.12; 8.28, 38; 9.38, 40; Acts 8.34; 21.39; 26.3). On the other hand, the verb seems to mean 'prayer' directed toward God—an activity more *urgent* than normal supplication (see 10.2; 21.36; Acts 4.31; 8.22, 24; 10.2).[77] The sense of crisis that forms the background to these latter employments of *deisthai* may be another indication of an eschatological concern.

Luke 22.32c—'turn around'. Jesus prophesies that Peter, after he is sifted by Satan, will 'turn around' (*epistrephein*). The same verb appears in the messianic prophecy at 1.16, 17. At other points in Luke–Acts the verb seems simply to imply the physical act of 'returning'. We may infer from 1.16, 17 and 22.32c that the verb can mean the act of *repentance*. This understanding of the verb is consistent with Luke's thought throughout Luke–Acts.

Luke 22.32d—'strengthen'. Luke is alone among the evangelists in his use of *stērizein*. His employment of the verb is striking. At 9.51, Jesus *sets* his face toward Jerusalem. In the parable of Lazarus and the rich man, there is a chasm *established* or *fixed* between the position of the rich man, on the one hand, and Abraham and Lazarus on the other. In Acts (18.23) one learns that Paul went about *strengthening* all the disciples. Thus, there is about this verb the sense of the working out of the will/plan of God. We will return to this notion below.

Luke 22.35b—'purse, bag, sandals'. Luke is the only NT writer to employ the word 'purse' (*ballantion*). The word appears in the Gospel four times. Luke uses it in combination with 'bag' (*pēra*) and 'sandals' (*hypodēma*) at 10.4.

Luke 22.37b—'be realized'. Luke's employment of the verb *telein* suggests action consistent with the will of God, i.e. activity that transpires because of divine necessity. At 2.39 one reads of Joseph and Mary (and Jesus?), 'And when they *had done* everything according to the Lord's law, they returned to Galilee, to their home town, Nazareth'. At 12.50, Jesus says, 'I have a baptism with which to be baptized, and oh how I am pressed until it *is realized*'. In 18.31, a passage similar in thought to 22.37b, Jesus tells the twelve, 'Look! we are going up to Jerusalem and everything written by the prophets about the Son of Man *is going to be realized*'. Again we encounter the eschatological dimension.

Conclusions. Prominent among the materials considered in this survey of so-called telltale Lukan language are 22.3a ('Satan'), 4a ('the chief priests and the officers'), 14b ('reclined at table'), 14c ('the apostles'), 15b ('yearned', 'before my suffering'), 18b ('from now on'),

20b ('new'), 23a ('to discuss among themselves'), 26c and 27b ('the one who serves'), 28 ('trials'), 32a ('begged'), 32c ('turn around'), 32d ('strengthen'), 35b ('purse, bag, sandals'), 37b ('be realized'). Two observations may be made: first, language characteristic of Luke is present in all portions of 22.1-38; second, several of these words may be viewed together under the rubric of *eschatology* ('Satan', 'from now on', 'new', 'trials', 'begged', 'turn around' [?], 'strengthen' [?], and 'be realized').

The Scope of the Special Lukan Passion Narrative Material in Luke 22.1-38
We are now in a position to suggest what portions of vv. 1-38 are special Lukan material. The strictest definition of this material includes only those portions of Luke's Passion Narrative that are completely different from the material in Mark's Passion account. According to this definition, 22.3a, 15a-16c, 19e-f, 24a-b, 27a-d, 28-30c, 31a-32d, 35a-38d are the lines of special Lukan material in this section.

Yet, one should see that there are portions of Luke's Passion Narrative that are similar to material in Mark, but are so thoroughly blended with special Lukan material, that they become different from their Markan parallels. These lines are 22.17a-18c, 19a-d, 20a-c, 25a-26c, 33a-34d. From this observation, it is perhaps best to regard 22.3a, 15a-18c, 19a-20c, 24a-27d, 28-30c, 31a-34d, 35a-38d as special Lukan material; although a final decision about the *scope* of the special Lukan Passion Narrative material will be possible only after consideration of the *origin* of the various lines in this list. In order to see this material printed out consecutively (not broken into lines), the reader should turn to Chapter 6. Now, this material may be examined in an attempt to understand the origin and purpose of the special Lukan material in 22.1-38.

Chapter 3

ANALYSIS OF THE SPECIAL LUKAN PASSION
NARRATIVE MATERIAL IN LUKE 22.1-38

The special Lukan Passion Narrative material will be analyzed in
two ways: namely as to origin and purpose.

The Origin of the Material

In this section, proceeding cautiously, one finds that Luke has
worked in a variety of ways to produce 22.1-38.

Luke 22.3a. As noted above, Schramm claims v. 3 is proven to be
traditional by the parallel in John 13.27;[1] but arguing against
Schramm's claim, Neirynck[2] demonstrates that the mention of Satan
entering into Judas at 3a could be the result of Luke's redactional
tendencies. One must recognize, however, that Neirynck does not
account for the occurrence of the same thought in John.

There are four possible explanations of this striking parallel
between Luke and John. First, both evangelists could have freely and
independently composed this detail—a very unlikely coincidence.
Second, Luke could have taken this idea from John—but most
scholars place the writing of Luke's Gospel at least a decade earlier
than John. Third, John could have derived this idea from Luke,[3] but
direct literary contact between the two evangelists is not proved.[4]
Fourth, both Luke and John derive this detail from an independent
tradition that was available to them.[5] This explanation seems
preferable since (a) Luke appears to have inserted the detail into
Markan material (22.1-13 par Mark 14.1-2, 10-16), and (b) John uses
the name *Satan* only at 13.27 instead of his usual *the devil* (three
times).[6]

In Luke the story of Jesus' ministry prior to his coming to
Jerusalem is a battle against Satan (see 10.18; 11.18; 13.16).[7]

Moreover, in the Lukan Passion Narrative (22.3a, 31, 53 [?]), Satan is once more on the offensive as he was in the trials of Jesus (4.1-13). Satan's presence emphasizes that the Passion is a time of eschatological crisis.

Luke 22.15a-18c. The parallels between the structure of 15a-16c and 17a-18c hold the four verses together as a unit (see pp. 27-28 above);[8] yet 17a-18c have parallels in Mark 14.23, 25, having been taken over from the eucharistic meal.

When Luke worked an additional tradition similar to 1 Cor 11.23-25 together with the Markan account, the Markan narrative structure for the bread and cup was destroyed. Luke created a new setting for the Markan material in 17a-18c by composing 15a-16c on the model of the dislocated Markan material.[9] The new position of 17a-18c and the new structure of 15a-18c emphasize the eschatological tone of the narrative.[10]

Luke 22.19a-20c. We saw that Luke, rather than substituting another source for Mark, let that tradition or source influence his handling of Mark. The bread symbolizing Jesus' body 'given in behalf of you' (19e) has no Markan parallel; but the words, 'in behalf of you', appear in 1 Cor 11.24. As for the cup symbolizing the new covenant by Jesus' blood 'poured out in behalf of you' (20c), the last words are in the same narrative position as Mark's 'in behalf of many'. Thus Luke has again created a parallel structure with balanced elements. But, strikingly, in these verses there is one other unbalanced element. After the breaking of bread, one reads, 'Do this in remembrance of me' (19f), words found in 1 Cor 11.24. Yet there is no balancing element after the cup. Therefore, the breaking of the bread becomes the high point of Luke's account.[11] That Luke created this structure is clear from comparision of 19a-20c with 24.30; Acts 2.42, 46; 20.7, 11; and 27.35.

Luke 22.24a-27d. Not all parts of 24a-27d have Markan parallels, but it appears that Luke has taken the basic material for 25a-26c from Mark 10.42-44. As he set this bit of Markan material in a new context, he gave it a new tone by composing 24a-b and 27a-d. Several factors lead to this understanding.

First, the connection between v. 23 and v. 24 is clear in light of our discussion of telltale Lukan language (p. 46 above).[12] The verb *sunzētein* for the discussing done by the disciples (23a) suggests an intermural debate from which it is a short step to the *contentiousness* that arose among the disciples.[13]

Second, Luke's description of the nature of this dispute is remarkably similar to that of the dispute he narrates at 9.46, 'An argument arose among them about which one of them was greatest'. Moreover, Luke tells the reader that Jesus responded to the dispute among the disciples at 9.46 by taking a child as a teaching example (9.47).[14] In turn, one should notice that in his version of Mark 10.42-44 (25a-26c), Luke has Jesus instruct the disciples to 'become like the youngest' (26b), an admonition not found in Mark. One can understand this difference as the result of Lukan redaction of Mark 10.42-44 under the influence of 9.47. Evidently Luke used the dispute at 9.46 as a model for composing 24b.

Luke 22.27a-d teaches three lessons about Luke's outlook. First, Luke avoids here as elsewhere the implication of *mere* 'ransom' theology that is seen in Mark 10.45.[15] While it certainly is no longer possible to deny the presence of sacrificial nuance in Luke's Gospel,[16] the emphasis here is on the *service of Jesus*. Jesus *serves* by giving his body and pouring out his blood. Second, the Lukan theme of table service is consistent with the mood and attitude of 12.37 and 17.7-10. Third, in the admonition to service (25a-26c) and in the self-designation of Jesus as 'the one who serves' (27d), there is an element of the eschatological reversal that permeates Luke's Gospel.[17]

Luke 22.28-30c. In 28-30c it seems Luke has included a Q tradition in the words of Jesus after the Last Supper, for a clear parallel to 28 and 30b-c exists at Matt 19.28.[18] Such incorporation was probably done by freely *editing* the tradition and by *composing* 29-30a.[19]

Luke's *editing* of the Q tradition can be seen by comparing v. 28 with Matt 19.28.[20] Matthew has Jesus refer to the disciples as 'you who have followed me'. Luke has Jesus call the disciples 'the ones who have remained with me throughout my trials'. As seen above Luke distinguishes himself from the other evangelists in the way he employs *peirasmos* with a clear, consistent eschatological dimension (see 22.28, 40, 46). Thus, the idea of *peirasmos* in this line is most likely Lukan.

That Luke composed 29-30a is probable because the messianic banquet described at 13.22-30 and anticipated at 22.16, 18 is

described here as a reality.[21] The Q tradition is set in the context of
the Last Supper by the inclusion of 30a,[22] which is an appeal to the
meal situation.[23] The pattern of thought in this unit is that of the
duality of *admonition and promise*. This design runs through the
whole of this section of the Passion Narrative.[24]

Luke 22.31a-34d. We noted that 31a-32d is without parallel in
Mark. Moreover, 33a-34d is internally different from the Markan
parallel, as well as being placed differently. How may we best
account for these findings?

First, one must recognize that certain information was not taken
over by Luke from Mark, e.g. Mark 14.27-28 (Jesus' quotation of
Zech 13.7 and Jesus' accompanying prophecy). These verses in Mark
intimate that after Jesus is arrested the disciples will abandon him.
Luke also did not take over Mark 14.31, the claim by Peter and the
other disciples that they will not abandon Jesus. These omissions are
usually accounted for as part of the typical Lukan tendency to cast
the disciples in a favorable light.[25]

As for material that Luke did take over from Mark, one can see
from 33a-34d that he reworked it. In Mark 14.29, Peter responds to
Jesus' prophecy that the disciples will abandon him with a boast that
even though the others may fail Jesus, he will not. In the place of this
statement, Luke has Peter respond to Jesus' prophecy and commission
(31a-32d) by saying that he is ready to go with Jesus to prison and to
death. A similar idea is found in Mark at 14.31a. The comparative
tone of Peter's statement in Mark 14.29 is not present in the Lukan
structural parallel, 33a-b—an omission highly appropriate after
Jesus' teaching in 24a-27d. By moving the statement of *readiness* into
the position of Peter's response to Jesus' prophecy, Luke alters the
order of Mark's material.

Yet in both Mark and Luke Peter is depicted as *responding* to Jesus'
prophecy. The particular prophecies in the two Gospels are,
however, completely different. Instead of Mark 14.27-28, with its
prediction of abandonment, we find 31a-32d, a prediction of the
sifting of the disciples and of Peter's 'turning around' and strengthening his brothers. Let us examine these verses to see if Luke *composed*
these verses to take the place of Mark 14.27-28.[26]

First, the double address, 'Simon, Simon', is typical of solemn
Lukan address (see 10.41). By having Jesus address this disciple as
Simon (see 5.4-5, 8, 10), Luke sets up the ensuing, deeply ironical

twist in 34b. *Peter*, who boasts of his steadfastness (33a-b), is himself fallible and will crack under pressure (34a-d); but he is *Simon*, the one for whom Jesus prayed and who will strengthen his brothers (32d). It is also important to notice that at 24.34, in a record of the risen Lord's appearing, the name Simon is used, not Peter.

Second, Satan is shown to be active in the *sifting* of the disciples at the time of the Passion. We learned earlier in this section (3a) of Satan's role in the betrayal of Jesus. The activity of sifting is consistent with both the image of Satan in the OT (Job 1.6-12; 2.1-6; Zech 3.1-2) and the role we saw him playing in the trials of Jesus at 4.1-13.[27]

Third, the prayerful intercession in 32a is typical of Luke's portrait of the praying Jesus.[28] As Fitzmyer says, 'Many of the major episodes of Jesus' ministry are explicitly linked with his prayer, occurring either before or during them'.[29]

Fourth, the Lukan ideas found in these verses are matched by Lukan words. As observed earlier, 'trials', 'begged', 'turn around', and 'strengthen' are all Lukan words expressive of Lukan ideas.

In summary, in the larger unit 22.31a-34d, one sees that in structure and thought 31a-32d is a Lukan composition designed to replace Mark 14.27-28.[30] Verses 33-34 are Luke's edited version of Mark 14.29-31.

Luke 22.35a-38d. We have seen that 35a-38d is without parallel in Mark and without parallel in Matthew or John. How then did Luke get the information in these verses? The following factors suggest that, in 35a-38d, Luke incorporated an independent saying attributed to Jesus (36d-f) into the setting of the Last Supper by composing the other lines that make up this unit of the Passion Narrative.[31]

First, there is a redactional parallel between 35b and 10.4, namely, *ballantion*, *pēra*, and *hypodēma*. Second, the temporal reference, 'but now' (*alla nyn*), at 36b constitutes a dramatic shift in time comparable to and in keeping with Jesus' earlier words, 'from now on' (*apo tou nyn*) at 18b, which is best understood as a Lukan addition to the basic Markan material. Third, 37b, with the eschatological *dei* indicating divine necessity, is part of a theme that permeates Luke's Gospel.[32] Fourth, the two-fold stress on fulfillment at 37b,d echoes 13.32 and 18.31.[33] Fifth, 37c is a formal citation of Isa 53.12.[34] The realization of this scripture may be understood in relation to either or both 22.49-50 and 23.32, 39-43.[35] Sixth, the mention of the sword at 36d-f brings about a misunderstanding among the disciples (38a-b) that elicits a brief, enigmatic rebuke from Jesus (38c-d). This misunderstanding anticipates the misguided behavior of the disciples and the rebuke of them by Jesus that Luke narrates in 22.49-50. Thus it appears that Luke composed 38a-d with 22.49-50 in mind.[36] Seventh, it is highly unlikely that either Luke or the early church would have created this sword logion.[37]

In summary, one may understand that Luke had available to him an independent statement by Jesus that lies behind 36d-f. By drawing on 10.4, Luke composed 35a-36c to lead into the saying. He set the saying in the context of the Passion Narrative by drawing on Isa 53.12 to provide a scriptural text that was realized in the Passion of Jesus by (a) referring to the use of the sword (at 22.49-50) and (b) associating Jesus with condemned criminals (23.32). Luke composed 38a-d to close the scene of the Last Supper and to anticipate the forthcoming events of the Passion Narrative.

Summary and Conclusions. We asked above about the origin of the lines determined to be special Lukan Passion Narrative material (22.3a, 15a-18c, 19a-20c, 24a-27d, 28-30c, 31a-34d, 35a-38d). Here are the conclusions deemed most probable.

Verse 3a is an independent tradition that Luke worked into his account of Jesus' Passion.

The unit 15a-16c is a Lukan composition that builds on the structure of reworked Markan material in 17a-18c. The Lukan composition and redaction form an integrated whole.

In 19a-20c Luke used both Mark's account of the Last Supper and a eucharistic tradition similar to that found in 1 Cor 11.23-25. Luke merged these two traditions into a structure that emphasizes the breaking of the bread.

Unit 24a-27d is Luke's edited version of Mark 10.42-44 (25a-26c), which Luke worked into his version of the Passion Narrative by composing 24a-b and 27a-d.

Unit 28-30c contains a Q tradition (28 and 30b-c). Luke appears to have edited this tradition freely and to have incorporated it into its present context by composing 29-30a.

Luke composed 31a-32d, and he merged these lines with 33a-34d, his edited version of Mark 14.29-31.

Finally Luke incorporated an independent saying of Jesus (36d-f) into the setting of the Last Supper. He did this by composing the other lines of this unit (35a-36c and 37a-38d).

The Purpose of the Material

Now that we have seen *what* material Luke used and *how* he employed it,[38] we can ask *why* Luke worked as he did.

A testamentary meal. This meal of Jesus with his disciples is one in a long series of meals that Luke narrates.[39] Two factors in Luke's portrait of this banquet are remarkable: First, in the context of the supper Luke includes material either found elsewhere in Mark or not in Mark at all. The extended dialogue between Jesus and his disciples in the context of the supper puts Luke's account of the meal, in many ways, closer to John's than to Mark's.[40] So one should not be surprised that scholars have frequently described Luke's version of the Last Supper as a *testamentary* banquet.[41] The literary genre of *testaments* is well attested in classical Greek literature;[42] the Old Testament, canonical[43] and apocryphal;[44] the pseudepigrapha;[45] the New Testament, canonical[46] and apocryphal.[47]

Second, Luke interprets the teaching of Jesus after the banquet meal in the framework of the supper.[48] Although testamentary literature is common in antiquity, no binding genre was employed by the authors of the *testaments*. But, in studying the various examples of this literary type, one can discern a common, loose format:[49] the main character is an ideal figure. Recognizing a special time, usually his own impending death, the main figure calls together his family or followers. When they are assembled, the central figure gives them special instructions. He often speaks of his own fatal flaw, predicts the future for them, and admonishes and/or instructs them in the ways of righteousness. Luke's account clearly fits into this pattern.[50]

The ideal figure: Jesus. The main character in 22.1–38 is Jesus. It is he who charges his disciples to go and prepare the Passover (8a–9b). The disciples do not show any initiative in these preparations; they are simply following orders (10a–12b). This role is quite different from that which the disciples play in Mark, where the disciples approach Jesus and his instructions come only in response to them.

Luke's reader has seen Jesus in charge of the events that transpire around him throughout the Gospel. At 4.30, he simply passed through the midst of a hostile crowd and went on his way. At 9.31 Jesus spoke with Moses and Elijah about his fate (*exodos*) that he was to fulfill in Jerusalem. Then, at 9.51, Jesus *set* his face toward Jerusalem. Later when Jesus learned that Herod wanted to kill him,

he answered that he was on his way and could not perish away from
Jerusalem (13.31-33). At 19.28, Luke tells us that Jesus 'went on
ahead, going up to Jerusalem'. In this vein Jesus directs his disciples
to prepare the Passover. It is with this sense of Jesus' being in charge
that Luke can have Jesus say, 'Now the Son of Man goes as it has
been appointed' (22.22a). One sees that Jesus enters into the time of
his Passion in full control of his destiny.

The special time: Jesus' Passion and death. Throughout the Gospel,
Jesus has been aware that he will die in a way related to his mission.
Like Mark, Luke includes three predictions by Jesus of his death:
9.22, 44; 18.31-33. In addition, at the scene of the Transfiguration
(9.31), Luke has Jesus talking with Moses and Elijah 'about his
exodos'. In 22.1-38, Luke has Jesus speak openly about his impending
death at least three times (15a-18c, 19a-20c, and 22a). Moreover, the
temporal references on the lips of Jesus at 18b and 36b suggest that a
special time has arrived.

The followers: the apostles. Since 5.30, Luke's reader has known
that Jesus has *disciples*. At 6.13, one learns that Jesus chose *twelve*
from among the apparent throng of disciples and named them
apostles. Jesus sends out this group of twelve followers on the first
authorized mission (9.1-6), and apparently this same group of twelve
followers, the apostles, is with Jesus at table during the Last Supper
(14b-c).[51]

Special instruction. The instruction that Jesus gives his followers
in the context of the Last Supper may be matched against the three
topics mentioned as typical of testamentary teaching. First, the main
character informs those around him of a fatal flaw. Since Luke thinks
of Jesus as the 'righteous' one (23.47), 'a savior, who is Christ the
Lord' (2.11), one should not be surprised that Jesus does not tell of a
fatal flaw. Yet one does find in the place of this type of information
Jesus' announcement (22.31b) that Satan is involved in his forthcoming Passion and death.

Second, the main testament usually predicts the future for those
around the ideal figure. In Luke Jesus opens the future by relating it
to his imminent death. He is about to suffer (15b), but somehow his
suffering moves toward the kingdom of God (16b-c, 18b-c). His
death provides a basis for the disciples' remembrance of him (19f)

and realizes the plan of God (37a-d). And, even though Jesus is slated to suffer and die, he can offer the disciples a portion of his own inheritance (28-30c). Still, he must warn the apostles of the trials that they will face (31a-b, 36a-f) even though he has made provision for their ultimate triumph (32a-d).

Third, the main testamentary character admonishes and instructs those around him in the ways of righteousness. Jesus prepares his disciples for the crisis ahead by giving them direction. He offers his Passion as the foundation for their future actions (19a-20c) and gives precepts for community conduct (24a-27d). He reminds the twelve that he sent them on a mission and tells them to prepare for hardship as they continue in the same activity (35a-36f).

Conclusions. We see that Luke has redacted some material and composed additional lines to develop the Markan Last Supper into the testamentary meal of Jesus with his followers. Luke seems to have reworked this portion of the Passion Narrative for at least three reasons: First, Luke shows Jesus to be in charge of the events of the Passion (8a-c, 15a-18c). Jesus charts his course and acts decisively (19a-20c). Presiding over the Last Supper, he knows the future and has made provision for it (28-38d).

Second, Luke reworked the Last Supper account in such a way as to heighten the eschatological character of the meal and the events that will follow. Satan is active (3a, 31b). Jesus reveals that the time has changed (18b, 36b). There is no more teaching 'along the way' as throughout 9.51-19.28. The plan of God is about to be realized (37a-d).

Third, the reader of 22.1-38 receives instruction along with the apostles. There is both implicit and explicit christological teaching. Jesus is the Son of Man (22a). He is 'the one who serves' (27d), but also the one to whom God has allotted a kingdom (29). Moreover, Jesus is the one who makes provision for his followers (30a) and intercedes in their behalf (32a-b). He identifies himself with the figure of Isaiah 53, and claims that God's plan is realized in him (37a-d). Finally, the reader receives instruction concerning Jesus' will for the life of the Christian community (24a-27d, 35a-36f). Thus 22.1-38 is a mini-course for the reader in christology, eschatology, and ecclesiology.

Chapter 4

SPECIAL LUKAN MATERIAL: FROM THE MOUNT OF OLIVES THROUGH JESUS' APPEARANCE BEFORE THE COUNCIL (22.39-71)

Chapters 4 and 5 focus on the events in Luke 22 that take place after Jesus and his disciples depart from the upstairs room where they have eaten the Last Supper. The occurrences narrated in this portion of Luke's Gospel transpire on the Mount of Olives, at the house of the high priest, and in the Council of the Jewish elders.[1]

Translation of Luke 22.39-71

39a	When he went out he proceeded, according to his custom, to the Mount of Olives
b	and just his disciples followed him.
40a	When he reached the place, he said to them,
b	'Pray not to enter into temptation!'
41a	And he withdrew from them,
b	about a stone's throw,
c	and going to his knees, he prayed,
42a	saying, 'Father, if you have it in mind,
b	take this cup away from me.
c	Only let not my will
d	but yours be done'.
45a	And when he arose from his prayer
b	and went to his disciples,
c	he found them sleeping because of their sad condition.
46a	And he said to them,
b	'Why are you sleeping?
c	Get up and pray so that you will not enter into temptation'.

47a   While he was still speaking
  b   a crowd appeared.
  c   Indeed, the one called Judas, one of the twelve, walked at the head of them;
  d   and he drew near to Jesus
  e   in order to kiss him.

48a   But Jesus said to him,
  b   'Judas, are you betraying the Son of Man by means of a kiss?'

49a   When those around him saw what was going to happen, they said,
  b   'Lord, are we to strike with a sword?'

50a   And one of them struck the high priest's servant
  b   and took off his right ear.

51a   But Jesus answered and said,
  b   'Let it be!
  c   That's enough of that!'
  d   And touching his ear,
  e   he healed him.

52a   Then Jesus said to those who came out for him:
  b   chief priests, officers of the Temple, and elders,
  c   'As if for a brigand,
  d   you came with swords and clubs.

53a   Day after day, when I was with you in the Temple,
  b   you did not stretch out your hand for me.
  c   But this is your hour,
  d   and the power of darkness.'

54a   Then they arrested him and led him away.
  b   They brought him to the house of the high priest;
  c   and Peter followed him at a distance.

55a   And when they lit a fire in the middle of the courtyard,
  b   and sat together,
  c   Peter sat among them.

56a   Then a maid saw him
  b   as he sat facing the light,
  c   and she stared at him and said,
  d   'This one was with him!'

57a   But he denied it saying,
  b   'I don't know him, woman!'

58a   And after a little while, another saw him and said,
  b   'You are one of them!'
  c   But Peter said,
  d   'Fellow, I am not!'

59a   About an hour passed
  b   and another one insisted (saying),
  c   'Of course this one was with him,
  d   after all, he is a Galilean!'

60a   But Peter said,
  b   'Fellow, I don't know what you are talking about!'
  c   And immediately, while he was still speaking,
  d   a cock crowed.

61a   And the Lord turned and looked straight at Peter;
  b   and Peter remembered th Lord's saying
  c   (how he said to him),
  d   'Before a cock crows today,
  e   you will deny me three times'.

62a   And he went out
  b   and wept bittely.

63a   And the men who were in charge of him (Jesus) mocked
         him;
  b   beating him
64a   and blindfolding him,
  b   they asked him (saying),
  c   'Prophesy!
  d   who is the one who hit you?'

65   And they said many other things, reviling him.

66a   And when it was day,
  b   the Assembly of the elders of the people came together,
  c   both chief priests and scribes,
  d   and they brought him into their Council;

67a   saying, 'If you are the Christ,
  b   tell us!'
  c   But he said to them,
  d   'If I tell you,
  e   you will not believe;

68a   and if I ask you,
  b   you will not answer.

69   Yet, from now on the Son of Man will be sitting at the right
        hand of the power of God.'

70a   Then they all said,
   b   'Are you then the Son of God?'
   c   But he said to them,
   d   'You yourselves say that I am'.

71a   Then they said,
   b   'What further need have we of testimony?
   c   For we heard it ourselves from his mouth!'

Identification of Material

This section focuses on the five types of material mentioned
above.

1. *Material Entirely without Parallel in Mark*
As was seen in Chapter 2, it is not always a simple matter to
determine whether a line in Luke's Passion Narrative is *entirely*
without a Markan parallel.[2]

Luke 22.39a-b. The relation of this verse to the comparable
portion of Mark's Passion Narrative (14.26, 32) is debatable.[3] We saw
above that Luke includes information in the context of the Last
Supper that is found in Mark *after* the group has gone out from the
upstairs room, and some of the material that Luke transposed is
between Mark 14.26 and 14.32.

Three observations may be made here. First, 39a-b should be
compared to both Mark 14.26 and 14.32. The notice that Jesus and
his disciples left the scene of the Last Supper in Mark 14.26 has them
going to a place (*chōrion*) called Gethsemane at Mark 14.32, a place
not mentioned in Luke. Second, the subject of the action differs. In
Mark the focus is on Jesus and his disciples as a group; but in Luke
the focus is on Jesus, with the band of disciples loosely appended in
39b.[4] Third, while 39a-b does not contain significant information
additional to that found in Mark's account, the relationship of this
verse to lines in Mark's Passion Narrative is complicated, for it is
without a simple Markan parallel. We will have occasion to consider
this verse further below.

Luke 22.40a-b. Verse 40a is similar to Mark 14.32 in the mention
of 'place', but Mark uses *chōrion* as the object of the preposition *eis*,

while Luke uses *topos* as the object of the preposition *epi*. Nevertheless, the next action attributed to Jesus in both Gospels is to speak to his disciples, giving them instructions. And so, 40a is probably Luke's restatement of information in Mark.

The relation of Luke 22.40b to Mark is more complex because in Luke there are two commands to pray but only one in Mark:

Luke 22.40b: *proseuchesthe mē eiselthein eis peirasmon*
Luke 22.46c: *proseuchesthe hina mē eiselthēte eis peirasmon*
Mark 14.38: *proseuchesthe hina mē elthēte eis peirasmon*

It is immediately apparent that, *pace* Finegan,[5] the parallelism is between 46c and Mark, not between 40b and Mark. Besides grammatical differences (Lukan infinitive in 40b vs. Markan subjunctive), 40b concerns the content of the prayer while Mark (and 46c) concerns the purpose. Therefore, 40b has no parallel in the Markan material.[6]

Luke 22.45a-c. These lines contain bits of narrative information not found in Mark's story: namely, in 45a the action 'he arose from his prayer'; and in 45c, the reason for the disciples' sleeping ('because of their sad condition'). One might argue that this information means 45a-c is without a Markan parallel.[7] But the real substance of the Lukan verse is in lines b and c, 'and he went to his disciples, and found them sleeping', which have clear parallels in Mark 14.37, 40, 41(?). Thus, it is best to understand that 45a-c is matched in Mark's account.[8]

Luke 22.48a-b. There is nothing in the Markan Passion Narrative that matches these lines of Luke's story. In Mark Jesus does not speak to Judas. Rather, Judas speaks to Jesus, and Jesus does not respond. In Luke Jesus takes the initiative and questions Judas, but we do not learn that Judas replied.

Luke 22.49a-b. These lines are without parallel in Mark's account. In Luke, we are told that 'those around' Jesus perceived what was going to happen—a perception absent from Mark. Luke reports that they asked Jesus whether they should strike with a sword,[9] while Mark has Jesus arrested before the swordsman strikes.

Luke 22.51a-e. In this verse Jesus addresses his disciples, rebuking them. He then heals the man whose ear has been severed as the disciples attempt to prevent the arrest of their *kyrios*. None of this information is related in Mark's Gospel, and so these lines clearly have no Markan parallel.[10]

Luke 22.52a-b. Two verses in each Gospel are involved, one at the beginning of the scene, one in the middle of the scene. At the beginning, Mark describes 'a crowd . . . *from* the chief priests and the scribes and the elders' (14.43), while Luke 22.47 describes simply 'a crowd', giving the reader no clue that they may have a hostile origin. In the middle of the scene Mark 14.48 has Jesus speak simply 'to them' (obviously those of 14.43). In the comparable position (22.52) Luke has Jesus speak to 'those who came out for him: chief priests, officers of the Temple, and elders'. Ultimately both Gospels think of a hostile crowd coming to where Jesus is, but Mark tells us from the start who sent them and Luke tells half-way through who they were. (Both Gospels mention chief priests and elders.) Thus to some extent Luke offers information not in Mark.[11]

Luke 22.53c-d. These two lines record a statement by Jesus not matched by Mark: 'But this is your hour and the power of darkness'. Comparing it to Mark 14.49, 'But let the scriptures be fulfilled', Finegan argues that with different words Luke and Mark make the same point, i.e. *it must be so*.[12] True, the statements in Mark and Luke are placed similarly and do perform the same narrative function;[13] but they are very different from one another. The polished statement in Luke is an enigmatic observation, while a clear imperative is expressed by the hortatory subjunctive in Mark. This striking Lukan pronouncement will receive further attention below.

Luke 22.56a-62b. Most scholars describe Luke's account of Peter's denials as borrowed Markan material;[14] but there are noticeable differences in the ways that Luke and Mark narrate the story. One may consider (A) the exchanges in which Peter denies Jesus and (B) the conclusions of the scenes.

(A) The three *exchanges* in which Peter denies Jesus may be compared under various headings. (To avoid duplication the following charts include John's account though it is considered later with references back to here.)

The Location of the Exchange

The first exchange:

> Mark: at the fire in the courtyard
> Luke: at the fire in the courtyard
> John: at the door as Peter enters the courtyard

The second exchange:

> Mark: in the gateway to the courtyard
> Luke: (no change indicated from previous location)
> John: at the fire in the courtyard

The third exchange:

> Mark: (no change indicated from previous location)
> Luke: (no change indicated from previous location)
> John: (no change indicated from previous location)

The Challenger

The first challenge:

> Mark: one of the maids
> Luke: a maid
> John: the maid who kept the door

The second challenge:

> Mark: the same maid
> Luke: another (a man [*heteros*])
> John: those at the fire: servants and officers

The third challenge:

> Mark: the bystanders at the gateway
> Luke: another one (a man [*allos tis*])
> John: one of the high priest's servants, a kinsman of Malchus

The Address of the Challenge

The first challenge:

> Mark: to Peter himself
> Luke: about Peter in the hearing of those around the fire
> John: to Peter himself

The second challenge:

> Mark: about Peter to the bystanders
> Luke: to Peter himself
> John: to Peter himself

The third challenge:

> Mark: to Peter himself
> Luke: about Peter in the hearing of those around the fire
> John: to Peter himself

The Form of the Challenge

The first challenge:

> Mark: with the Nazarene, Jesus
> Luke: with him
> John: one of this man's disciples

The second challenge:

> Mark: one of them
> Luke: one of them
> John: one of his disciples

The third challenge:

> Mark: one of them, for . . . a Galilean
> Luke: with him, for . . . a Galilean
> John: in the garden with him

The Form of Peter's Denial

The first denial:

> Mark: 'I neither know nor understand what you mean'
> Luke: 'I don't know him'
> John: 'I am not'

The second denial:

> Mark: 'But again he denied it'
> Luke: 'Fellow, I am not'
> John: 'He denied it and said, "I am not"'

The third denial:

> Mark: 'I don't know this man of whom you speak'
> Luke: 'Fellow, I don't know what you're talking about'
> John: 'Then again Peter denied it'

Clearly Mark and Luke narrate in different ways the exchanges in which Peter denied Jesus, although the structure of the accounts and the narrative components are remarkably similar.

(B) A similar assessment may be made of the conclusions to the accounts of Peter's denials (Mark 14.72; Luke 22.60c-62b), which have similar elements in the same sequence, thus:

A temporal reference:

> Mark: and immediately (*euthys*)
> Luke: and immediately (*parachrēma*) while he was still speaking
> John: and immediately (*eutheōs*)

What occurred:

> Mark: the cock crowed a second time
> Luke: the cock crowed
> John: the cock crowed

The impact on Peter:

> Mark: Peter remembered how Jesus said to him
>   (+ earlier prophecy quoted)
> Luke: Peter remembered the Lord's saying
>   (+ earlier prophecy quoted)
> John: (nothing)

Peter's reaction:

> Mark: he broke down and cried
> Luke: he went out and wept bitterly
> John: (nothing)

Luke alone (61a) adds that the Lord turned toward Peter after the crowing of the cock (see the next section).

By way of summary, it appears that Luke 22.56a-62b (with the exception of 61a) is Lukan material with a clear parallel in Mark 14.66-71, even if details of the narrative are different. The differences will be discussed further below.

Luke 22.61a. There is nothing in Mark's version of the denials of Peter that even approximates Luke's indication that Jesus looked at Peter during these exchanges.[15] In Mark's account, Jesus is above the courtyard in the council hall of the Jewish leaders, and no visual contact is mentioned or presumably possible.

Luke 22.63a-65. There is no exact parallel in Mark's Passion Narrative to these lines in Luke's story, although a similar incident is narrated in Mark 14.65.[16] One may compare the two accounts of Jesus' being mocked as follows:

Where the mockery took place:

> Mark: in the council
> Luke: (apparently) in the courtyard

Who mocked Jesus:

> Mark: some (of the council members [?])
> Luke: the men who were in charge of him

What the mockers did:

> Mark: spat on him, blindfolded his face, struck him, and said
> Luke: mocked him (by) beating him, and blindfolding him, and saying

The demand they made:

> Mark: 'Prophesy!'
> Luke: 'Prophesy! who is the one who hit you?'

The conclusion to the incident:

> Mark: and the attendants slapped him around
> Luke: and they said many other things, reviling him

Parts of the stories told by Mark and Luke are different, amidst striking similarities. If Luke had not thought the similarities were more important than the differences he could have narrated another mocking scene exactly like Mark's in the context of the Council meeting. So Luke himself probably regarded these stories as parallels.

Two further observations should be made at this point: First, whole lines in Luke's account (64d and 65) are not matched in Mark's story and should be designated as Lukan material without a Markan parallel. Second, while vv. 63a-64c narrate an event similar to that related in Mark 14.65, noticeable differences exist between the way the mocking is portrayed. Because of the presence of unparalleled lines and dissimilarities between the stories of Luke and Mark, we will consider the whole of 22.63a-65 below.

Luke 22.66a-d. Some scholars compare 66a-d to Mark 14.53b and Mark 15.1;[17] others conclude the lines come from an old non-Markan tradition that related a meeting of the Council only on the morning following the arrest of Jesus.[18] The following factors indicate that the verse is probably best designated as Lukan material without a Markan parallel.

Verse 66a gives a temporal reference indicating that 'day' had begun. But the completely different wording, context, and purpose of this line do not allow comparison with Mark 15.1 which mentions 'morning'.

Verse 66b names a group, 'the Assembly of the elders of the people', not 'the elders' of Mark 14.53b.

Verse 66c defines that group as 'both chief priests and scribes', but Mark 14.53 and 15.1 name 'the chief priests and the elders and the scribes'.[19]

Verse 66d makes the statement, 'and they brought him into their Council'. Mark's statement, 'and they led Jesus to the high priest' (14.53), even if similar in idea, is not the same and is made at a different point in the story.

Luke 22.67a-b. At Mark 14.61 Jesus is asked a question similar to this one. But for the following reasons, it seems best to understand that these Lukan lines are not simply taken over from Mark.

First, in Mark the high priest poses the question; in Luke the whole Assembly questions Jesus. Second, the way the question is put in Mark and Luke is noticeably different (Mark: 'are you the Christ?'; Luke: 'if you are the Christ'). Third, only one part of Mark's two-part question is posed here; Luke does not add 'the son of the blessed one' after 'the Christ'. Fourth, the material before and after the asking of the questions in Mark and Luke is not alike. Before the question, witnesses appear in Mark's account and Jesus refuses to answer their charges; but in Luke the question is the first event in the Council's meeting. After the question in Mark, Jesus answers, 'I am'; but in Luke Jesus refuses to answer by advancing a dilemma against the Assembly.

Luke 22.67c-68b. The bold answer that Jesus gives to the Assembly is reminiscent of prophetic statements of judgment.[20] It is not comparable to anything in Mark's account, where Jesus is silent.[21] We will return to these lines below.

Luke 22.70a-b. For the same reasons that we judged 67a-b as best designated Lukan material without a patent Markan parallel, we do the same here, noticing, however, that there is a similar question posed in Mark 14.61.

Luke 22.70c-d. Finegan argues that Luke united Mark 14.62 (*egō eimi*) and 15.2 (*sy legeis*) to form this line (*hymeis legete hoti egō eimi*).[22] Even if Finegan is correct, these lines, in their present form and setting, have no simple parallel in Mark's Passion Narrative.

Conclusions. From this survey we have identified certain lines in Luke 22.39-71 as material *entirely* without parallel in Mark's Passion Narrative. These are 22.39a-b, 40b, 48a-b, 49a-b, 51a-e, 52b, 53c-d, 61a, 64d-65, 66a-68b, 70a-d.

Moreover, other lines in 22.39-71 that appear to have parallels in Mark's story are still different from Mark's version of the lines. These include: 22.45a,c, 55a-60d, 61b-62b, 63a-64c.

2. Material Representing an Agreement of Luke with Matthew or John against Mark
We will give primary attention to similar ideas and thought patterns but will also consider significant verbal parallels.[23]

Luke 22.39b. Luke, Matthew (26.36),[24] and John (18.1-2)[25] agree at this point in the way they narrate their stories. All three mention Jesus separately ('he . . . and the disciples'), while Mark 14.32 simply speaks of the group ('they'). But this agreement is not so striking when compared to dissimilar names for the place to which Jesus and his disciples went, namely, Mount of Olives (Luke), Gethsemane (Matthew—from Mark), and across the Kidron to a garden (John). The agreement, then, reflects only similar narrative technique and is not significant for defining special Lukan material.

An additional similarity is shared by Luke and John here, for both portray the 'place' as being a regularly visited, known spot.[26] Luke, however, tells the reader it was *Jesus'* custom to go to the Mount of Olives, while John relates that *Judas* was familiar with the garden spot because Jesus often met there with his disciples. Luke's statement, related to earlier material at 21.37, emphasizes that Jesus acted in his customary fashion. John's statement is more directly concerned with accounting for how Judas could have found Jesus. This similarity is probably mere coincidence.

Luke 22.40b. All four evangelists speak of the 'place' to which Jesus and the disciples went. John (18.2) and Luke use the word *topos*, while Mark (14.32) and Matthew (26.36) use *chōrion*. This minor agreement in vocabulary between Luke and John is more than offset by the different names Luke and John give for the 'place' (see under 22.39b above). And so, one should not consider this agreement between Luke and John to be *against* Mark.

Luke 22.42a-d. These lines are comparable to material in Matt 26.39 and 26.42 in three ways. First, 42a and Matt 26.39 agree in the way they cast the opening of Jesus' prayer.[27] Instead of Mark's imperfect verb, *elegen*, both use the participle *legōn*. Both have the vocative *pater* as the address to God, whereas Mark has *abba* with the nominative, *ho patēr*. Both Luke and Matthew begin the prayer with *ei* + a present active indicative verb, casting the prayer as a present simple conditional sentence. Mark portrays Jesus as speaking in the imperative, giving a different force to the statement.

Although the language and form of 42a and Matt 26.39 are remarkably similar, in one way Luke's statement is more like Mark's than Matthew's. Mark's 'all things are possible' for God implies that God can do whatever is in the divine mind, as does Luke's 'Father, if you have it in mind'. But Matthew presents a query, 'My Father, if it is possible' (compare, however, Mark 14.35). A complicated situation exists whereby the agreements between Luke and Matthew may be simply the results of similar methods of writing or may be significant for locating special Lukan material.

A second agreement between Luke 22.42 and Matt 26.39 is in the use of *plēn*[28] to begin the apodosis of the simple conditional sentences in these verses. *Plēn* is not a common word in Matthew's Gospel; it appears only five times. Luke, on the other hand, uses the word fifteen times in his Gospel and four times in Acts.[29] This agreement between Matthew and Luke is the only common point at which they use the word. What follows the *plēn* in Luke 22.42 and Matt 26.39 communicates the same basic, imperatival idea, but the words and syntax of the respective statements are not alike.

A third agreement exists between 42c-d and Matt 26.42.[30] Matthew reads, 'let your will be done' (*genēthētō to thelēma sou*), the exact words of the Matthean Lord's Prayer (Matt 6.10). Luke does not include this statement in his Lord's Prayer (11.2-4). Yet 42c-d employs similar language to express a similar thought: 'let not my will but yours be done', *mē to thelēma mou alla to son ginesthō*.

One may consider these similarities between Luke and Matthew together. That Luke and Matthew agree at three separate points suggests these similarities are indeed agreements of Luke and Matthew *against* Mark. But are they chance occurrences or signs of special Lukan material? Viewed together, these agreements are most easily understood as the result of a common oral tradition (see further below in Chapter 5).

Luke 22.45b. Luke 22.45b agrees with Matt 26.40 in using the phrase 'to his disciples' (*pros tous mathētas*) to clarify where Jesus went when he arose from prayer.[31] Mark 14.37 simply says that Jesus 'came and found them sleeping'. Since Jesus departed from the disciples earlier and has been off at prayer, it does not seem significant that Luke and Matthew add the phrase, 'to his disciples', to specify Jesus' motion.

A comparison of the sequence confirms this assessment, for Luke and Matthew continue their stories from this point differently. Luke says the disciples were sleeping 'because of their sad condition'; Matthew has no comparable remark. Luke has Jesus address all of the disciples; Matthew, like Mark, has Jesus speak to Peter. In Luke Jesus asks a short, simple question of the group and issues a direct command; but in Matthew Jesus asks Peter a polemical question, then gives a command to the group, and utters a proverb. Thus, when one sees the different material following the matching phrases, the agreement does not seem significant for identifying special Lukan material.

Luke 22.47b. Both Luke and Matt 26.47 include the exclamatory imperative *idou* when they give notice that the crowd arrived.[32] This word is a common way to vivify narrative in each of the Synoptic Gospels and is an agreement of minor importance.

Luke 22.47c. Osty compares this line of Luke with John 18.3: both portray Judas as the leader of the crowd in a more emphatic fashion than do Mark and Matthew.[33] For Luke this is true, exemplified only in the verb, *proerchesthai*, which seems stronger than Mark's *paraginesthai* or Matthew's simple *erchesthai*. But John 18.3 says that Judas procured a cohort of soldiers and officers from the Jewish authorities and went (*erchetai*, singular) to the garden equipped with lanterns, torches, and weapons. There is no significant agreement between Luke and John here.[34]

Luke 22.48a-53d. Both Luke and John depict Jesus as more thoroughly in control of the events comprising the arrest scene than do Mark and Matthew[35]—an extremely general similarity. In considering the purposes that motivated Luke in this section, we will, however, give detailed attention to the manner of Jesus below.

Luke 22.48a-b. These lines may be compared to both Matt 26.50 and John 18.5. First, 48a-b agrees with Matt 26.50 in having Jesus speak directly to Judas in order to ask him a question.[36] The questions, however, are not at all alike:[37]

> Luke: 'Judas, are you betraying the Son of Man by means of a kiss?'
> Matt: 'Friend, why are you here?'

The contexts in Luke and Matthew in which Jesus questions Judas are also different. In Luke Judas draws near to Jesus to kiss him; Jesus poses his question; then the unnamed disciple strikes with the sword. In Matthew Judas comes up to Jesus and says, 'Greetings, Rabbi!' and kisses Jesus. Then, Jesus questions Judas and the members of the crowd arrest Jesus. Amid the marked differences in the narratives of Luke and Matthew, the factual agreement that Jesus questioned Judas is striking.[38] The similarities and dissimilarities here are probably best accounted for as evidence of the continued influence of oral tradition alongside and upon the written Gospel. But because of this agreement, 48a-b will be considered in the analysis of the special Lukan material.

Second, Luke and John 18.5 agree in not saying explicitly that Judas kissed Jesus. (It remains unclear whether Judas did or did not kiss Jesus in Luke.)[39] At 47e, however, Luke tells his readers that Judas intended to kiss Jesus, and he has Jesus mention the kiss in 48b. In John there is never a mention of a kiss. One is probably safest to see no agreement of significance between Luke and John at this point.[40]

Luke 22.49a-50b. Both Luke and John 18.10 record the blow with the sword prior to the arrest of Jesus,[41] as apparently the disciples attempt to prevent that arrest.[42] The significance of this agreement in order will inform the discussion of Luke's redactional and compositional technique below.

Luke 22.49b-50a. Luke and Matt 26.51 agree in using the verb, *patassein* ('to strike'), instead of the verb in Mark 14.47, *paiein* (also in John 18.10).[43] Luke uses *patassein* twice (49b and 50a) and Matthew once, but the particular forms in which they put the verb do not match. One should notice that at this point in their stories, both Luke and Matthew offer information beyond that found in Mark. Matthew gives a more elaborate description of how the unnamed disciple drew his sword. Luke has the disciples question Jesus. Granted that the additional material differs, it seems safest to understand their agreement in choosing a verb to be a matter of chance.

Luke 22.50b. Luke and John 18.10 agree that it was the *right* (*dexios*) ear that was cut off of the high priest's servant. Two observations should be made: First, different words for 'ear' are used by Luke (*ous*) and John (*ōtarion*). Second, this item is but one of different pieces of information that Luke and John have that are not found in Mark. For example, Luke also records that Jesus healed the man whose ear was lost; and John knows that Simon Peter wielded the sword and Malchus was the slave who lost his ear.

The mere designation of the ear as the 'right' ear is not a significant agreement in any case;[44] and there is telling evidence that Luke and John may agree merely by chance in giving this detail.[45] It is fairly clear that at 6.6-11 Luke is dependent on Mark 3.1-6. Both evangelists relate the story of how Jesus healed a man with a withered hand. In his version of the incident Luke (6.6, compare Mark 3.1) adds the detail that the withered hand was the man's 'right' one.

Luke 22.51a-c. Factually Luke, Matthew (26.52-54), and John (18.11) all record a rebuke of the disciples by Jesus, but disagree on the words Jesus speaks. The three-way factual agreement is best described as a general narrative agreement,[46] perhaps to be accounted for as reflecting the continued existence and influence of oral tradition (see the discussion in Chapter 5).

Luke 22.52a-b. Osty suggests that Luke and John 18.3, 12 are similar, for in both the crowd is described in a more imposing fashion than in Mark and Matthew.[47] Luke's crowd is awesome because of its composition: chief priests, officers of the Temple, and elders. But John's crowd is impressive because of its size: a detachment of two hundred or six hundred men.[48] This creative suggestion of similarity is not helpful in locating special Lukan material.

Luke 22.53c-d. We have already seen that these lines are without a Markan parallel. Several scholars, however, compare these lines to Johannine thought.

For example, Osty suggests that the *hour* reminds one of John 13.1; 16.4; and 16.21.[49] But comparison of Luke and John shows there is not an agreement between the Gospels here. We saw above that the word *hour* is a Johannine technical term for the Passion, death, resurrection, and ascension of Jesus, and that Luke does not use the word in a set fashion. In fact, Luke's use of *hour* in 53c is dissimilar from John's employment of the term, because it is not the positive hour of Jesus (see John 12.23) but the negative, '*your hour*', in conjunction with *the power of darkness*. A better comparison for the Lukan *hour* mentioned in 53c would be Mark 14.35 ('the hour might pass') or 14.41 ('the hour has come—the Son of Man is betrayed into the hands of sinners'). The implication in both of these verses is that the hour is a less-than-desirable time.[50]

Osty also compares the 'power of darkness' to Johannine language and thought. He suggests *power* is depicted as a metaphysical entity both here and in John 5.27; 10.18; 17.2.[51] He suggests the idea of *darkness* as a realm of evil may be seen here and in John 1.5; 12.46; 1 John 1.5; 2.9, 11; 3.19. Four items undermine the validity of this comparison: First, the word translated 'power' is *exousia*, used fifteen times in Luke and seven times in Acts. It consistently implies the idea of *authority*. Indeed, in Acts 26.18 *exousia* is used in a statement that describes the turning of humanity 'from the power of Satan to God'. Second, since as early as 1.79 the reader of Luke's Gospel has been aware that *darkness* is a metaphorical reference to evil, and at

11.35 *darkness* seems to mean evil per se. Third, a natural comparison of 53c-d can be made with 22.3a and 22.31b where the mention of Satan gave notice that Jesus and his disciples have entered into an ominous time. The line, 'This is your hour, and the power of darkness', brings to mind the malicious intent of Satan and the request of Satan to sift the disciples.[52] Thus, Luke is not an entire stranger to the language and imagery of 53c-d. Fourth, in the context of Jesus' trial, the single line of John closest to 22.53 is 18.20, which has no mention of the 'hour' or 'the power of darkness'. In summary, there is not a strong case for the necessary comparison of 53c-d with Johannine thought.

Luke 22.53d. Luke and John agree in not mentioning a flight of the disciples.[53] Arguments from silence are always weak, but even more so when the agreement may be understood simply in terms of the individual tendencies of both evangelists. With regard to Luke, 'the conduct of Jesus' disciples and friends towards him in Mark can easily be improved on, and Luke improves it'.[54] With regard to John, a careful comparison of the account of the arrest in John and the Synoptic Gospels 'causes us to favor the theory of Johannine independence'.[55] That leaves it possible but unnecessary to posit that Luke was influenced by John.

Luke 22.54a. Luke and John may be compared at this point both generally and specifically. By way of general comparison, the arrest of Jesus comes only at the end of the arrest scene in both Gospels. This agreement is similar to two general narrative 'agreements' noted above in reference to 22.48a-53d compared with John 18.1-11 (Jesus as more thoroughly in control of the events surrounding the arrest) and Luke 22.49a-50b compared with John 18.10 (the blow with the sword prior to the arrest). We will consider these general narrative agreements when we discuss Luke's redactional and compositional technique.

By way of specific comparision, Luke uses two verbs in this line: *syllambanein* and *agein*. One finds *syllambanein* in John 18.12; and *agein* occurs in John 18.13.[56] Close examination does not allow much interpretative weight to this seemingly striking vocabulary 'agreement'. First, neither Luke nor John says anything substantively different from what is said in Mark 14.46 (Jesus was arrested) and Mark 14.53 (the captors led Jesus away). Second, Mark has the verb *syllambanein* (used by both Luke and John)[57] at 14.48 when Jesus asks, 'Have you come out . . . *to capture me?*' Third, when Jesus is led away in Mark 14.53, Mark uses the verb *apagein*, a compound form of the same verb that occurs in Luke and John. When one gathers all the evidence, the agreement between Luke and John does not seem terribly striking. Indeed, the easiest way to account for this agreement is to attribute it to chance[58] (or possibly, although not probably, to the influence of Mark on both).

Luke 22.55a-60b. These lines in Luke may be compared broadly with John's story of Peter's denial in at least three ways. First, 55a and John 18.18 both mention the making of the fire at which Peter warmed himself.[59] Although the words used in each Gospel are different, the idea is the same. One sees that Mark (14.54) and Matthew (26.58) also know there was a fire in the courtyard of the high priest's house; true, they do not mention the making of the fire, but all fires must be started. So, there is a small agreement of Luke and John here. It is offset, however, by an agreement of Luke with Mark and Matthew against John. In the verses mentioned, Luke, Mark, and Matthew say that Peter *sat* at the fire. John says that Peter was *standing*. Overall, Luke's story seems closer to Mark's than to John's.

The second and third comparisons are general narrative agreements and may be considered together: only one woman interrogator appears in Luke and John; and Peter neither invokes a curse on himself nor swears. One may understand these agreements as the results of either a similar narrative technique or the influence of oral tradition. The many differences between John and Luke at this point do not suggest the use of a common written source.[60] Although we will consider these narrative agreements below, it may be helpful at this point to compare John's account of Peter's denials with the versions of the story that appear in Mark and Luke.[61] The reader is requested to look back to pp. 65-67 where John was included (even though there we were comparing only Mark and Luke) precisely so that this might be done.

A careful study of the charts makes it difficult to understand why interpreters, like Perry and Osty,[62] maintain that Luke 22.55-60 is closer to John 18.15-18, 25-27 than to Mark's version of the denials. At the points that may be compared, Luke's story is more like Mark's account than like that of John; and even when one brings into consideration the unparalleled material that John adds,[63] it becomes impossible to suggest that Luke is more like John than like Mark. But some specific verses demand further attention.

Luke 22.60d. Luke agrees with both Matt 26.74 and John 18.27 in mentioning only one cock crow. This is probably the result of either similar narrative techniques or the continued influence of oral tradition alongside and upon the written Gospel. We considered the roots of this agreement above.

Luke 22.62a-b. Luke's *kai exelthōn exō eklausen pikrōs* has an *exact* match in Matt 26.75; Mark's parallel reads, *kai epibalōn eklaien*. It is a complicated task to account for this agreement,[64] but we will undertake this chore when we analyze the special Lukan material in 22.39-71.

Luke 22.64d. Once again one finds an exact verbal parallel for this line in Matthew at 26.68 in the question the mockers pose to Jesus, 'Who is the one who hit you?' (*tis estin ho paisas se*). Mark's story has nothing comparable. This line will also receive attention when we analyze the special Lukan material below.

Luke 22.66a-71e. Taylor cites Buse, agreeing with him, saying that in these verses there is nothing in common between Luke and John.[65] Yet other scholars compare the general narrative presentation of the inquisition scene in Luke and John in at least eight ways:

1. The scene does not portray a formal trial.[66]
2. The hearing is not at night.[67]
3. There are no witnesses against Jesus.[68]
4. Jesus is not silent.[69]
5. The high priest does not tear his robe.[70]
6. There is no statement that Jesus blasphemes.[71]
7. No verdict is pronounced.[72]
8. Jesus is not abused by the Council members.[73]

At best, a series of arguments from silence are advanced here. But examination of the eight so-called similarities shows that they will not bear scrutiny.

First, it is true that neither Luke nor John presents a formal trial. But it seems illegitimate to compare a meeting of and inquisition by the Jewish Assembly (Luke) with the audience of Jesus before the high priest (John).

Second, the questioning of Jesus by the high priest in John does occur at night, for the cock-crow is narrated after the questioning. Even if John's intercalation of the questioning of Jesus into the denials of Peter is designed to portray simultaneous action, the questioning occurs at night.[74]

Third, in light of the first response, it seems illegitimate to speak of witnesses. John's story of a conversation between Jesus and the high priest does not easily allow for them, even if Luke's account does.

Fourth, it is true that Jesus is not silent before either the Assembly or the high priest. But the completely different stories told in 66a-71c and John 18.19-24 render such an observation almost meaningless. Moreover, Jesus does refuse to answer Herod at Luke 23.9, while he is never silent in John.

Fifth, John's story mentions two high priests and so one could have torn a robe. But the high priest does not do the questioning in Luke's story (as he does in Mark and John); indeed, he is not even mentioned in 66a-71c; consequently it is not surprising that Luke does not say he tore his robe. Here the difference between Luke and John is what is noteworthy.

Sixth, there is no statement that Jesus blasphemes in either Luke or John. But, Luke says, 'We have heard it ourselves from his mouth' (71c). The phrase *apo tou stomatos autou* is a Lukanism for *speech*. (At 11.24 a similar phrase [*ek tou stomatos autou*] appears in reference to the speech of Jesus by which the Pharisees hope to entrap him.) Thus, while Luke does not have the Assembly members explicitly charge that Jesus blasphemes, he probably indicates that Jesus said something they considered worthy of condemnation. Furthermore, even though John does not mention blasphemy, Jesus is struck for what he said.

Seventh and eighth, that no verdict is pronounced and that Jesus is not abused *by the Council* is not unusual in John since the Council is not in session. The absence of the verdict in the Assembly meeting is one way in which Luke differs from Mark, but scarcely comparable to the story in John. Moreover, Luke does record that Jesus was abused at both 22.63-65 and 23.11, while John (18.22) indicates that Jesus was slapped when he appeared before Annas.

Luke 22.66b. 66b agrees with Matt 27.1 in using the genitive *tou laou* to qualify similar nouns.[75] Luke uses the noun *to presbyterion*, 'the Assembly of the elders of the people' (consisting of chief priests and scribes). Matthew agrees with Mark 15.1 in mentioning *hoi presbyteroi*, qualifying these men as 'the elders of the people'. This minor agreement between Luke and Matthew in the use of a qualifying genitive does not seem to be significant for locating special Lukan material.

Luke 22.67a-68b. Scholars frequently compare these lines with Matt 26.63 and material found in John outside the Passion account, namely, John 10.24-26.[76] One may first compare Luke and Matt 26.63.

The Question Put to Jesus

Luke: *ei sy ei ho christos, eipon hēmin*
Matt: *hina hēmin eipēs, ei sy ei ho christos,*
     ho huios tou theou

The Answer Jesus Gives

Luke: *ean hymin eipō, ou mē pisteusete*
Matt: *sy eipas*

Some of the words employed by Luke and Matthew are similar, especially the clause, 'If you are the Christ, tell us'. But, there are marked differences as well. First, the demand in Matthew is made by the high priest alone, whereas in Luke it is made by the Assembly of the elders. Second, Matthew casts the demand in the form of an indirect question, whereas the question is put directly in Luke. Moreover, Matthew includes here the title 'the Son of God'. Third, the response of Jesus is completely different.[77] So, no significant agreement between Luke and Matthew appears here.

One may next compare these portions of Luke with John 10.24-26.

The Question Put to Jesus

Luke: *ei sy ei ho christos, eipon hēmin*
John: *ei sy ei ho christos, eipe hēmin parrēsia*

The Answer Jesus Gives

Luke: *ean hymin eipō, ou mē pisteusēte*
John: *eipon hymin kai ou pisteuete*

Two observations may be made: First, the lines being viewed from John 10 are but part of an elaborate, but typical, Johannine conversation between Jesus and the Jews. Second, the remarkable similarity between these lines in Luke and John makes it likely that Luke and John had a similar tradition available to them. We will need to give careful attention to 67a-e in our analysis of the special Lukan Passion Narrative material.

Scholars often compare 67c-68b with John 18.23.[78] In both places Jesus is said to give an evasive answer:

Luke	John
If I tell you,	If I have spoken ill,
you will not believe;	testify to the wrong;
and if I ask you,	but if correctly,
you will not answer.	why do you hit me?

Klein observes that the answer in Luke could be drawn from a source common to Luke and John or it may be a Lukan construction.[79] It seems better to understand this so-called agreement as the independent result of a similar narrative technique for three reasons. First, the statement in John ends in a question; in Luke it does not. Second, the context in which Jesus makes these statements is different. In Luke Jesus speaks to the Council, but in John he speaks to the high priest and some officers. Third, we saw above that John 10.24-26 forms a much closer parallel to the words spoken by Jesus in 67c-e.

Luke 22.69. The scholarly consensus contends that this line of Luke's Passion Narrative reflects Luke's use of Mark's Passion account.[80] Luke and Matthew agree here, however, in two ways that differ from Mark: in the addition of a temporal reference in the Son of Man saying and in basic word order.[81]

At Mark 14.62 the high priest's question is 'Are you the Christ, the Son of the blessed one?' Jesus answers, 'I am; and you will see the Son of Man sitting at the right hand of power and coming with the clouds of heaven'.

In the question posed by the Assembly, Luke does not have 'the Son of the blessed one'. In the answer Luke has the statement in 67c-68b rather than 'I am'. Then he has Jesus continue, 'From now on (*apo tou nyn*) the Son of Man will be sitting at the right hand of the power of God'.

In the question Matthew has 'the Son of God' instead of 'the Son of the blessed one'. In the answer Matthew has 'You say yourself' instead of 'I am'. Then, he has Jesus continue, 'But I say to you, hereafter *(ap' arti)* you will see the Son of Man sitting at the right hand of power and coming upon the clouds of heaven'.

We examined a similar agreement between Luke 22.18b and Matt 26.29 above. There we saw that Luke and Matthew agreed in adding a temporal qualifer to a line they knew from Mark. That agreement was the result of both evangelists' *making sense* of Mark's statement in a similar fashion. The same type of alteration seems to take place here.

Mark, Luke, and Matthew all mention the Son of Man sitting in an exalted position, but Luke and Matthew agree in having a different word order from Mark:

> Mark: *ton huion tou anthrōpou ek dexiōn kathēmenon tēs dynameōs*
> Luke: *ho huios tou anthrōpou kathēmenos ek dexiōn tēs dynameōs*
> *tou theou*
> Matt: *ton huion tou anthrōpou kathēmenon ek dexiōn tēs dynameōs*

This agreement between Luke and Matthew is a stylistic improvement. Despite this similarity, Matthew's statement is closer to Mark's than to Luke's, for the 'Son of Man' is the subject in Luke, but the object in Mark and Matthew; and Luke clarifies *tēs dynameōs* with *tou theou*, but Mark and Matthew do not.

Comparison of the three accounts shows that while Matthew's version is somewhat different from Mark's, it is more like Mark's account than like Luke's. The minor agreements between Luke and Matthew at this point are much less striking than the obvious similarities between Matthew and Mark.

Luke 22.70d. A portion of the answer given by Jesus in this line is compared to Matt 26.64. Luke has Jesus say, 'You yourselves say . . . ' *(hymeis legete)*; and Matthew reads, 'You say yourself' *(sy eipas)*.[82] These lines differ in at least three ways: First, Luke has Jesus address the Assembly as a group, thus the plural forms; but Matthew has Jesus speak directly to the high priest, thus the singular forms. Second, Luke and Matthew use different verbs (Luke: *legein*; Matt: *eirein*). Third, the words, *hymeis legete*, are but part of a larger statement in Luke *(hymeis legete hoti egō eimi)*; Matthew's 'you say' is the whole answer. In summary, the agreement between 70b and Matt 26.64 is not significant.

Conclusions. From this survey, we have identified certain lines in Luke 22.39-71 as material representing a significant agreement of Luke with Matthew or John against Mark. These are 22.42a-d, 48a-b, 51a-c, 60d, 62a-b, 64d, 67a-e. We also recognized an agreement between Luke and John in narrative order concerning the blow with the sword occurring prior to the arrest of Jesus (22.49a-50b).

3. *Material Forming a Story Sequence Different from that of Mark*
The primary concern here is with thought patterns and ideas in what is sometimes known as *transposed* sentences and lines.

Luke 22.39a-b. Some scholars reckon 39a-b to be a transposition of Markan material.[83] Examination of this understanding does not support its validity. The notice that Jesus and his disciples went out to the 'Mount of Olives' at the conclusion of their meal appears in Luke 22.39 and Mark 14.26. Later in his account Mark (14.32) records that the band went to 'Gethsemane'. Between Mark 14.26 and 14.32 one finds (a) Jesus' quotation of Zech 13.7 and his prophecies that accompany that scripture (14.27-28); (b) Peter's boast (14.29); (c) Jesus' prediction that Peter will deny him three times (14.30); and (d) the claim by Peter and the other disciples that they will die with Jesus rather than abandon him (14.31). Luke's story includes no information that matches Mark 14.27-29, and Luke's version of Mark 14.31, 30 is in 22.33a-34d, transposed into the setting of the Last Supper. Leaving aside these lines, one finds that 22.39a-b is not transposed material.

Luke 22.40b. Finegan understands the command by Jesus in 40b to come from Mark 14.38.[84] Yet, as we saw above, a closer match for Mark's text is 22.46c, so that 22.40b is material without a parallel in Mark's text—not a transposition of Markan material.[85]

Luke 22.54a-71c. Before considering specific differences, it is helpful to summarize the issue of the order of Peter's denials, the mockery, and the Jewish interrogation thus:

Mark	Luke
Trial (14.53-64)	Denials (22.54-62)
Mockery (14.65)	Mockery (22.63-65)
Denials (14.66-72)	Examination (22.66-71)

Luke 22.54a. In Mark (14.46) the unnamed disciple strikes with the sword (14.47) and Jesus confronts those who have come to arrest him *after* he has been arrested (14.46). The blow with the sword is apparently an effort to liberate Jesus. But in Luke the unnamed disciple wields his weapon (22.50a-b) and Jesus speaks (22.51a-53d) *before* the arrest (54a). The use of the sword in Luke seems aimed at preventing the arrest (see 22.49a-b). Luke's order of events is clearly different from that of Mark.[86]

Luke 22.56a-62b (minus 61a).[87] In Luke's Passion Narrative Peter's three denials of Jesus come *before* the Assembly of the elders of the people examines Jesus (66-71c). In Mark's account Peter's denials (14.66-72) follow the trial of Jesus by the chief priests and the council.[88] The material in 56a-62b is clearly in an order different from that of Mark.[89]

Luke 22.57b and 60b. The variation in sequence in 56a-62b is itself striking, but further comparison of this block of material with Mark's account shows an internal difference in order.

Peter's first answer:

Mark:	*oute oida oute epistamai sy ti legeis* 'I neither know nor understand *what you are talking about*'
Luke:	*ouk oida auton* 'I don't know *him*'

Peter's third answer:

Mark:	*ouk oida ton anthropon touton hon legete* 'I don't know *this man of whom you speak*'
Luke:	*ouk oida ho legeis* 'I don't know *what you are talking about*'

In summary, Mark's first answer equals Luke's third and vice versa.

Luke 22.63a-64c. In the larger unit 63a-65, we saw that 64d-65 has no parallel in Mark, although 64d has an exact verbal parallel in Matt 26.68. As part of this complexity, the origin of 63a-64c must be studied. At this point we wish only to recognize that although in both Mark and Luke Jesus is mocked prior to being handed over to Pilate, the mocking occurs at different points in their story sequences. In Mark Jesus is mocked *after* the trial by the Jewish officials. In Luke Jesus is mocked *prior to* his being called before the Jewish Assembly.[90]

Luke 22.67a-71c.[91] The questioning of Jesus by the Jewish authorities obviously takes place in different positions in the narrative sequences of Mark and Luke. But further comparison reveals an internal difference. In Mark 14.61 the high priest asks Jesus, 'Are you the Christ, the Son of the blessed one?' and Jesus answers, 'I am; and you will see the Son of Man sitting at the right hand of power and coming with the clouds of heaven' (14.62). In Luke 22.67a-b the Assembly demands of Jesus, 'If you are the Christ tell us!' and Jesus answers with the statement in 67d-68b. He then continues in 22.69, 'Yet, from now on the Son of Man will be sitting at the right hand of the power of God'; subsequently the Assembly poses a question, 'Are you then the Son of God?' (22.70a-b).

In summary, in Mark's story, the Son of Man saying follows the two-part question, 'Are you the Christ, the Son of the blessed one?' But in Luke's story, the Son of Man saying appears between the demand, 'If you are the Christ, tell us!' and the question, 'Are you then the Son of God?'[92]

Conclusions. From this survey we have identified certain sentences and lines in Luke 22.39-71 as material forming a story sequence different from that of Mark. This material is 22.54a, 56a-62b (minus 61a), 63a-64c, 67a-71c. We saw internal differences between Luke and Mark in two of the larger units of 'transposed' material. These double differences are in 56a-62b at lines 57b and 60b and in 67a-71c at lines 69 and 70b. We recognized once more the complicated nature of 39a-b and 40b.

4. *Material with a Low Level of Verbal Correspondence between Luke and Mark*
The focus is on the *thought* and *content* of the lines that we have found to be prominent in our three previous surveys, as in the similar section of Chapter 2.

Luke 22.39a-b. We argued above that these lines are best understood as special Lukan Passion Narrative material. But we also saw that 39a-b may be compared to both Mark 14.26 and Mark 14.32. Eight of Luke's seventeen words in 39a (47%) are matched by words in Mark; but 39b, the mention of the disciples following Jesus, has no vocabulary parallel in Mark. Yet this line is included in this comparison since Mark 14.26 and 14.32 refer to Jesus and the disciples as a group.

Luke 22.40a-46c. This section of the Lukan Passion Narrative seems to contain a variety of material. 40a is similar to Mark 14.32. 40b is without a Markan parallel, but the vocabulary is similar to both 46c and its parallel, Mark 14.38. 41a-42d is similar to Mark 14.35-36; but there are noticeable agreements between 42a-d and Matt 26.39, 42 against Mark. 45a-46c is similar to Mark 14.37-38.

Line	Number of Words	Markan Matches
40a	7	3
40b	5	5
41a	5	1
41b	3	0
41c	5	2
42a	4	2
42b	6	6
42c	5	0
42d	4	1
45a	5	0
45b	4	1
45c	6	2
46a	3	1
46b	2	1
46c	7	6

31 of Luke's 71 words, or 44%, are matched by words in Mark. After recognizing the apparent variety of the material in this section, it is surprising to find even this level of verbal correspondence between Luke and Mark.

Luke 22.54a-62b. We saw that 54a is in a different position in Luke's account from the place it occupies in Mark's Passion Narrative (14.53-54). The same is true of 56a-62b (Mark 14.66-72). We also saw that 61a presents an idea that has no match in Mark's story.

Line	Number of Words	Markan Matches
54a	4	1
54b	7	3
54c	5	4
55a	7	2
55b	2	0
55c	5	1
56a	5	2
56b	4	3
56c	4	1
56d	5	2
57a	4	4
57b	4	2
58a	7	3
58b	5	3
58c	4	2
58d	3	0
59a	5	1
59b	4	1
59c	7	1
59d	4	4
60a	4	2
60b	5	4
60c	5	1
60d	2	2
61a	7	0
61b	8	4
61c	3	3
61d	5	4
61e	3	3
62a	3	1
62b	2	1

65 of Luke's 142 words, or 46%, have Markan matches. If one does not include 61a in the comparison, the agreement is 48%.

Luke 22.63a-64c. We saw that the mocking of Jesus occurs in a different position in Luke's narrative sequence from the order found in Mark's account (14.65). These lines form a part of the larger unit 63a-65. We saw that 64d-65 has no Markan parallel; but we also saw that 64d has an exact verbal parallel in Matt 26.68.

Line	Number of Words	Markan Matches
63a	8	2
63b	1	0
64a	3	2
64b	2	1
64c	1	1

6 of Luke's 15 words, or 40%, are matched by words in Mark.

Luke 22.67a-71c. The questioning of Jesus by the Jewish authorities occurs in Luke's narrative order in a different sequence from that of Mark (14.61-64a); there seems to be a variety of material in these lines. The larger unit 67a-68b has no simple Markan parallel, but one may compare 67a-c with Mark 14.61-62. We saw that 67a-e is similar to material found in John's Gospel outside the Passion Narrative of that Gospel. In its present position 22.69 is in a different position from that which it occupies in Mark. Finally, we saw that 70a-d has no simple Markan parallel, but the lines may be compared to Mark 14.61.

Line	Number of Words	Markan Matches
67a	6	5
67b	2	0
67c	3	1
67d	3	0
67e	3	0
68a	3	0
68b	3	0
69	16	9
70a	3	0
70b	7	3
70c	5	2
70d	5	2
71a	3	0
71b	5	4
71c	7	1

27 of Luke's 74 words, or 36%, are matched by words in Mark. If one does not bring the unparalleled material in 67d-68b into this comparison, 27 of Luke's 62 words, or 44%, have Markan matches.

Summary

Luke	Mark	Level of Agreement
22.39a-b	14.26, 32	47%
22.40a-46c	14.32, 35-38	44%
22.54-62b	14.53-54, 66-72	46%
(minus 61a)		(48%)
22.63a-64c	14.65	40%
22.67a-71c	14.61-64a	36%
(minus 67c-68b)		(44%)

Conclusions. There are at least two ways in which one may view the results of this survey: either by including or excluding the obviously unparalleled material. We will set aside the unparalleled material for the purposes of this discussion. Doing so, one finds one item to be particularly striking, namely, the homogeneity of this unit. The average percentage of agreement for the five units is remarkably consistent. In Chapter 5 we will return to certain of the findings of this survey.

5. Material Containing So-called Telltale Lukan Language

Using the results of other earlier studies here, we will go further to suggest that certain words are typical of Luke.[93] To do this we shall prefix a general section that lists words, with brief explanations, that appear to be preferred Lukan vocabulary.

A list of Lukan words and terms. At least 21 words in 22.39-71 in one way or another imply the hand of Luke. In the order of their appearance, they are:

1. *Withdrew* (41a). Luke uses the verb *apospan* 3 of the 4 times that it is used in the NT. Luke uses this verb only for people. See Acts 20.30; 21.1.

2. *About* (41b). Luke commonly uses *hōsei* to qualify statements. The word occurs 9 times in Luke and 7 times in Acts, whereas Mark uses the word once and Matthew 3 times.[94]

3. *Arose* (45a)/*get up* (46c). The use of *anistanai* and the balanced employment of the word in 45a and 46c are described as Lukan usage and style.[95] The verb occurs 29 times in Luke and 36 in Acts, but only 17 times in Mark and 6 in Matthew.

4. *The one called* (47c). The participial phrase *ho legomenos* occurs at 22.1 and Acts 6.9.[96] This construction occurs frequently in Matthew but never in Mark.

5. *Drew near* (47d). The word *engizein* occurs 18 times in Luke and 6 in Acts, but only 3 times in Mark and 7 in Matthew.[97]

6. *Right* (50b). In 6.6 Luke adds *dexios* ('right') to the mention of the withered hand of a man whom Jesus healed. Luke's tendency is to specify.[98]

7. *Chief priests, officers of the Temple* [*strategos*], *and elders* (52b). This is the only time these three groups are named together. Luke does have the chief priests with the officers at 22.4; Acts 4.1; 5.24; and the elders with the chief priests and scribes at 9.22; 20.1. He is the only NT author who uses the word *strategos*, twice in the Gospel and 8 times in Acts.

8. *Stretch out your hand* (53b). Luke uses the verb *ekteinein* 6 times: 3 times in Luke and 3 times in Acts. In 5 of the 6 uses it is coupled with 'hand' in an idiom meaning 'to take hold of' or 'touch.'

9. *Arrest* (54a). *Syllambanein* occurs in Mark, Matthew, and John once each. It appears in Luke 7 times and in Acts 4 times. In Luke the verb means 'conceive', 'help', or 'arrest'. But, in Acts, all four employments mean 'arrest'.

10. *Stare at* (56c). Luke alone uses *atenizein* in the NT (4.20; 22.54; Acts 1.10; 7.55). The use of the verb at the point where Mark has *emblepein* is said to be a vivification of language and is attributed to Luke's story-telling style.[99]

11. *Woman* (57b). The vocative address *gynai* is described by Schneider as revealing Luke's hand,[100] since Mark never employs this form. It occurs here and in unparalleled material at 13.12.

12. *After a little while* (58a). The temporal phrase *meta brachy* appears here and at Acts 5.34; 27.28[101]—exclusively Lukan in NT as a temporal usage.

13. *Immediately* (60c). Luke uses *parachrēma* 10 times in the Gospel and 6 times in Acts. It does not appear in Mark, and Matthew has it only twice. At four points where Mark has *euthys*, Luke uses *parachrēma*.[102]

14. *While he was still speaking* (60c). The genitive absolute phrase *eti lalountos autou* is found here and at 8.49; 22.47; Acts 10.44.

15. *Beat* (63b). The verb *derein* appears 5 times in Luke and 3 times in Acts. While the verb is in Mark 3 times and in Matthew once, in 4 of the 5 usages in Luke the word is unparalleled.[103]

16. *Many other things* (65). The construction, *hetera polla* + a participle, appears here and at 3.18. It is called Lukan.[104] Even

heteros is typical of Luke,[105] who uses the word 34 times in the Gospel and 18 times in Acts—whereas Matthew uses *heteros* 9 times and Mark never.

17. *When* (66a). Luke is fond of using *hōs* to mean 'when',[106] using the words in this manner 19 times in the Gospel and 29 times in Acts.

18. *People* (66a). *Laos* is called typical Lukan vocabulary.[107] It occurs 37 times in Luke and 47 times in Acts, but only 3 times in Mark and 14 in Matthew.

19. *Ask* (68a). The verb *erōtan* is typical Lukan vocabulary,[108] occurring 16 times in Luke and 7 in Acts, but only 3 times in Mark and 4 in Matthew.

20. *They all said* (70a). The hyperbolic phrase *eipan de pantes* is referred to as a Lukanism.[109] *Eipan* occurs 27 times in Luke and 18 in Acts, whereas Mark uses the verb 7 times and Matthew 14. In the Passion Luke uses *eipan* 6 times while Mark never uses the verb. Furthermore, Luke alone uses *eipan de* (Luke 18.26; Acts 21.20).[110] Luke is also fond of *pas* (*pantes*), using it 152 times compared with Mark's 67. In the Passion Narrative Luke employs *pas* 27 times and Mark 15.[111]

21. *From his mouth* (71c). The word *stoma*, which never appears in Mark, occurs 9 times in Luke and 12 times in Acts. The phrase 'something out of one's mouth' frequently appears in Luke (and consistently in Acts) as a designation for one's speech.

Language suggestive of Lukan thought. We turn now to what is the greater concern, the words and phrases that seem particularly suggestive of Lukan thought and concerns, following the pattern employed in Chapter 2.

Luke 22.39a—'*according to his custom*'. The word *ethos*, meaning *custom*, appears 3 times in Luke and 6 times in Acts. Here it is in a prepositional phrase with *kata*, just as it is at Acts 26.3. Scholars debate whether *ethos* is typical of Luke or his alleged source 'L',[112] but the use of the word in Acts suggests that it is characteristic of Luke.

By speaking of the 'custom' of Jesus, Luke probably refers to his statement at 21.37 that at night Jesus lodged on the Mount of Olives. But the other uses of *ethos* suggest that Luke probably means to indicate that Jesus was doing that which was normal for him, that is, in accordance with the basic governing principle of his life. See Luke 1.9; 2.42; and Acts 6.14; 15.1; 16.21; 25.16; 26.3; 28.17.

Luke 22.39b—'his disciples followed him'. If Jesus is depicted as acting according to custom, so are the disciples. Luke uses *akolouthein* 18 times in the Gospel to refer to the activity of the disciples,[113] who (since 5.11) have been 'followers' of Jesus. Luke probably means to indicate more followers here than the (eleven) apostles, for in 22.49a he will refer to them as 'those around' Jesus. At Acts 13.13 Luke refers to the companions of Paul as *hoi peri Paulon*, so that the phrase 'those around' is a Lukanism for 'followers'.[114]

Luke 22.40a—'he reached the place'. Only Luke among the Synoptic Gospels uses *ginesthai* + *epi* (see 3.2; 24.22; Acts 21.35). Here, the object of *epi* is *topos*, 'place', a common word in Luke, and used to name the location where Jesus prays (as he is about to do here) in 4.42 and 11.1.

Luke 22.40b, 41c, 45a, 46c—'pray/prayer'. Throughout his Gospel Luke depicts Jesus as regularly at prayer. Only in Luke (11.1) do the disciples ask Jesus during his ministry to teach them to pray.[115] Thus, the repeated references to prayer in this section are consistent with the Lukan interest in prayer.[116]

Luke 22.40b, 46c—'temptation'. Luke distinguishes himself among the evangelists in his use of *peirasmos* (see above p. 46)—especially as an eschatological struggle against the evil one. That same sense seems present in the urgency of Jesus' command in these lines.

Luke 22.41c—'going to his knees'. The phrase *theis ta gonata* is a typical Lukan way of describing the position in which persons pray, particularly significant prayers. Stephen goes to his knees in his death prayer (Acts 7.60); Peter does so before raising Tabitha from the dead (Acts 9.40); as does Paul when he parts from the elders at Miletus (Acts 20.36); and the disciples at Tyre bidding farewell to Paul (Acts 21.5).

Luke 22.42a—'have it in mind'. The verb *boulesthai* is used only once in Luke (10.22 of the Son *choosing* to reveal the Father), but 14 times in Acts, where it is related to the noun *boulē* ('plan'). At Acts 2.23, one reads about 'the plan of God'.

Luke 22.43c—'will'. The word *thelēma* is another word Luke uses for the 'plan' of God. The significance of this word becomes clear in the three times it appears in Acts: God's will (13.22), the Lord's will (21.14), and God's will (22.14).

Luke 22.45c—'because of their sad condition'. This explanation of why the disciples slept (unique among the Gospels) is similar to Luke's explanation of why the disciples did not or could not believe at 24.41, 'because of their joy' (*apo tēs charas*).[117] These explanations are often thought to be part of Luke's tendency to improve the image of the disciples.[118] But it may be that here Luke intends to contrast the behavior of the disciples with that of Jesus.[119]

Luke 22.48b—'Son of Man'. One sees clearly in 9.44; 18.32; 22.22; and 24.7 that in one way 'Son of Man' was a fixed term for Luke,[120] namely, in the Passion predictions to refer to Jesus' forthcoming suffering and death. But it may not be possible to say exactly how he understood this term, since its use was set in the Gospel tradition prior to his writing.[121] Luke, however, may have even *introduced the title himself* (here; 6.22; 12.8). In the two earlier instances, Son of Man appears in Q material where Matthew does not have the title (Luke 6.22 par Matt 5.11; Luke 12.8 par Matt 10.32). At 6.22 the disciples are blessed when they suffer because of their association with the Son of Man (Jesus?). At 12.8 Luke has Jesus promise that the Son of Man (probably another) will acknowledge those who acknowledge him (Jesus). Here, in the statement to Judas, Luke clearly identifies Jesus as the Son of Man, particularly in his role as the one who fulfills the Passion predictions (see 22.37).

Luke 22.49b—'Lord'. Luke has the disciples address Jesus as 'Lord' (*kyrie*) throughout the Gospel. In the Passion Narrative Peter addresses Jesus as 'Lord' at 22.33. Then, the twelve address Jesus as 'Lord' when they tell him they have two swords (22.38b). In these instances, the disciples are portrayed as recognizing the leadership of Jesus.

Luke 22.51b—'Let it be!'. These words translate the imperative, *eate*—from the verb *ean*, used twice in the Gospel and 7 times in Acts. The other occurrence of the verb in the Gospel is at 4.41, where

Jesus exercises his authority over the forces of evil by not *allowing* the demoniacs to speak. A similar show of authority is portrayed here in Jesus' issuing this command.

Luke 22.51d—'touching'. This is a typical act of Jesus in Luke.[122] Luke uses the verb *aptesthai* 13 times in the Gospel. 5 of the uses are instances where others touch Jesus and are healed (6.14; 8.44, 45, 46, 47). 4 of the uses are instances where Jesus touches someone and produces a miracle of healing (5.13; 7.14; 18.15; 22.51).

Luke 22.51e—'healed'. Luke is particularly fond of the verb *iasthai*: 11 times in the Gospel and 4 times in Acts. (Mark uses the verb once and Matthew has it 4 times.) Moreover, the act of healing the man whose ear was cut off is an incident consistent with Jesus' activity in the rest of Luke. This particular healing gives evidence that Jesus was not powerless at the time of his arrest,[123] rather, he has the same authority he has exercised throughout the course of his ministry.

Luke 22.53c-d—'hour . . . power of darkness'. Luke sometimes uses language such as that found in these lines (above pp. 75-76), especially as regards the power of Satan (see Acts 26.18).

Luke 22.61a—'the Lord'. 'Lord' is the most frequently used title for Jesus in the Gospel and Acts.[124] 16 times in Luke Jesus is called *ho kyrios* in the narrative portions of the Gospel, compared to only once each in Mark and Matthew. Since *ho kyrios* appears throughout Acts, this title is probably the best clue to perceiving Luke's own understanding of Jesus,[125] using a title current in his day.

Luke 22.61a—'turned'. Luke uses the verb *strephein* 7 times in the Gospel (7.9, 44; 9.55; 10.23; 14.25; 22.61; 23.28) and 3 times in Acts. Although the word can simply mean physical turning toward someone or something, the only subject of this verb in Luke's Gospel is Jesus. Furthermore, the theological importance of this verb may be detected by observing the three uses of *strephein* in Acts. At 7.39 the fathers of Israel are said to have refused to obey God and to have *turned* to Egypt. Then at 7.42, one reads that *God turned and gave them over* to the worship of the host of heaven. Finally, at Acts 13.46, after Paul and Barnabas are reviled by certain Jews, they say, 'Behold! we *turn* to the Gentiles'. Notice that when Jesus *turns*, the verb leads to another verb (*look*). In Acts God alone turns and then does something else. Plausibly, then, *to turn and act* is to act positively with regard to the will of God, and here Jesus' *turning* to Peter may be significant activity in the planned way of God.

Luke 22.61b—*'saying'*. Luke uses *rēma* 19 times in the Gospel and 14 times in Acts, whereas Mark uses it twice and Matthew 5 times. Here the word seemingly signifies the prophetic speech of Jesus as also at 24.8 and at Acts 11.16 (the same phrase as here). The phrase calls to the readers' attention the certain dependability of what Jesus says and so emphasizes Jesus' authority.

Luke 22.62b—*'wept'*. Luke uses the verb *klaiein* 10 times in the Gospel and 3 times in Acts. The verb indicates crying expressive of earnest remorse, as in Luke 7.38 where the woman who was a sinner wept, wetting Jesus' feet. Thus, in the present context, one should probably understand the verb to indicate *repentance*.[126]

Luke 22.69—*'from now on'*. This frequent Lukan phrase (5 times in Luke, once in Acts; see p. 45 above) marks a turning point in the story orienting the reader toward the ensuing narrative events.[127] It emphasizes the eschatological nature of the time and events.

Conclusions. In this survey we have discussed so-called Lukan language in two ways: first, a list of twenty-one preferred Lukan vocabulary items; second, an examination of words/phrases expressive of Lukan thought and concerns. By way of evaluation, every portion of 22.39-71 contains language that is characteristic of the evangelist, Luke. The items studied in the second portion may be grouped under five headings:

(1) *Jesus in authority*: 'according to his custom' (39a); 'Lord' (49b); 'Let it be!' (51b); 'touching' (51d); 'healed' (51e); 'the Lord' (61a); 'saying' (61b).

(2) *the plan of God*: 'have it in mind' (42a); 'will' (42c); 'Son of Man' (48b); 'turned' (61a).

(3) *eschatology*: 'temptation' (40b and 46c); 'hour' (53c); 'power of darkness' (53d); 'from now on' (69).

(4) *prayer*: 'he reached the place' (40a); 'pray' (40b, 41c, 46c); 'prayer' (45a); 'going to his knees' (41c).

(5) *information about the disciples*: 'his disciples followed him' (39b); 'because of their sad condition' (45c); and 'wept' (62a).

These observations become useful in Chapter 5 in analyzing the special Lukan Passion Narrative material in 22.39-71.

The Scope of the Special Lukan Passion Narrative Material in Luke 22.39-71

We are now prepared to suggest what portions of vv. 39-71 are special Lukan material. The strictest definition allows only those Lukan sentences and lines completely different from the material in Mark's Passion Narrative to be designated as *special Lukan material*. Under this definition come 22.39a-b, 40b, 48a-b, 49a-b, 51a-c, 51d-e, 52b, 53c-d, 61a, 64d-65, 66a-68b, 70a-d. But, because of the thorough agreement between Luke and Matthew against Mark at certain points, one should also include 42a-d and 62a-b.

There are also, however, portions of Luke's account that are similar to material in Mark but are so thoroughly blended with special Lukan material that they become different from their Markan parallels. These lines are 63a-64c, 69, 71a-c. So it is perhaps best to consider 22.39a-b, 40b, 42a-d, 48a-b, 49a-b, 51a-c, 51d-e, 52b, 53c-d, 61a, 62a-b, 63a-65, 66a-71c as special Lukan Passion Narrative material; although, again, a final decision about the *scope* of the special Lukan Passion Narrative material will be possible only after a consideration of the *origin* of the various lines in the list. These lines will receive attention in Chapter 5 as we attempt to understand the origin and purpose of the special Lukan material in 22.39-71. Once more, in order to see this material printed out consecutively, the reader should turn to Chapter 6.

Chapter 5

ANALYSIS OF THE SPECIAL LUKAN PASSION NARRATIVE MATERIAL IN LUKE 22.39-71

As in Chapter 3 we will first consider the *origin* of this material and then the *purpose*.

The Origin of the Material

Through analysis of the special material in 22.39-71, we again see that Luke worked in a variety of ways in order to produce this section of his Passion account.

Luke 22.39a-b. Luke has redacted Mark 14.26 (*departs* from upstairs room to Mount of Olives) and 14.32 (*goes* to Gethsemane), transposing or deleting material in between.[1] The result is a re-focus centered on Jesus' action (according to his custom) with the disciples only following.[2] This shift is consistent with the emphasis that we saw Luke expressing in 22.1-38, i.e. Jesus acts authoritatively in approaching his Passion.[3]

Luke 22.40b. This line has no match in Mark's Passion, but it is similar to 22.46c, which does match Mark 14.38 exactly. While 40b is probably best understood as Luke's redactional composition based on the model of 46c/Mark 14.38,[4] one should distinguish 40b from 46c and Mark 14.38. 40b indicates what the *content* of the disciples' prayer is to be, while 46c and Mark 14.38 indicate the *purpose* of their prayer.[5]

By composing 40b, Luke created an *inclusio* (40b and 46c) that frames the prayer of Jesus in 22.42a-d. This frame seems to provide commentary upon that prayer, prompting the reader to understand that the content of Jesus' prayer was that he should not enter into temptation. Thus, the temptation would be to do his own will instead of God's. Moreover, one may understand that the activity of praying was the weapon that Jesus employed in order that he might not enter into temptation.

Luke 22.42a-d. Even though on the whole Matthew is much closer to Mark than to Luke in this section,[6] there are significant agreements between Matthew and Luke in the prayer uttered by Jesus before his arrest. These agreements are probably the result of oral tradition,[7] because there remain striking differences—scarcely the sign of a written common tradition. Also, among the points of agreement between Luke and Matthew are the use of the vocative *pater*, 'Father', and of a similar phrase about God's will (Luke: *mē to thelēma mou alla to son ginesthō*; and Matt: *genēthētō to thelēma sou*). The *pater* is parallelled in both the respective forms of the Lord's Prayer and the phrase in Matthew's form.[8]

Probably an oral tradition of the prayer Jesus uttered before he died existed in the first century, even after the pre-Markan and Markan moves to write down the tradition (Heb 5.7 may be a sign of this). The wording of the prayer was influenced by the oral recitation of the Lord's Prayer or vice versa.[9]

Luke 22.48a-b. Although Luke and Matt 26.50 agree *that Jesus confronted Judas*, the form of Jesus' statement differs as does the respective course of events surrounding the saying. Matthew's account follows Mark's story almost exactly with the exception of the inclusion of Jesus' speaking to Judas. The differences between Luke and Matthew do not suggest a common written source. Matthew's close agreement with Mark and Luke's disagreement with Mark's order make it unlikely that independently each evangelist simply added a Judas saying to the Markan material, working totally from his own reflective imagination. Probably independently Luke and Matthew reflect the influence of oral tradition. It would have been a natural tendency in the re-*telling* of the Passion story to declare that Jesus said something to Judas, and each evangelist may have filled in the statement. The phrasing of Jesus' saying in each Gospel reflects the respective evangelists' outlook: Matt 26.50a is described by D.P. Senior as 'characteristically Matthaean' in vocabulary and christology.[10] Luke introduces 'the Son of Man' here as he does at 6.22 and 12.8, and his wording may be influenced by the Passion predictions, especially 22.22.

Luke 22.49a-b and 51a-c.[11] In 51a-c Luke agrees with Matthew (26.52-54) and John (18.11) in having Jesus rebuke his disciples after one of them had struck the servant of the high priest with a sword. The forms of the rebuke are so different that one should not understand the evangelists to depend upon a common written tradition. Rather, in the re-*telling* of the story of the arrest of Jesus, oral tradition probably developed in such a way that it became known *that* Jesus rebuked his disciples.

Three factors make it likely that Luke himself composed the particular form of the rebuke found in 51a-c. First, the verb *ean* is highly characteristic of Luke. Second, the rebuke here is reminiscent of the rebuke composed by Luke at 22.38d when the disciples boasted they had two swords.[12] Third, the general pattern of Jesus rebuking the disciples goes back as far as 9.52-56, a scene without counterpart in the other Gospels.[13] Luke 9.51 is the point in Luke's Gospel where one learns Jesus deliberately set a course toward Jerusalem:[14] coming to a Samaritan village, he sent his messengers ahead, but the villagers refused to receive them because Jesus was going to Jerusalem. James and John asked whether they should call down fire from heaven to consume the Samaritans, and Jesus rebuked them. This brief story is similar to the information in 22.49a-b, 51a-c. Viewing 22.49a-b and 9.54 together, one sees that 49a-b is peculiar to Luke's Passion Narrative. In 49a and in 9.54, the disciples *see* (*idontes*) what is taking place; then they question Jesus calling him 'Lord' (*kyrie*); finally, they ask, in 49b and 9.54, whether they are to act in order to bring retribution upon those who have set themselves in opposition to Jesus. Comparing 9.55 and 22.51a-c, one is only told *that* Jesus rebuked his disciples at 9.55, while 51a-c has the actual rebuke.

In summary, it was argued above that 51a-c is a Lukan composition filling in the oral tradition that Jesus rebuked his disciples when one of them used a sword at the time of his arrest. We may now suggest that 49a-b is also a Lukan composition, not from oral tradition, but based upon a pattern of thought like that in 9.54-55. Luke knew from Mark (and oral tradition) that a disciple assaulted the servant of the high priest at the time of the arrest of Jesus. Luke added the detail about the ear being the right one. He filled in the wording of a rebuke and composed 49a-b as an introduction to the 'sword scene', perhaps using 9.54-55 as a model.[15] We will consider Luke's purpose for working in this fashion below, but one gains insight for that consideration by analyzing the remaining portion of v. 51.

Luke 22.51d-e. After Jesus rebuked his disciples, he healed the man who suffered the ear injury. The detail is unmatched in the other Gospels and there is no reason for omission were it known to their authors. While it is possible to attribute this information to a source,[16] most scholars plausibly contend that the lines come from Luke's own composition. First, the healing is consistent with Luke's style as a story-teller.[17] Second, the healing serves an apologetic motif: (a) that Jesus shunned violence[18] and/or (b) that Jesus was 'the great physician'.[19] Third, as seen above, the vocabulary used to describe Jesus' activity is typical of Luke. Fourth, the healing serves a theological motive: (a) that Jesus brings salvation[20] and/or (b) that Jesus refused to yield to temptation and interfere with the arrival of the appointed hour of suffering.[21]

Luke 22.52b. Why is the makeup of Luke's crowd different from that of the crowd described by Mark at 14.43? The words of the reproach in Mark 14.48-49, which match Luke's words in 52c-53b, seem better suited for Luke's crowd of leaders (22.52b) than the crowd *from* the leaders described by Mark (14.43).[22] The change of audience in Luke is most likely editorial,[23] since it is unlikely that the chief priests and elders themselves performed the arrest,[24] and since John 18.3 also says the crowd was *from* the Jewish authorities. Luke most likely made this alteration from his own reflection in order to have Jesus' words direct the shame of the event, not to a group of subordinates, but to those responsible for the arrest.[25]

Luke 22.53c-d. Jesus' full closing statement is in lines 52c-53d, the first part of which (52c-53b) is taken from Mark's account.[26] But Mark's *hina plērōthōsin hai graphai* offers no parallel to lines 53c-d, *all' autē estin hymōn hē hōra hē exousia tou skotous*. The Luke who altered the composition of the arresting crowd in order to make the crowd more nearly suited to the rebuke alters further here again for the sake of clarity. Mark's Greek is difficult, having either imperatival force (RSV: 'Let the scriptures be fulfilled!') or indicative force (if one supplies *gegonen*, as does Matthew: 'This happens in order that the scriptures may be fulfilled').[27] Moreover, it is not clear what scripture Mark meant to indicate. Luke's statement is composed of his typical eschatological language (see Acts 26.18) and the negative concept of 'the hour' which he may have borrowed from Mark 14.35 and 41, verses not previously cited. As he moved earlier to fit the crowd to the rebuke, so now, Luke works to make explicit the diabolical nature of the opponents' deed. Although they act inappropriately (52c-53b), the chief priests, officers of the Temple, and the elders are merely puppets in the hand of Satan. 53c-d clearly sounds the eschatological tone that has played through the story since 22.3a.[28]

Luke 22.61a. The Lukan addition of the detail that immediately after the cockcrow Jesus turned and looked at Peter subtly differs from the story in Mark. In Mark (14.72) the cock-crow stirs Peter's memory and moves him to break down and cry; but in Luke the cock-crow becomes the confirmation of Jesus' prediction concerning Peter's denial. In Luke Jesus' look, not the cock-crow, causes Peter's going out and weeping bitterly. How is one to account for this line? Scholars usually understand 61a either to be a Lukan composition[29] or to stem from a pre-Lukan source.[30] One may add to these two possibilities that 61a betrays the influence of oral tradition. It seems best, however, to understand 61a as a piece of Lukan composition. There is no similar tradition in another source to indicate the influence of oral tradition. This does not completely rule out the possibility of 61a coming from oral tradition, but no basis exists for such an interpretation. There is also nothing in 61a to suggest that Luke depends on a pre-Lukan source. Indeed, the converse appears to be true. In saying that Jesus turned, *strephein*, toward Peter, and by having Jesus' gaze motivate Peter's remembrance of Jesus' prophecy, Luke employs typical vocabulary and develops characteristic thoughts. Jesus acts here in an authoritative manner, a characteristic Lukan concern in the Passion Narrative.

Luke 22.62a-b.[31] There are at least two ways to understand the agreement between Luke and Matt 26.75. First, Matthew and Luke agree here because they independently altered Mark's story in exactly the same fashion. One might reason that when two writers employ the same source in producing their own versions of the story told by the common source, agreements are bound to occur. But that Luke and Matthew agree here *exactly*, in five words which are strikingly different from Mark's three words, seems to be too significant an agreement to be reasonably attributed to chance.

Second, these lines may be evidence of the continued existence and influence of oral tradition alongside and upon the written Gospel.

Marked differences exist between Luke and Matthew in their recounting of Peter's denials. Except for the information in these lines, Matthew followed Mark's story closely. We saw above that Luke made alterations in Mark's account. Therefore, the soundest way to understand the agreement between Luke and Matthew is that both evangelists heard, 'And he went out and wept bitterly', in the retelling of the story and preferred this simple and dramatic line over Mark's *kai epibalōn eklaien*.[32]

Luke 22.63a-65. Scholars often argue that the differences here between Luke and Mark (14.65) are so great as to suggest that Luke followed another source.[33]

The analysis of this scene will begin with 64d. How may one account for the agreement between Luke and Matt 26.68? Verse 64d should be understood as were 42a-d and 62a-b.[34] The differences between the basic narratives of Luke and Matthew are striking. Except for this line, which is not found in Mark's story, Matthew closely follows Mark's order and action; but Luke differs from Mark's story in both narrative order and detail. The differences between Luke and Matthew make it unlikely that independently they used a common written source. It is even more unlikely that independently Luke and Matthew composed and added exactly the same five-word question (*tis estin ho paisas se*) to the account of the mockery of Jesus. Thus, one best understands this striking agreement by inferring that Luke and Matthew knew the same non-Markan tradition;[35] and the dissimilarities between the accounts of Luke and Matthew make it unlikely this tradition was written. Therefore, it seems justified to conclude that Luke and Matthew had access to the same oral tradition in Greek. We may infer that in retelling the incident of Jesus' mockery, after the challenge to Jesus to prophesy was narrated, early Christians made clear *what* Jesus was dared to say. Luke and Matthew had heard this clarification of the command to prophesy and independently added *tis estin ho paisas se* to their versions of the story.[36] (This obviously differs from previous instances where oral tradition created the idea that Jesus spoke but the evangelists filled in the words.)

This line of reasoning brings us to an important observation. Since Luke and Matthew include the same non-Markan tradition[37] in their versions of Jesus' mockery, we may conclude that they were narrating the same event. The implication of this conclusion is that 22.63-65 is Luke's redacted version of Mark 14.65.

Working from these inferences, one may understand 63a-65 in the following manner: Verse 64d comes from oral tradition. The unmatched material in 65 is Luke's general redactional summary of what Mark tells explicitly in 14.55-61a.[38] Other instances of this type of editorial summarizing are found throughout Luke, e.g., 3.18 and 21.37-38.[39] Verses 63a-64c are Luke's thorough redaction of Mark 14.65.[40] Luke transposed the mockery of Jesus out of the context of the Assembly meeting and appropriately altered the description of the group doing the mocking. Mark's account distinguishes 'certain ones' who spat on Jesus, slapped him, and challenged him to prophesy from 'the guards' who received Jesus with blows after the mockery. But Luke says that prior to the Assembly meeting 'the men who were in charge of' Jesus mocked him. Luke seems to indicate the same group here that came out to the Mount of Olives to arrest Jesus, members of the crowd of 'chief priest, officers of the Temple, and elders' (52b). And so Luke portrays the same group mocking Jesus *before* the Assembly meeting that Mark depicts as mocking Jesus *during* the Assembly meeting.[41]

The alteration in order brings the sequence of Luke's narrative into compliance with the order delineated in the first Passion prediction at Luke 9.22. The differences between Luke and Mark achieve at least three results: (1) Jesus' courage is accentuated by having Peter's cowardice precede.[42] (2) Deep irony is inherent in Luke's narrative when Peter remembers that Jesus prophesied his denials, and then, the men holding Jesus imply he is no prophet with their mocking game.[43] (3) After Peter's denials and the treatment that Jesus suffers, the readers might expect him to be easy prey for the Assembly.[44]

Luke 22.66a-71c.[45] Portions of 66a-71c may be compared to portions of both Mark and John; but, *as a whole*, this unit is different from both Mark and John. How then may one best imagine that Luke came to record the information he communicates here?

Analysis suggests that, in 66a-71c, Luke reworked Mark 14.53–15.1 using an independent tradition and composing other lines of this unit. The factors that lead to this conclusion include the following.

First, one may easily compare 66a-d with Mark 14.53b and perhaps 15.1.[46] Such comparison is justified since Luke's story clearly reflects that of Mark at 22.67a (par Mark 14.61), 69 (par Mark 14.62), 70b (par Mark 14.61), 71 (par Mark 14.63b-64a).[47] That Luke records the meeting of the Assembly in the morning may be no more than a narrative device to continue the action of the story and to indicate a narrative time from which the Assembly may *immediately* take Jesus to Pilate.[48]

Second, the coherent, polished unit, 67a-68b, forms a key to the interpretation of this passage. Verse 67a-b may be compared to both Mark 14.61 and John 10.24; v. 67c-e may be compared to John 10.25; but there is no statement outside Luke comparable to 68a-b. How should one understand these phenomena? In the light of John 10.24-26 it appears that Luke knew of an exchange between Jesus and the Jews wherein Jesus was challenged to declare whether he was the Messiah. Using this tradition, Luke thoroughly reworked Mark to allow Jesus to answer the first part of the High Priest's question at Mark 14.61. Then, working as he did at 22.15-18, 19-20, Luke composed 68a-b to provide a balancing statement for 67d-e.[49] By providing this extra element in Jesus' answer, Luke accentuated the stubborn refusal of those questioning Jesus to listen to what Jesus has to say.

Third, Luke redacted the statement in Mark 14.62 concerning the Son of Man for at least these reasons: (a) He sounds once more the eschatological note heard throughout his narrative by saying '*apo tou nyn* the Son of Man will be sitting at the right hand of God's power'. (b) He makes clear for his (Gentile) readers the meaning of the circumlocution for God in Mark's text ('the right hand of Power'). (c) He separates the two parts of Mark's appositional inquiry ('the Christ'/'the son of the blessed one'), bringing the Son of Man saying between the 'Christ' question (22.67a-b) and the 'Son of God' question (22.70a- b), and makes clear how the Assembly came to ask Jesus whether he was the Son of God.[50]

Fourth, after separating the *Christ* question from the *Son of God* question by moving the *Son of Man* saying to a new narrative position, Luke composed a new answer to the second question ('You yourselves say that I am'). He may have written this line drawing on the answers given by Jesus to his inquisitors at Mark 14.62 (*egō eimi*) and Mark 15.2 (*sy legeis*). But Matthew, who follows Mark closely in this part of his Passion story, has Jesus respond to the High Priest by saying, *sy eipas*. And so perhaps the answer, 'you say', had made its way into the retelling of this story from oral tradition. Here, however, there can be no real certainty.

Fifth, as noted above, it appears that at 71a-c Luke's story reflects Mark's account. Virtually all scholars understand these lines to come from Mark.[51]

In summary, Luke knew an independent oral tradition that lies behind 67a-e, and he reworked Mark in conjunction with this tradition by composing 68a-b. He transposed and edited the saying in 69. He formed a separate, climactic question at 70a-b using transposed Markan material (14.61) and at 70c-d he composed an answer to this second question using ideas from Mark 14.62 and 15.2, perhaps under the influence of oral tradition. It seems most likely that Luke introduced this section by composing 66a-d using ideas from Mark 14.53b and perhaps 15.1.

Summary and conclusions. We asked above about the origin of the lines determined to be special Lukan Passion Narrative material in 22.39-71. That material is 22.39a-b, 40b, 42a-d, 48a-b, 49a-b, 51a-c, 51d-e, 52b, 53c-d, 61a, 62a-b, 63a-65, 66a-71c.

Verse 39a-b is Luke's redactional composition. He employed ideas from Mark 14.26 and 14.32 for these lines.

Verse 40b is also Luke's redactional composition. He wrote this line employing the model of Mark 14.38 that is matched by 22.46c, but there is a subtle difference between the focuses of the 40b and 46c.

Verse 42a-d is Luke's redacted version of Jesus' prayer prior to his arrest. Luke used Mark 14.36 and an oral tradition as the basis of his redaction.

Verse 48a-b also shows Luke's access to an oral tradition that influenced his handling of Mark's account.

Verse 49a-b is Luke's composition to introduce the sword scene.

Verse 51a-c is Luke's version of an oral tradition that told of Jesus rebuking his disciples after one of them struck with the sword.

Verse 51d-e is a Lukan composition, developed from the evangelist's own reflection.

Verse 52b is Luke's modification of Mark's account, wherein Luke himself brought the Jewish officials to the scene of the arrest of Jesus.

Verse 53c-d is also a Lukan composition, replacing a line in Mark's narrative that was not entirely clear with these lines that bring an eschatological tone to the Passion Narrative.

Verse 61a was composed by Luke. The line is part of a prominent Lukan Passion Narrative theme according to which Jesus acts authoritatively.

Verse 62a-b stems from oral tradition and functions in the Passion Narrative to develop the Lukan idea of repentance.

Verses 63a-65 are made up of various materials: 63a-64c is Luke's radically redacted version of Mark 14.65. 64d is based on an oral tradition. 65 is a Lukan redactional composition that condenses Mark 14.55-61a.

Verses 66a-71c are also composed of various material: 66a-d appears to be an introduction composed by Luke using ideas from Mark 14.53b and perhaps 15.1. 67a-e is Luke's redacted version of Mark 14.61 based upon an oral tradition that is also reflected in John 10.24-26. 68a-b is a Lukan composition that balances 67d-e and emphasizes the obstinacy of those questioning Jesus. 69 is a redacted version of Mark 14.62. 70a-b is Luke's redacted version of the second part of the question in Mark 14.61. 70c-d appears to be a Lukan redactional composition using ideas from Mark 14.62 and 15.2. Finally, 71a-c is Luke's version of Mark 14.63b-64a.

The Purpose of the Material

Having seen *what* material Luke employed and *how* he used it, we will now ask *why* Luke worked as he did.[52]

The presentation of the section. In considering the purpose of Luke 22.1-38, we saw that Luke worked deliberately to shape the Last Supper into the testamentary meal of Jesus with his followers. He developed that section of the Passion Narrative as he did for at least these reasons: (a) Jesus is portrayed as clearly in command of the events of the Passion. (b) The eschatological character of the meal and the postprandial conversation is heightened. (c) As Jesus speaks to the apostles, instruction is given to the readers.

In 22.39-71, Luke appears to have continued to work in a deliberate fashion developing the themes he made prominent in 22.1-38. He does not mold the scenes in this portion of his Passion in the form of a particular literary genre,[53] but he does employ recognizable narrative features and devices that we may compare to other literature of his day.

Jesus: The one in whom God's plan is realized. As the ideal figure at the testamentary meal, Jesus dominates the scene and enters into his Passion in full control of his destiny. Luke continues to develop and expand this theme in 22.39-71. First, Luke shows Jesus acting deliberately in this section of the Passion Narrative. He moves from the scene of the Last Supper and sets a course that the disciples only follow (39a-b), and the readers are told that Jesus acted as was his custom (39a). In Luke's Gospel Jesus has moved in this authoritative manner since 4.30.[54] Luke repeatedly records that Jesus' goal was Jerusalem (9.51; 13.33-34; 19.11; 19.28) and he overtly associates a meaningful death with Jesus' goal at 9.31 and 13.33.

When he arrives at the Mount of Olives, Jesus issues a command to his disciples to pray (40a-b). He tells those who follow him to 'pray not to enter into temptation' and separates himself from the disciples and fulfills the command by praying himself (41a-42d). When he returns from prayer, Jesus issues a second command to pray, but this order is to 'pray *so that* you [the disciples] will not enter into temptation' (46c). By his own activity, Jesus not only fulfills the order that he gave, but his words reveal that the motive for his prayer was to combat temptation. In his own praying Jesus apparently is fortified for the trials that he is about to undergo.[55]

When Judas and the crowd come out to arrest Jesus, Jesus acts so that he is clearly in control of the events.[56] In Mark's account Jesus does not speak to Judas; but Luke includes a statement by Jesus to Judas that leaves the readers uncertain whether or not Judas delivered the kiss he intended to give Jesus (48a-b). After the unnamed disciple strikes the servant of the High Priest, Jesus dominates the scene in word and deed. He orders the disciples to desist from their efforts to prevent his arrest (51a-c). Then, with the power and compassion exhibited throughout his ministry, Jesus heals the man whose ear was severed (51d-e). Still in control of himself and the events around him, Jesus confronts the crowd of priests, officers, and elders, questioning their clandestine actions and, in an elevated style, identifying the truly satanic nature of what they are about to do (52a-53d).

Even while he is held prisoner, Jesus dominates the events. When Peter has acted exactly as Jesus prophesied, Jesus turns toward him (61a). Jesus' action produces Peter's reactions: Peter remembers, and, with proper remorse, he repents (61b-62b).

Luke's arrangement of the scenes reinforces the image of Jesus' determination. When Jesus stands before the Assembly (66a-71c) he has already witnessed Peter's denying him three times (54a-62b), and he has already suffered the indignity of injurious, mocking treatment from his captors (63a-65). Despite being abandoned and abused, Jesus is not intimidated as he faces the Assembly. Rather, he displays the equanimity that comes from knowing that his destiny is the realization of the will of God (42a-d).[57] Throughout 22.39-71—in prayer, at his arrest, during Peter's denials, while he is mocked, and in his appearance before the Assembly—Jesus is absolutely *steadfast*. He acts in his customary fashion and thereby assures that the plan of God will come to proper realization.

Second, Jesus' statements in 22.39-71 demonstrate his authority and reveal his awareness of the extraordinary significance of the events which are about to transpire. His commands to the disciples to pray not to enter into temptation indicate a time of serious testing is at hand (40b, 46c). Moreover, his own prayer reveals that as the events of the Passion unfold, Jesus will realize the very will of God (42a-d).

In his rebuke to the disciples, Jesus commands that there be no interference with the machinations of the arresting party (51a-c). Indeed, in the closing lines of his remarks to the members of the crowd that come to arrest him, Jesus recognizes the diabolic nature of their intention, but he also seems to authorize the carrying out of their treachery (53c-d).

The truth and value of Jesus' word is emphasized when Peter remembers 'the Lord's saying' (61b-c). This fulfillment of Jesus' prophecy demonstrates the authenticity and dependability of his statements.

Therefore, when one hears Jesus speak in the Assembly meeting, one knows his words are neither nervous chatter nor hollow boasts. When he is charged to tell the Assembly whether he is the Christ (67a-b), Jesus again exposes the faults of the leaders rather than yield to their demand (67c-68b). He tells the Assembly members that although their minds are made up (to do the wrong), the outcome of their evil purpose will be the exaltation of the Son of Man (69).

Luke has again arranged the story in such a way that there is logical, purposeful development in the narrative. The Assembly's questioning is moved from the level of Jesus' status as Messiah (67a-b) through his statement about the Son of Man (69) to the inquiry whether Jesus is the Son of God (70b). By separating the Christ-question from the Son-of-God-question, Luke emphasized Jesus' true identity to the readers, who have been aware of Jesus' status as Son of God from the time of Gabriel's visit to Mary in the first chapter of the Gospel (1.26-38).[58] And, in his development of the scene, Luke makes the self-understanding expressed by Jesus in 22.67a-70d (esp. 70a-d) the sole basis for the Assembly's condemnation of him.[59]

Third, one understands that Jesus acts in full control of his destiny and, thereby, fulfills God's plan by means of the *irony* that Luke developed in this portion of the Passion account.[60] Luke built into his narrative an unstated communication between himself and his readers. He created a two-storey phenomenon wherein there exists a sharp contrast between appearance and reality. The readers are invited to participate with Luke in the higher level of the narrative. Such participation provides a covert corrective to a false understanding of the story based merely on appearance. This claim must be illustrated.

In appearance, Jesus is the victim of those 'in charge of him' as he waits to go before the Assembly (63a-65). This group plays a cruel game. They blindfold Jesus, take turns hitting him, and as they strike him, they dare him to reveal exactly who delivered the blow. The implication of their taunt is that Jesus is incapable of prophesying.

The readers of this story enjoy a privileged position. If they take their cues from Luke, they move to the higher level of the narrative from which they gain a new perspective on the events of the Passion. From this vantage point, it is possible to know what the members of the group have yet to discover, i.e. *Jesus is a prophet*. In the episode that precedes the mockery, Peter denies Jesus three times, fulfilling exactly the prophecy of Jesus. Luke arranged the scenes of the Passion in 22.54-71 so that the readers have information that allows them to contrast Jesus' implied inability to prophesy with his true power as a prophet. They see that Jesus is no mere victim; indeed, he is the true prophet who sees and does God's will. Those 'in charge' of Jesus are ignorant and their false assumption about Jesus' prophetic impotence causes them to suffer the brunt of their crude joke. The effect of Luke's narrative technique is that the apparent victim becomes *the one in charge* and the apparent authorities become the victims of their own ignorance. It would be only the dim-witted reader who would not at least perceive the implications of Luke's carefully managed plot.

The special time: Inaugurated eschatology. In 22.39-71, the time of the Passion of Jesus is portrayed as having eschatological significance in at least four ways. First, Jesus' prayer on the Mount of Olives makes clear that the time of his suffering and death moves history to a new level. When he prays prior to his arrest, Jesus goes to his knees (41c), assuming a posture Luke associates with prayers of uncommon significance (see Acts 7.60; 9.40; 20.36; 21.5). In this praying position, Jesus utters a prayer that explicitly acknowledges the eschatological nature of the Passion (42a-d). He refers to God's plan ('if you have it in mind') and speaks of his imminent suffering and death as 'this cup', calling to the minds of the readers the two cups at the Last Supper. The first of those cups marked the moment from which it was shared as a time of new beginnings and anticipated the coming of the kingdom of God (22.17-18). The second cup shared at the Last Supper was similar in that it was said to be symbolic of the new covenant formed by the death of Jesus (22.20). Finally, in his prayer (22.42c-d) Jesus resolves, in the face of his suffering and death, to bring to fulfillment the plan of God ('not my will but yours be done').

Second, Jesus' statements throughout 22.39-71 recognize the eschatological dimension of the time of the Passion. He commands his disciples to pray (40b and 46c), saying their prayer is to guard them from entering into *temptation*, i.e. a struggle against the evil one.

When Jesus confronts Judas (48b) and the members of the Assembly (69), he speaks about the Son of Man, a title with clear eschatological connotations. The title alone should register the eschatological significance of the moment by showing that the Passion predictions were being fulfilled; but, if the readers do not perceive the connotations of this title, Luke added the words *apo tou nyn* to Jesus' Son of Man statement to the Assembly. This phrase dramatically marks the time and directs the readers to look toward the fulfillment of God's plan and the coming of the kingdom of God (see 22.18).

Furthermore, in 53c-d Jesus speaks metaphorically about his Passion as the 'hour' of his adversaries and 'the power of darkness'. There is an unmistakable eschatological tone to these words.

Third, when Jesus' betrayer and the members of the crowd arrive the readers recognize that the time of fulfillment for Jesus' Passion predictions is at hand (47a-c, 52b). Throughout the Gospel Jesus has said that the Son of Man will be betrayed (9.44; 18.32; 19.22). Moreover, in the first Passion prediction (9.22) Jesus names 'the elders and chief priests and scribes' as those who will reject the Son of Man. The crowd members named in 52b ('chief priests, officers of the Temple, and elders') and the members of the 'assembly of the elders of the people' at 66b-c ('both chief priests and scribes') are those who the readers understand will reject the Son of Man.

Fourth, at the Last Supper Jesus warns the apostles that Satan has demanded to sift them like wheat (22.31b). In 22.39-62 the readers see Jesus' prophecy come true. When the crowd comes the disciples react violently, attempting to prevent Jesus' arrest (49a-50b). They succumb to the temptation to interfere with the fulfillment of God's plan. Later, Peter is sifted in the special way that Jesus predicted (55a-60d). This temptation marks the time as that toward which Jesus has looked and about which he has spoken.

In Chapter 6 we will consider the parameters of Luke's eschatology. In anticipation of that treatment, Luke's eschatology may be described here as 'inaugurated eschatology'. The Passion of Jesus is the culmination of the Lukan pattern of *acceptance or rejection* that has characterized the response of people to the earthly ministry of Jesus. This pattern was first seen in the Birth Narratives of Luke's Gospel in Simeon's second oracle (2.34- 35),[61] where Luke reveals Jesus was *set* for a judgment which divides, i.e. Jesus himself is the criterion for distinguishing between people. Some accept him while others reject him. Indeed, the pattern of acceptance or rejection does not end at the Passion; rather, it reaches the high point with regard to Jesus' *earthly* ministry. In Acts (2.17; 3.22), it becomes apparent that the Passion of Jesus *inaugurated* the penultimate eschatological era of the Last Days. Following the Passion, Jesus resides in heaven until the time for the establishment of *all* that God plans,[62] although he continues what he began by working in and through his disciples (Acts 1.1 says the Gospel had to do with *hōn ērxato ho Iēsous poiein te kai didaskein*). Luke can say at Acts 9.34 that Jesus Christ heals and at 26.22-23 that Christ proclaims light to his own people and to the Gentiles. Thus the patterns of human response to Jesus that were seen throughout his earthly ministry, and which culminated in the events of the Passion, continue after Jesus' death and resurrection; for, while Jesus is exalted into heaven, humanity continues to accept or reject him as he ministers among and through the disciples.

The followers. The followers of Jesus seem to serve two narrative functions in 22.39-71. First, they are *those in whom Jesus' words are fulfilled*. Jesus told the disciples they would be sifted, and when, at the arrest, they perceive what is about to happen, they are thoroughly sifted. In typical fashion, they ask Jesus if they are to act, here violently. Unlike their Lord, the disciples panic; they do not wait for Jesus' reply but take matters into their own hands.

Therefore, Jesus condemns their behavior. The inappropriateness of the disciples' action reveals they did their own will rather than God's. They have been sifted, and so Jesus' words are fulfilled in them. At this point the disciples fade out of the story, although they do seem to reappear later as witnesses to the events of Jesus' Passion (23.49).

One disciple, Peter, does continue to follow Jesus, though 'at a distance' (54c). The extent of the distance between Peter and Jesus becomes clear in 55a-60, when Peter performs exactly as Jesus prophesied, denying Jesus three times. Yet Jesus said at 32a-d that he had prayed for Peter—he begged that Peter's faith might not fail and that when Peter turned around he might strengthen his brothers (who have temporarily disappeared from the story). After Peter has denied Jesus, 'the Lord' turns and looks at Peter. One should understand that the *turning of the Lord* assured the *turning around of Peter*. Moreover, it is possible that the mention of the presence of 'all' of Jesus' 'acquaintances' at the crucifixion (23.49) is Luke's notation of the beginning of the strengthening that Jesus said Peter would do.

Second, the disciples are *those through whom Luke has Jesus instruct the readers*. In this portion of Luke's Passion Narrative Jesus commands the disciples to pray. We saw that the content of the prayer is *not to enter into temptation*, and the purpose of the prayer is *so that they will not enter into temptation*. There is a clear lesson in these commands of Jesus: Through prayer those who follow him may combat the evil one, and through prayer they commit themselves to finding and doing the will of God.

Jesus also rebukes his disciples for their use of violence at the time of his arrest. It may be that Luke recorded that Jesus did not tolerate violence for several reasons,[63] but the readers see plainly that he did not condone the use of the sword.

The readers of 22.39-71 also learn that 'the Lord' actively supports repentance. He not only desires that his followers should not fail him completely, he intercedes (22.32) for them and, when necessary, acts to insure their turning around (61a).

Conclusions. In 22.1-38 we saw that Luke provided a mini-course for his readers in christology, eschatology, and ecclesiology. In 22.39-71 Luke built upon the foundation he laid in the first part of ch. 22, and so the mini-course is developed into a full program of study.

First, Jesus appears here as the one in whom the plan of God is fulfilled. Second, the eschatological dimensions of the events in 22.39-71 are highlighted. Third, the followers of Jesus are portrayed in such a way that they serve two narrative functions: they are those in whom Jesus' prophecies are fulfilled, and they are those through whom Luke allowed Jesus to address the readers of his Gospel.

Chapter 6

CONCLUSIONS

Throughout this study summary sections have stated the results of the various portions of this investigation of the scope, origin, and purpose of the special Lukan Passion Narrative material in Luke 22, and so, there is no need to reiterate those earlier sections here. Instead, the reader is referred with regard to *scope* to pp. 48, 96; with regard to *origin* to pp. 54, 105-106; and with regard to *purpose* to pp. 57, 112-13.

Luke's Redactional and Compositional Technique

At this juncture it may be helpful to view the special material in the context of the whole of Luke's presentation. Accordingly, the text of Luke 22 is printed out and the special Lukan material is underscored with a variety of symbols that express the suggestions made above about the origin of the material. This viewing may provide a basis for defining the scope of the special Lukan Passion Narrative material more precisely than before (pp. 48, 96).

The emphasis calls attention to special Lukan material or activity of the following types:

oblique	Markan material redacted (thoroughly) by Luke
underlined	Oral tradition drawn on by Luke
bold	Lukan composition
italics	Markan material that Luke has combined with oral tradition.

Unemphasized text presents material taken from Mark with little or no redaction by Luke.

Luke 22.1-71

(1a) Now the Festival of Unleavened Bread drew near, (b) which is called Passover. (2a) And the chief priests and the scribes were looking for a way to put him to death, (b) because they were afraid of the people. (3a) Then Satan entered Judas, (b) the one called Iscariot, (c) who belonged to the number of the twelve; (4a) and he went out and conferred with the chief priests and the officers (b) how he might hand him over to them. (5a) Now they were delighted, (b) and they agreed to pay him. (6a) So he agreed (b) and he sought an opportunity to hand him over to them (c) apart from a crowd. (7a) The Day of Unleavened Bread came (b) on which the paschal lamb had to be sacrificed. (8a) So he [Jesus] sent Peter and John, saying, (b) 'Go prepare the Passover for us (c) so that we may eat it'. (9a) And they said to him, (b) 'Where do you want us to prepare it?' (10a) And he said to them, (b) 'Look! when you have entered the city, a man carrying a clay water jar will meet you. (c) Follow him into the house that he enters. (11a) And you shall say to the master of the house, (b) "The Teacher says to you, (c) Where is the guest room (d) where I may eat the Passover with my disciples?" (12a) And he will show you a large upstairs room that has been furnished. (b) Prepare it there.' (13a) They went and found it exactly as he had told them; (b) and they prepared the Passover. (14a) When the hour came (b) he reclined at table, (c) and the apostles with him. (15a) **He said to them,** (b) '**I have eagerly yearned to eat this Passover with you before I suffer;** (16a) **for I say to you** (b) **that I will surely not eat it** (c) **until it is fulfilled in the kingdom of God'.** (17a) *And when had taken a cup and given thanks* (b) *he said, 'Take this and divide it among yourselves;* (18a) *for I say to you* (b) *that from now on I will surely not drink from the fruit of vine* (c) *until the kingdom of God comes'.* (19a) *And when* he had taken bread and given thanks (b) *he broke it* (c) *and gave it to them* **saying,** (d) *'This is my body* (e) which **is given** in behalf of you. (f) Do this in remembrance of me'. (20a) *And* in the same way *the cup* after the dinner, saying, (b) 'This cup *is a* new *covenant by my blood* (c) *which is poured out in behalf of you.* (21) But look! the hand of the one betraying me is with me on the table. (22a) Now the Son of Man goes as it has been appointed; (b) but woe to that man through whom he is betrayed.' (23a) And they began to discuss among themselves (b) who then from among them intended to do this thing. (24a) **And indeed contentiousness arose among them** (b) **which of them was to be thought of as the greatest**. (25a) *So he* [Jesus] said to them, (b) *'The Kings of the Gentiles lord it over one another,* (c) *and the ones of them who wield authority call themselves benefactors;* (26a) *but you shall not be that way.* (b) *Rather let the greatest among you become like the youngest.* (c) *Indeed the one who has authority must be like the one who serves.* (27a) **For who** is greater, (b) **the one reclining at table or the one serving?** (c) **Is it not the one who reclines?** (d) **Yet in your midst I am like the one who serves.** (28) Now you are the ones who have remained with me throughout my trials. (29) **So I allot to you, as my Father allotted to me, a kingdom;** (30a) **so that you may eat and drink at my table in my kingdom,** (b) and you may sit on thrones (c) judging the twelve tribes of Israel. (31a) **Simon, Simon, look!** (b) **Satan demanded to sift you all like wheat.** (32a) **But I begged concerning you** (b) **that your faith might not fail,** (c) **and when you yourself turn around** (d) **strengthen your brothers.'** (33a) *But he* [Simon] *said to him,* (b) *'Lord, I am ready to go with you both to prison and to death'.* (34a) *Then he* [Jesus] *said,* (b) *'I tell you, Peter,* (c) *the cock will not crow today* (d) *until three times you deny that you know me'.* (35a) **And he said to them,** (b) **'When I sent you without a purse, bag, or sandals,** (c) **did you lack anything?'** (d) **And they said,** (e) **'Nothing'.** (36a) **Then he said to them,** (b) **'But now, let the one who has a purse carry it** (c) **and likewise a bag;** (d) and whoever does not have one, (e) let him sell his mantle (f) and buy a sword. (37a) **For I tell you** (b) **that this scripture must be realized in me** (c) **"Indeed he was reckoned among the lawless"** (d) **for in fact that which is about me has its fulfillment.'** (38a) **Then they said,** (b) **'Lord, look, here are two swords'.** (c) **But he said to them,** (d) **'That's enough'.** (39a) *When he went out he proceeded, according to his custom, to the Mount of Olives* (b) *and just his disciples followed him.* (40a) When he reached the place, he said to them, (b) **'Pray not to enter into temptation!'** (41a) And he withdrew from them, (b) about a stone's throw, (c) and going to his knees, he prayed, (42a) *saying, 'Father, if you have it in mind,* (b) *take this cup away from me.* (c) *Only let not my will* (d) *but yours be done.'* (45a) And when he arose from his prayer (b) and went to his disciples, (c) he found them sleeping because of their sad condition. (46a) And he said to them, (b) 'Why are you sleeping? (c) Get up and pray so that you will not enter into temptation.' (47a) While he was still speaking (b) a crowd appeared. (c) Indeed, the one called Judas, one of the twelve, walked at the head of them; (d) and he drew near to Jesus (e) in order to kiss him. (48a) But Jesus said to him, (b) 'Judas, are you giving over the Son of Man by means of a kiss?' (49a) **When those around him saw what was going to happen, they said,** (b) **'Lord, are we to strike with a sword?'** (50a) And one of them struck the high priest's servant (b) and took off his right ear. (51a) But Jesus answered and said, (b) 'Let it be! (c) That's enough of that!' (d) **And touching his ear,** (e) **he healed him.** (52a)

Then Jesus said to those who came out for him: (b) **chief priests, officers of the Temple, and elders,** (c) 'As if for a brigand, (d) you came with swords and clubs. (53a) Day after day, when I was with you in the Temple, (b) you did not stretch out your hand for me. (c) **But this is your hour,** (d) **and the power of darkness.**' (54a) Then they arrested him and led him away. (b) They brought him to the house of the high priest; (c) and Peter followed him at a distance. (55a) And when they lit a fire in the middle of the courtyard, (b) and sat together, (c) Peter sat among them. (56a) Then a maid saw him (b) as he sat facing the light, (c) and she stared at him and said, (d) 'Hey, this one was with him!' (57a) But he denied it saying, (b) 'I don't know him, woman!' (58a) And after a little while, another saw him and said, (b) 'Hey, you are one of them!' (c) But Peter said, (d) 'Fellow, I am not!' (59a) About an hour passed (b) and another one insisted (saying), (c) 'Of course this one was with him, (d) after all, he is a Galilean!' (60a) But Peter said, (b) 'Fellow, I don't know what you are talking about!' (c) And immediately, while he was still speaking, (d) a cock crowed. (61a) **And the Lord turned and looked straight at Peter**; (b) and Peter remembered the Lord's saying (c) (how he said to him), (d) 'Before a cock crows today, (e) you will deny me three times'. (62a) And he went out (b) and wept bitterly. (63a) *And the men who were in charge of him* [Jesus] *mocked him:* (b) *beating him* (64a) *and blindfolding him,* (b) *they asked him (saying),* (c) *'Prophesy!* (d) *who is the one who hit you?'* (65) And they said many other things, reviling him. (66a) **And when it was day,** (b) **the Assembly of the elders of the people came together,** (c) **both chief priests and scribes,** (d) **and they brought him into their Council;** (67a) *saying, 'If you are the Christ,* (b) *tell us!'* (c) But he said to them, (d) 'If I tell you, (e) you will not believe; (68a) and if I ask you, (b) you will not answer. (69) *Yet, from now on the Son of Man will be sitting at the right hand of the power of God.'* (70a) *Then they all said,* (b) *'Are you then the Son of God?'* (c) *But he said to them,* (d) *'You yourselves say that I am'.* (71a) *Then they said,* (b) *'What further need have we of testimony?* (c) *For we heard it ourselves from his mouth!'*

By viewing the special Lukan material in the context in which Luke placed it and by taking into consideration the suggestions regarding the origin of that material, what further may one say about *how* Luke worked?

1.   Mark is the basic source for Luke's work in ch. 22 of his Gospel.

2. Luke had recourse to oral tradition that went beyond Mark, and he included some of that information in ch. 22 by smoothly blending it with the basic Markan narrative.
3. In the course of writing ch. 22, Luke freely composed additional material of his own, and he thoroughly integrated his composition into the blended material from Mark and oral tradition.

Verses 19-20 of ch. 22 provide the best single support for this overall interpretation. In comparing 22.19-20 with Mark 14.22-23 and 1 Cor 11.23-25, we saw that Luke did not simply follow Mark in narrating the institution of the Lord's Supper; indeed, he clearly departed from it, agreeing with 1 Corinthians at several points. But both Mark and 1 Corinthians (or more likely a tradition like it—see above ch. 2 n. 13) will not fully account for Luke 22.19-20; for in blending Mark and this Corinthians-like tradition, Luke created touches of poetic balance (a) by reiterating the verb *didonai* from 19c in 19e and (b) by altering Mark's phrase *hyper pollōn* (14.24) to *hyper hymōn* in 20c so that it matches the phrase in 19e from the Corinthians-like tradition.

A Further Word Concerning the Scope of the Special Lukan Passion Narrative Material in Luke 22

By eliminating the thoroughly redacted Markan material, one may define the special Lukan Passion Narrative material more precisely now than has been possible before. When the Markan material is taken out of consideration, the following lines and units remain as *special Lukan Passion Narrative material*: 22.3a, 15a-16c, 19a-20c, 24a-b, 27a-32d, 35a-38d, 39b, 40b, 42a-d, 48a-49b, 51a-e, 52b, 53c-d, 61a, 62a-b, 64d, 66a-68b. Viewed as a continuous piece, this material appears as follows:

The Special Lukan Passion Narrative Material in Luke 22.1-71

(3a) Then Satan entered Judas. (15a) He [Jesus] said to them, (b) 'I have eagerly yearned to eat this Passover with you before I suffer; (16a) for I say to you (b) that I will surely not eat it (c) until it is fulfilled in the kingdom of God'. (19a) And when he had taken bread and given thanks (b) he broke it (c) and gave it to them saying, (d) 'This is my body (e) which is given in behalf of you. (f) Do this in remembrance of me.' (20a) And in the same way the cup after the dinner, saying, (b) 'This cup is a new covenant by my blood (c) which is poured out in behalf of you'. (24a) And indeed contentiousness arose among them (b) which of them was to be thought of as the greatest. (27a) 'For who is greater, (b) the one reclining at table or the one serving? (c) Is it not the one who reclines? (d) Yet in your midst I am like the one who serves. (28) Now you are the ones who have remained with me throughout my trials. (29) So I allot to you, as my Father allotted to me, a kingdom; (30a) so that you may eat and drink at my table in my kingdom, (b) and you may sit on thrones (c) judging the twelve tribes of Israel. (31a) Simon, Simon, look! (b) Satan demanded to sift you all like wheat. (32a) But I begged concerning you (b) that your faith might not fail, (c) and when you yourself turn around (d) strengthen your brothers.' (35a) And he said to them, (b) 'When I sent you without a purse, bag, or sandals, (c) did you lack anything?' (d) And they said, (e) 'Nothing'. (36a) Then he said to them, (b) 'But now, let the one who has a purse carry it (c) and likewise a bag; (d) and whoever does not have one, (e) let him sell his mantle (f) and buy a sword. (37a) For I tell you (b) that this scripture must be realized in me, (c) "Indeed he was reckoned among the lawless", (d) for in fact that which is about me has its fulfillment.' (38a) Then they said, (b) 'Lord, look, here are two swords'. (c) But he said to them, (d) 'That's enough'. (40b) 'Pray not to enter into temptation!' (42a) saying, 'Father, if you have it in mind, (b) take this cup away from me. (c) Only let not my will (d) but yours be done.' (48a) But Jesus said to him, (b) 'Judas, are you giving over the Son of Man by means of a kiss?' (49a) When those around him saw what was going to happen, they said, (b) 'Lord, are we to strike with a sword?' (51a) But Jesus answered and said, (b) 'Let it be! (c) That's enough of that!' (d) And touching his ear, (e) he healed him. (52b) chief priests, officers of the Temple, and elders (53c) But this is your hour, (d) and the power of darkness.' (61a) And the Lord turned and looked straight at Peter (62a) And he went out (b) and wept bitterly. (64d) 'Who is the one who hit you?' (66a) And when it was day, (b) the Assembly of the elders of the people came together, (c) both chief priests and scribes, (d) and they brought him into their Council; (67a) saying, 'If you are the Christ, (b) tell us!' (c) But he said to them, (d) 'If I tell you, (e) you will not believe; (68a) and if I ask you, (b) you will not answer'.

Overall, two observations may be made. While some creative rearrangement of this material might produce a *continuous* narrative, in its present form, isolated from the other portions of Luke 22, *this is not a continuous narrative*. Moreover, this material seems to fall naturally into many independent units; namely, 22.3a, 15a-16c, 19a-20c, 24a-b, 27a-d, 28-30c, 31a-32d, 35a-38d, 40b, 42a-d, 48a-b, 49a-b, 51a-e, 52b, 53c-d, 61a-62b, 66a-d, 67a-68b. In other words, careful examination of the special Lukan material in Luke 22 supports neither the contention that Luke's Gospel is based upon a proto-Luke nor the claim that Luke had recourse to a written, integrated special Passion Narrative source that was itself an independent form of the Passion story. Furthermore the findings of this study suggest it is artificially restrictive to think only in terms of written sources. The variety of oral materials which Luke employs shows that early Christians continued to *tell* of Jesus' last days after that story was committed to writing. Confirmation of this point appears in Eusebius's quotation of Papias which says, 'For I did not suppose that information from books would help me so much as the word of a living and surviving voice' (*Hist. eccl.* 3.39.4). This statement testifies to the lively and highly regarded oral transmission of tradition among early Christians. Perhaps it is not only artificial but even misleading to think of *an* oral and *a* written Passion account, for Luke could have known twenty-five or more Passion Narratives, one of which was written and which he used as the basis of his own writing, namely the Gospel according to Mark. This usage, however, does not imply that Luke viewed Mark's Passion Narrative as inherently more authoritative than the other oral (and written?) accounts to which he had access.

At this juncture, if one understands that Luke is not using a single, continuous, written, special source, one must attempt to answer two related questions: (1) Why does the resultant Passion Narrative in Luke differ so much from Mark's (in percentage terms), whereas, elsewhere when Luke is not using a special source, he follows Mark much more closely?[1] (2) Why is the manner in which Luke arranged the order of pericopes in the Passion Narrative markedly different from his manner elsewhere in the Gospel when he is using Mark?[2]

Both these questions have been considered by some scholars to be more-or-less unanswerable apart from the hypothesis of a special Lukan source (at least in the Passion Narrative). It should be recognized at the outset that possibly no completely satisfactory answers exist to these questions, but the results of the present study do imply certain conclusions. We have seen a theological harmony between Luke's Passion Narrative and the rest of his Gospel, and it is possible, even preferable, to understand Luke's adaptation of Mark's

Passion account upon the basis of theological motives rather than to take recourse to a hypothetical, special source to explain the differences between Luke and Mark. Moreover, if one successfully explains these differences as redactional activity for theological purposes (as was done above), then one may respond with confidence to these questions by means of a series of observations and assertions.

There are places throughout Luke's Gospel wherein the level of verbal agreement between Luke and Mark is as low, and often lower, than in the Passion Narrative. One well-known example is the story of the Transfiguration (Luke 9.28-36 par Mark 9.2-8). For convenience Luke and Mark may be compared in terms of verbal agreement in a chart:

Verse	Number of Words	Markan Matches
9.28	20	9
9.29	18	4
9.30	11	5 or 6
9.31	13	0
9.32	23	0
9.33	36	22 to 26
9.34	18	4
9.35	16	14
9.38	22	2

60 to 65 of Luke's 177 words, or between 33.9 and 36.7%, are matched by words in Mark. Interestingly, while the words agree, in v. 28 Luke has 'John and James', whereas Mark 9.2 reads 'James and John'; and in v. 30 Luke has 'Moses and Elijah', whereas Mark 9.4 reads 'Elijah and Moses'. The low verbal correspondence (represented especially in whole Lukan verses without matches in Mark) and the different arrangements of the material cause some scholars to speak of Luke's use of a special source for the Transfiguration account.[3] But, as others demonstrate, most of the differences between Luke and Mark 'may be regarded as expressing Lukan motifs'.[4]

The concern here is not to enter into the discussion of Luke's account of the Transfiguration, but to illustrate a fallacious assumption in the questions posed above, namely, that the Passion Narrative is qualitatively different from the rest of Luke's Gospel. While the differences between Luke and Mark in their Passion accounts may extend through a larger segment of narrative than elsewhere in the stories (at best a quantitative difference), one should not view Luke's

Passion Narrative as really different from important portions of the rest of his Gospel.[5] Indeed, at times Luke does follow Mark closely, and he does so often in his Passion Narrative (see the *unemphasized* material in the chart above); but at other times Luke's narrative is strikingly different from Mark's, as it is frequently in the Passion Narrative.

This leads to a further observation. That Luke often follows Mark closely should not create a maxim that he always must do so, as if Luke wrote in a rigidly uniform manner. Given the pattern of agreement and disagreement between Luke and Mark, especially as observed in the Passion Narrative, the most reasonable question to pose here seems to be neither of those above, but rather, Why does Luke sometimes take over Mark with little change and at other times (esp. in the Passion Narrative) differ from him significantly? One possible answer, of course, is that he is using a special source. But unless one is prepared to posit that source for every significant difference between Luke and Mark (proto-Luke?), and unless one is prepared to go against the clear finding of the investigation above, that the special Lukan Passion Narrative material does not form a coherent story (a finding that undermines proto-Luke), one must seek another, more plausible solution.

In light of the evidence assembled in the present investigation, it is reasonable to assert that *the greatest differences between Luke and Mark may be the result of Luke's strongest motive(s) for writing his Gospel*. Indeed, the focus on percentage of agreement and order of pericopes as primary exegetical principles may have kept interpreters from discovering Luke's true concerns by leading to the postulation of a hypothetical, special source to explain the differences between Luke and Mark—differences that may be the best evidence for determining Luke's theological concerns.[6] Scholars have long since recognized that Luke's Gospel is 'revisionist', and the findings of this investigation of Luke 22 support that description; yet no consensus exists concerning the motive for Luke's writing a 'second edition' of the Gospel.[7] Perhaps one result of the attempt to answer the question just posed is the recognition of one of the main motives for Luke's efforts, namely, he wrote his Gospel, rewriting Mark, in order to alter subtly the image of Jesus and the impact of his Passion. This explanation is particularly persuasive because it takes into account the theological harmony between the Lukan Passion Narrative and the rest of Luke's Gospel.

Luke's Attitude toward Tradition and his Theological Tendencies

At the conclusion of this study, how are we to understand the remarkable freedom Luke displays in his employment, or better, appropriation, of traditions, both oral and written, about Jesus? The following series of observations and suggestions builds upon the detailed work in the foregoing study in an attempt to address this broad question.[8]

Luke obviously reveres the tradition, otherwise he would not have preserved it. Yet, as one analyzes his method of working, it becomes clear that he does not merely produce a pastiche, taking over Markan material and supplementing it with additional, complementary information. Indeed, the freedom Luke exhibits in appropriating tradition suggests his motivation is to be attributed partly to his reverence of the tradition and partly to his concern with something else that caused him to reshape that tradition. Taken together these observations imply that Luke's freedom is not the result of license; rather, the traditions are preserved and employed for a purpose, i.e. to serve some function and/or to meet some need.[9] In other words, Luke's *use* of tradition is the result of his effort to respond to his perception of the situation of some community or communities of believers in his own day;[10] and, in his use of tradition, he reveals an *attitude toward* the material that suggests he regards it as 'penultimate'.

To explicate and illustrate, the (a) elevated christology, (b) heightened eschatology, and (c) articulated ecclesiology in Luke 22 are probably aimed at meeting specific needs. Luke worked to merge the horizons of the past and the present. The horizon of the past was found in all of the traditions he employed; the horizon of the present was located among the readers whom Luke envisioned for his work. Luke presented Jesus in such a manner as to cause those readers to gather that Jesus was/is both authoritative and trustworthy (see above pp. 55-56, 57, 106-109). Throughout the material in ch. 22 Luke sounded an eschatological tone which cued the reader that the events he narrated were of ultimate significance: time had been reoriented (see above pp. 56, 57, 109-11); but simultaneously Luke clearly implied that human, earthly existence would continue. And so Luke had Jesus instruct, interact with, and correct the disciples in such a manner that Luke's readers would gain a focused vision of what it meant to live as followers of Jesus (see above pp. 56, 57, 111-13). Taken together, these emphases appear to be Luke's attempt to *engender confidence*—in Jesus as the agent of God's salvation and in Christianity as the result of God's plan—a goal consistent with the aim stated in the prologue to the Third Gospel.

In relating these horizons to one another, Luke reveals his belief that the story of the life, death, and resurrection of Jesus Christ did not belong simply to the past; it belonged also to his present and the present of his readers. Moreover, he labored to narrate the events of Jesus' Passion not merely because they were worthy of being remembered, but because they had the capacity to influence or determine the course of his own time. Luke believed the story he told somehow transcended the realm of the ephemeral, for the events had inaugurated and defined the final days. Thus, the story of Jesus' Passion continued to be meaningful as it enabled Luke's readers to find and do the will of God.

Appendix

IMPLICATIONS OF THE PRESENT INVESTIGATION
FOR FUTURE STUDY

The method of inquiry defined and practiced in this study may be used in studying ch. 23 of Luke's Gospel. There is in Luke 23 a striking array of non-Markan material. A survey of ch. 23 suggests that 23.1-16, 18-25, 27-33, 35-43, 45-49, 51-52, 54-56 should be investigated as possible special Lukan Passion Narrative material.

A broad and preliminary application to Luke 23 of the method employed in this study shows that much of the material in this portion of Luke's Passion account may be without parallel in Mark's Gospel, e.g. 23.1-2, 4-16, 18-25(?), 36-37, 39-43, 45, 46(?), 48, 49a, 51, 55-56. Agreements between Luke and Matthew and/or John against Mark may occur in 23.4, 9, 18-19, 46, 52. The information in 23.2, 19, 32, 33, 35, 36, 37, 38, 45, 54, 56 may appear in a story sequence different from that found in Mark. Furthermore, the entire chapter, especially the non-Markan material, should be studied (a) in terms of verbal correspondence between Luke and Mark and (b) for telltale Lukan language.

A *Habilitationsschrift* by F.G. Untergassmair[1] studying Luke 23.26-49 and a paper by F.J. Matera[2] comparing Luke 23.44-48 to Mark 15.33-39 anticipate the application of the present method of study to Luke 23. Both scholars argue that the differences between Luke and Mark may be understood without taking recourse to a coherent special Lukan source.[3] Rather, Untergassmair and Matera conclude (as does this study of Luke 22) that the 'special' portions of Luke's Passion Narrative represent Luke's own theological vision. Having seen Luke work as he does in 22.1-71, one should be surprised to find him doing anything different in ch. 23; but this presupposition demands testing.

NOTES

Notes to Chapter 1

1. F.C. Burkitt, *The Gospel History and its Transmission* (Edinburgh: Clark, 1906), 135; R. Bultmann, *The History of the Synoptic Tradition* (New York: Harper & Row, 1963; German original 1921), 362; W.G. Kümmel, *Introduction to the New Testament* (17th edn; Nashville: Abingdon, 1975; German original 1973), 130-31; and F. Neirynck, 'The Argument from Order and St. Luke's Transpositions', *ETL* 49 (1973), 784-815.

A modified form of the Two-Document Hypothesis (i.e. Mark and Q plus L and M) is the solution to the so-called Synoptic Problem that informs this study of the *special Lukan Passion Narrative material*. This way of understanding the relationship of the Synoptic Gospels to one another has not gone without criticism from scholars like W.R. Farmer, a vigorous opponent of either the Two-Document or modified Two-Document Hypothesis and an energetic advocate of the Griesbach Hypothesis that Mark is an abridgment of Matthew and Luke. Farmer's position, as representative of those defending the validity of the Griesbach Hypothesis, may be seen in his book, *The Synoptic Problem. A Critical Analysis* (rev. edn; New York: Macmillan, 1964; Dillsboro, NC: Western North Carolina Press, 1976) or his article, 'A "Skeleton in the Closet" of Gospel Research', *BR* 9 (1961), 18-42. Some of the most recent investigations related to the questions comprising the Synoptic Problem are found in *New Synoptic Studies: The Cambridge Gospel Conference and Beyond*, ed. W.R. Farmer (Macon, GA: Mercer University, 1983).

Kümmel includes a thorough survey of the Synoptic Problem and the various solutions that have been offered to it in his *Introduction* (38-80). For the purposes of the present study, a careful and persuasive espousal of the legitimacy of the modified Two-Document Hypothesis for the study of Luke is J.A. Fitzmyer's article, 'The Priority of Mark and the "Q" Source in Luke', *Perspectives* 11 (1970; also entitled *Jesus and Man's Hope*, I), I, 131-70; reprinted in *To Advance the Gospel: New Testament Studies* (New York: Crossroad, 1981), 3-40.

2. J.C. Hawkins ('Three Limitations to St Luke's Use of St Mark's Gospel', *Studies in the Synoptic Problem by Members of the University of Oxford*, ed. W. Sanday [Oxford: Clarendon, 1911], 29-94) gives a list of twelve *variations in order* in Luke's Passion Narrative as compared with Mark's. A.M. Perry (*The Sources of Luke's Passion-Narrative* [Chicago: University, 1920], 107) claims that twenty-three passages are introduced in Luke's Passion Narrative in a position different from that given them in

Mark. Of these items, twenty-one fall within the boundaries established for this study, i.e. chs. 22 and 23. V. Taylor (*The Passion Narrative of St Luke* [SNTSMS, 19; Cambridge: Cambridge University Press, 1972], 122 n. 2) describes thirteen differences in order between the Markan and Lukan Passion accounts. E. Schweizer (*Das Evangelium nach Lukas* [NTD, 3; Göttingen: Vandenhoeck & Ruprecht, 1982], 235) mentions eight transpositions. Here as in many other places scholars are not at one concerning the Lukan Passion Narrative. See also on this point, J. Jeremias, 'Perikopen-Umstellung bei Lukas?', *NTS* 4 (1957-58), 115-19.

3. Some of these differences of detail may be understood as the results of Luke's not using particular Markan material. Other such differences of detail may be the results of Luke's use of traditions not found in Mark. (We will consider both of these matters below.) J. Finegan (*Die Überlieferung der Leidens- und Auferstehungsgeschichte Jesu* [BZNW, 15; Giessen: Töpelmann, 1934], 27) suggests that Luke omits certain Markan incidents from their original narrative positions and incorporates those incidents in another context in his own narrative. J.A. Fitzmyer (*The Gospel according to Luke, I–IX* [AB, 28; Garden City, NY: Doubleday, 1981], 92-96) discusses at length the characteristics of Lukan redaction.

4. It should be noted that while different names are given for what appears to be the same place in the parallel accounts of Mark and Luke (see Mark 14.32 and Luke 22.39), Luke may have picked up the name, Mount of Olives, from Mark 14.26. In any case, Luke does not refer to Gethsemane in his narrative.

5. The differences in detail among apparently parallel stories in the various Gospels (canonical and non-canonical) provide much of the fodder for scholarly study of scripture. Methods are devised to analyze details in a 'scientific' fashion. Taylor (*Passion*, 30-37) suggests there are four methods available for investigating the problems of the Lukan Passion Narrative: (1) the numerical or statistical method, (2) the literary of stylistic study, (3) the form-critical approach, and (4) the use of historical criticism. Taylor describes, illustrates, and critiques each of these methods in a helpful way. One may argue, however, that his recourse (and that of others) to source theories may be too quick and reflect a presupposition that affects the value of his 'scientific' analysis.

6. Scholars do not agree concerning which verses in the Markan Passion Narrative lack parallels in the Lukan Passion Narrative. Perry (*Sources*, 107) claims these include 14.3-9, 20, (23-34), 26-29, 31c, 33-34, 38b-42, 44, 46, 50-52, 55-61, 64; 15.1a, 4-6, 8, 10, 16-20, 23, 25, 29, 34-36, 44-45. In identical lists (!) G. Schneider (*Das Evangelium nach Lukas* [Ökumenischer Taschenbuchkommentar zum Neuen Testament 3/1 & 2; Gütersloh/Würzburg: Mohn/Echter, 1977], II, 436) and J. Ernst (*Das Evangelium nach Lukas* [RNT; Regensburg: Pustet, 1977] 643), enumerate 14.3-9, 27, 33-34, 38b-42, 44, 46, 49b-52, 55-61a, 64; 15.4-5, 16-20a, 23, 25, 29-30, 34– 35, 44–

45. Schweizer (*Evangelium*, 235) offers still another list of Markan elements missing in Luke: 14.3-9, 26-28, 33f., 38b-42, 55-61a, 64b; 15.3-5, 6-10, 16-20a, 23, 25, 29f., 34f., 44f. The list offered here draws from these lists but differs from all of them for reasons that will be explained below.

The phenomenon of Luke *omitting* portions of Mark is discussed by Fitzmyer (*Gospel*, 92-94). The reason usually given by scholars for most of these omissions is described as Luke's 'principle of economy', i.e. Luke avoids redundant materials and he omits items that might detract from his overall literary plan.

7. *Horae Synopticae* (2nd edn; Oxford: Clarendon, 1909), 15.

8. *Sources*, 107.

9. *Passion*, 124.

10. Ernst judges the agreements between Mark and Luke to be insignificant when compared to the differences between their Passion accounts. He claims that the parts of Luke that represent Markan material worked into Luke's special source are 22.13, 34, 46b, 50b, 52b-53a, 54b-61; 23.3, 26, 34b, 38, 44-45, 49, 50-54. See *Evangelium*, 643.

11. *Evangelium*, II, 436.

12. *Gospel*, 67, 84.

13. *Evangelium*, 236.

14. In general the distinction between 'composition' and 'redaction' is clearly described by Fitzmyer (*Gospel*, 85) who defines *composition* as 'verses [Luke] wrote to present the story about Jesus and the sequel thereto in the form that he was interested in' and *redaction* as 'the editorial modifications of source-material that Luke had taken over'.

Often various authors will judge that in one place Luke is freely composing while in another place Luke is redacting tradition. For example, Bultmann (*History*, 282-83) claims that the healing of the ear cut off from the servant of the high priest (22.51) 'goes back to Luke himself'. Yet, for the Lukan account of the Last Supper, esp. 22.14-18, Bultmann (279) claims that Luke 'has another and indeed older report than Mark'. Bultmann even suggests that here Luke draws upon a special source that was written.

15. This line of thought is represented in Schneider's statement that 'if one takes into account the continuation of oral tradition both at the time of and following the composition of the Gospels, then one needs to postulate no connected special source for the special material of the third evangelist' (*Evangelium*, II, 436).

16. The history of this position is admirably surveyed by Taylor (*Passion*, 3-27). Since Taylor's work appeared in 1972, Ernst (*Evangelium*, see esp. 643-44) has taken this position. In 1982, Schweizer (who admits that the question about a special source cannot be finally answered) made a case for a special source (*Evangelium*, 235-36). Schweizer's position is generally consistent with his earlier argument for a 'hebraizing' source in Luke (see 'Eine hebraisierende Sonderquelle des Lukas?', *TZ* [1950], 161-85).

17. See nn. 14, 15, and 16.

18. In a paper entitled 'Luke's Account of Jesus before Herod Antipas' which was presented in the Catholic Biblical Association Luke–Acts Task Force at the annual meeting of the Catholic Biblical Association of America, August, 14–18, 1983, I studied a portion of the Lukan Passion Narrative that is universally recognized to go beyond Mark: Luke 23.6-12. In that paper (in revision as 'Tradition, Composition, and Theology in Luke's Account of Jesus before Herod Antipas', *Bib* 66 [1985], 344-64 I analyzed Luke's compositional and redactional technique. In 23.6-12, Luke appears to have composed a story upon the basis of two pieces of information that were available to him and that went beyond Mark, namely, that Herod Antipas was involved in the trial of Jesus and that Herod and Pilate were hostile toward one another. I argued that Luke composed this story and worked it into his Passion Narrative for at least two discernible reasons: (1) to emphasize the innocence of Jesus, and (2) to show his readers that Jesus' involvement in events brings about something good.

19. *Passion*, 41.

20. *Passion*, 41.

21. *Passion*, 42.

22. *Passion*, 44.

23. *Passion*, 59.

24. *Passion*, 119-26.

25. *Behind the Third Gospel: A Study of the Proto-Luke Hypothesis* (Oxford: Clarendon, 1926).

26. *Passion*, 87.

27. Certain of these writings are only relevant to Luke 23.

28. See R. Scroggs, 'Section IV: Markan Stylistic Characteristics in Introductory and Concluding Phrases and Sentences', in W. Kelber, A. Kolenkow, and R. Scroggs, 'Reflections on the Question: Was there a pre-Markan Passion Narrative?', *SBLASP 1971*, 503-85, esp. 529-37.

29. This judgment is shared by R.E. Brown (*The Birth of the Messiah* [Garden City, NY: Doubleday, 1977], 246) and is illustrated by the editorial comments of O.E. Evans in Taylor's *Passion* (27-30).

30. Prominent among those doing such study are B.S. Easton ('Linguistic Evidence for the Lucan Source L', *JBL* 29 [1910], 139-80), Hawkins (*Horae* and 'Limitations'), Perry (*Sources*), F. Rehkopf (*Die lukanische Sonderquelle: ihr Umfang und Sprachgebrauch* [WUNT, 5; Tübingen: Mohr, 1959]), G. Schneider (*Verleugnung, Verspottung und Verhör Jesu nach Lukas 22,54-71* [SANT, 22; München: Kösel, 1969], esp. 16), H. Schürmann (*Quellenkritische Untersuchung des lukanischen Abendmahlberichtes* [NTAbh 19/5, 20/4 & 5; Münster: Aschendorff, 1953/1955/1957]), and Taylor (*Passion*).

31. In 'The Question of a Pre-Markan Passion Narrative' (*Bible Bhashyam* 11 [1985], 144-69) I describe, illustrate, and criticize the methods or criteria used to distinguish sources and redaction in Gospel narrative. The criteria

discussed are (1) parallels, (2) internal tensions, (3) vocabulary and style, (4) theological themes and literary motifs, and (5) conceptual clusters. Some of these criteria become useful for analyzing the special Lukan Passion Narrative material from the perspective of thought-content.

32. To illustrate this process Luke 23.6-12 will be used as an example.

33. The story of Jesus' appearance before Herod Antipas is found only in Luke. The story begins in v. 6 with Pilate's unpredictable reaction to the charge leveled against Jesus in v. 5. A clear ending to the episode comes with the editorial report in v. 12.

34. Luke 23.6-12 has no parallel in Mark.

35. Luke 23.6-7 ties the scene of Jesus before Pilate to the story of Jesus before Herod.

36. Different parallels are suggested for various aspects of the account of Jesus before Herod. The idea of Herod Antipas being involved in the trial of Jesus finds parallels in both Acts 4 and *Gos. Pet.* 1 and 2. In Acts 4.25-27 we see early Christians depicted as employing Psalm 2 as a proof-from-prophecy. The Psalm portrays *kings* and *rulers* taking counsel together against the Lord and his anointed. The Psalm seems to have been employed merely because it provided a set of catchwords, *hoi basileis* and *hoi archontes*. The sense of the Psalm and the exegesis of it in Acts regarding the involvement of the kings and rulers are contrary to the scene in Luke 23. In Luke 23 Herod is a witness to Jesus' innocence. In Acts 4 he is depicted as aligned with Pilate against Jesus. The discrepancy between Luke 23 and Acts 4 suggests a basic historical remembrance of Herod's involvement in the trial of Jesus that was put to different uses in different places.

The narratives of Luke 23 and *Gos. Pet.* 1 and 2 are also different. In the *Gospel of Peter* Herod is responsible for the condemnation and execution of Jesus. A study of the *Gospel of Peter* (esp. focused on *Gos. Pet.* 1, 2, 5, 7, 13, 25, 28) shows numerous similarities to the tradition in Luke's Gospel. From a comparison of these points it appears that the *Gospel of Peter* reflects a later (though independent) anti-Jewish development of the earlier tradition found in or behind Luke 23.

Different parallels are suggested for the notice of Jesus' silence before Herod (23.9), e.g. Isa 53.7, *Mithras Liturgy* 6.42, or Mark 14.60-61 and 15.4-5. Similarly the mistreatment and dressing of Jesus at 23.11 find loose parallels in Mark 15.16-20.

Further, Herod's desire to see Jesus (23.8) is consistent with the statement at Luke 9.9. Moreover, the intense accusation by the Jewish leaders (23.10) is similar to Luke 23.3 and 18.

Finally, 23.12 relates that Pilate and Herod Antipas had been hostile toward one another. This statement is in agreement with information in Philo (*Embassy to Gaius* 28.299-305).

37. The statement at 23.12 that Pilate and Herod Antipas became friends after sending Jesus back and forth is unique to Luke.

38. See as examples B.S. Childs, *Introduction to the Old Testament as Scripture* (Philadelphia: Fortress, 1979); R.A. Culpepper, *Anatomy of the Fourth Gospel: A Study in Literary Design* (Phildelphia: Fortress, 1983); H. Frei, *The Eclipse of Biblical Narrative: A Study in Eighteenth and Nineteenth Century Hermeneutics* (New Haven: Yale University, 1974); N. Frye, *The Great Code: The Bible and Literature* (New York and London: Harcourt, Brace, Jovanovich, 1982); R.M. Frye, 'A Literary Perspective for the Criticism of the Gospels', in *Perspectives* 11 (1970; also entitled *Jesus and Man's Hope*, II), II, 193-221; F. Kermode, *The Genesis of Secrecy: On the Interpretation of Narrative* (Cambridge, MA: Harvard University, 1979); N. Petersen, *Literary Criticism for New Testament Critics* (Philadelphia: Fortress, 1978); and D. Rhoads and D. Michie, *Mark as Story: An Introduction to the Narrative of a Gospel* (Philadelphia: Fortress, 1982).

Notes to Chapter 2

1. A variety of answers is given by scholars to the question, 'Where does the Lukan Passion Narrative begin?' Most scholars designate Luke 22.1 as the starting point for the Lukan Passion Narrative. See W.F. Arndt, *The Gospel according to St. Luke* (St. Louis: Concordia, 1956); F.W. Danker, *Jesus and the New Age: According to Luke—A Commentary on the Third Gospel* (St. Louis: Clayton, 1972); Fitzmyer, *Gospel*; F.C. Grant, *The New Testament: The Gospels and the Acts of the Apostles* (Nelson's Bible Commentary, 6; New York: Nelson, 1962); W. Grundmann, *Das Evangelium nach Lukas* (THKNT, 3; 9th edn; Berlin: Evangelischer Verlag, 1981); J.H. Holtzmann, *Die Synoptiker—Die Apostelgeschichte* (HKNT, 1; Freiburg: Mohr, 1889); M.-J. Lagrange, *Evangile selon Saint Luc* (4th edn; Paris: Gabalda, 1927); E. LaVerdiere, *Luke* (New Testament Message, 5; Wilmington: Michael Glazier, 1980); W. Manson, *The Gospel of Luke* (MNTC; Hodder & Stoughton, 1930); I.H. Marshall, *The Gospel of Luke: A Commentary on the Greek Text* (New International Greek Testament Commentary; Grand Rapids: Eerdmans, 1978); A. Plummer, *The Gospel according to S. Luke* (ICC; 5th edn; Edinburgh: Clark, 1922); K.H. Rengstorf, *Das Evangelium nach Lukas* (NTD, 3; 13th edn; Göttingen: Vandenhoeck & Ruprecht, 1968); A. Schlatter, *Das Evangelium nach Markus und Lukas* (Schlatters Erläuterungen zum Neuen Testament, 2; Stuttgart: Calwer, 1947); A. Stöger, *The Gospel according to St. Luke*, I/II (New York: Crossroad, 1981; German original 1964); J. Weiss, *Die Schriften des Neuen Testaments*, I (Göttingen: Vandenhoeck & Ruprecht, 1906); and T. Zahn, *Das Evangelium des Lucas* (3rd & 4th edns; Leipzig: Deichert, 1920).

Other scholars who designate a unit wherein Luke tells of the activity of Jesus in Jerusalem, suggest that Luke introduced the final major section of the ministry of Jesus at 19.28. This final section is usually called Jesus' ministry in Jerusalem. Yet even the so-called Jerusalem ministry is divided into units, and the Passion is reckoned to begin at 22.1. See Ernst, *Evangelium*; J. Schmid, *Das Evangelium nach Lukas* (Regensburg: Pustet, 1951); Schneider, *Evangelium*; Schweizer, *Evangelium*; F. Stagg, *Studies in Luke's Gospel* (Nashville: Convention, 1967).

2. The translation follows the so-called longer text of the Lukan Last Supper, including 19e-20c as an authentic part of the original text. Since 1950, with the discovery of P^{75}, the inclusion of these lines has increasingly been the practice of textual critics. As early as 1951, Schürmann ('Lk 22,19b-20 als ursprüngliche Textüberlieferung', *Bib* 32 [1951], 364-92, 522-41) demonstrated the virtual impossibility of the originality of the shorter text. B.M. Metzger (*A Textual Commentary on the New Testament* [United Bible Society, 1971], 174-77) covers the problem thoroughly and makes a clear case for the authenticity of the 'longer' text.

3. Perry (*Sources*, 107) suggests that only a remote parallel exists between Mark 14.10 and Luke 22.3. Easton ('Evidence', 169) includes 22.3 in a list of special Lukan material that is mixed with other sources.

4. Scholars who maintain that 14a-c is Luke's redacted version of Mark 14.17 include Finegan, *Überlieferung*, 9; Schürmann, *Paschamahlbericht*, 104-10, esp. 110; and Schneider, *Evangelium*, II, 444. Scholars who deny that Luke has redacted Mark and is rather following a non-Markan source include Taylor, *Passion*, 47-58, 48-49; and Jeremias, *The Eucharistic Words of Jesus* (rev. edn; New York: Scribner's, 1966), 99 n. 1.

5. There is consistent support for this position among scholars. Those who understand Luke to be following a special source here include Easton, 'Evidence', 169; Hawkins, *Horae*, 15; Perry, *Sources*, 107; Schürmann, *Paschamahlbericht*, 3-14; Rehkopf, *Sonderquelle*, 30; Jeremias, *Words*, 96-100, 160-64; Taylor, *Passion*, 47-58; Ernst, *Evangelium*, 643; and Schweizer, *Evangelium*, 236. Others who do not judge that Luke follows a source in v. 15 (e.g. Schneider, *Evangelium*, II, 436) still contend that the verse is special Lukan material.

6. The positions taken by critics on v. 16 are the same as for v. 15 except for Hawkins (*Horae*) who does not designate v. 16 as special Lukan material.

7. *Passion*, 47.

8. *Sources*, 39-40.

9. Five of the eleven words in 17a-b are matched in Mark 14.23-24. Taylor (*Passion*, 47) shows the parallels but does not make anything of them in his discussion. Both Finegan (*Überlieferung*, 12) and X. Léon-Dufour ('Das letzte Mahl Jesu und die testamentarische Tradition nach Lk 22', *ZTK* 103 [1981], 35) do argue, however, that Luke 22.17 is a parallel to Mark 14.23-24.

10. Taylor follows Schürmann (*Paschamahlbericht*, 46-74) here.

11. See Schürmann, *Paschamahlbericht*, 14-23, 34-46, 50-52.

12. A position similar to the one taken here is argued by R. Pesch (*Das Abendmahl und Jesu Todesverständnis* [Quaestiones Disputatae, 80; Freiburg: Herder, 1978], 31-34).

13. This position is at least as old as A. Schweitzer, *Das Abendmahlsproblem auf Grund der wissenschaftlichen Forschung des neunzehnten Jahrhunderts und der historischen Berichte* (Tübingen: Mohr, 1901). Schürmann devotes the entire volume, *Einsetzungsbericht*, to the analysis of 22.19-20; see esp. 7-14, 17-42. See Jeremias, *Words*, 138-203.

14. Perry (*Sources*, 107) recognized 24a-27d as a remote parallel to Mark 10.41-45. Others (e.g. Schweizer, *Evangelium*, 222) restrict the focus and suggest that there is a parallel to 25a-27d in Mark 10.42b-45. Still others (e.g. J.A. Bailey, *The Traditions Common to the Gospels of Luke and John* [NovTSup, 7; Leiden: Brill, 1963], 35) argue that only 25a-26c are matched by Mark 10.42b-44.

15. With regard to the relationship of Luke 22.27 to Mark 10.45, M. Rese (*Alttestamentliche Motive in der Christologie des Lukas* [SNT, 1; Gütersloh: Mohn, 1969], 161-64) suggests there are three possible solutions. First, 22.27 offers the primitive form of a saying that was filled out from a dogmatic perspective in Mark. Second, 22.27 is a dogmatically motivated shortening of the statement in Mark. Third, Luke and Mark are literarily independent from one another, but they depend upon a commonly held *Vorform*. Rese claims to follow the work of E. Lohse (*Märtyrer und Gottesknecht. Untersuchungen zur urchristlichen Verkündigung vom Sühntod Jesu Christi* [FRLANT, 64; Göttingen: Vandenhoeck & Ruprecht, 1955], 117-22) in deciding in favor of the third of these options. He relates the *Vorform* to 'allusions' to Isa 53.10-12 in both Mark and Luke. He argues that the existence of the *Vorform* explains not only the relationship of Mark 10.45 and Luke 22.27 but also the explicit citation of Isa 53.12 in Luke 22.37.

16. Compare E. Klostermann (*Das Lukasevangelium* [HNT, 5; 2nd edn; Tübingen: Mohr, 1929], 209-11) who points to the sharp differences between Mark 10.42b-44 and Luke 22.25-26. He shows that Mark teaches that the way to greatness is through service while Luke enjoins *noblesse oblige* on those who are already great.

17. We will give further attention below to the pattern of addressing Simon Peter in this section.

18. In a careful study of the question of whether or not there was a pre-canonical Passion Narrative ('Das Problem einer vorcanonischen Passionserzählung', *BZ* 16 [1972], 222-44), G. Schneider concludes, 'In my opinion, only the following Lukan units from Luke 22 can be reckoned with certainty as pre-Lukan and non-Markan: 22.19-20a (anamnesis with the bread-word); 24-26, 28-30 (dispute over rank; reward of discipleship); 31-32 (statement to Peter); 35-38 (two swords); 63-64, 66-68 (scoffing; examination)' (236).

19. Many studies campare Luke to Matthew and/or John. Prominent among these are E. Osty, 'Les points de contact entre les récits de la Passion

dans Saint Luc et Saint Jean', *RSR* 39 (1951), 146-54; P. Borgen, 'John and the Synoptics in the Passion Narrative', *NTS* 5 (1958-59), 246-59; N. Turner, 'The Minor Verbal Agreements of Mt. and Lk. against Mk.', in *Studia Evangelica*, K. Aland *et al.*, eds. (Berlin: Akademie, 1959), 223-34; R.McL. Wilson, 'Farrer and Streeter on the Minor Agreements of Matthew and Luke against Mark', in *Studia Evangelica*, K. Aland *et al.*, eds. (Berlin: Akademie, 1959), 254-57; X. Léon-Dufour, 'Passion (Récits de la)', *DBS* 6 (1960), cols. 1419-92; I. Buse, 'St John and the Passion Narratives of St Matthew and St Luke', *NTS* 7 (1960-61), 65-76; S. Temple, 'Two Traditions of the Last Supper, Betrayal, and Arrest', *NTS* 7 (1960-61), 77-85; P. Parker, 'Luke and the Fourth Evangelist', *NTS* 9 (1962-63), 317-36; Bailey, *Traditions*, 29-46; Schneider, 'Problem'; F. Neirynck, 'La matière marcienne dans l'évangile de Luc' in *L'Evangile de Luc: Problèmes littéraires et théologiques*, F. Neirynck ed. (BETL, 32; Gembloux: Duculot, 1973), 157-201; Neirynck, *The Minor Agreements of Matthew and Luke against Mark with a Cumulative List* (BETL 37; Gembloux: Duculot, 1973); and H. Klein, 'Die lukanisch-johanneische Passionstradition', *ZNW* 67 (1976), 155-86.

20. Neirynck, *Agreements*, 169.

21. We see at 22.47, that Luke can use *ho legomenos* to make explicit reference to 'Judas'. That he does not use this participial phrase at 3b weakens further the possibility that there is an 'agreement' between Matt 26.14 and Luke 22.3b.

22. Neirynck (*Agreements*, 169) records this parallel as did earlier Léon-Dufour ('Passion', col. 1446).

23. Léon-Dufour, 'Passion', col. 1446; Neirynck, *Agreements*, 169.

24. T. Schramm, *Der Markus-Stoff bei Lukas: Eine literarkritische und redaktionsgeschichtliche Untersuchung* (SNTSMS, 14; Cambridge: Cambridge University Press, 1971), 182 n. 8.

25. See R.E. Brown, *The Gospel according to John, XIII–XXI* (AB, 29A; Garden City, NY: Doubleday, 1970), 563.

26. See R.E. Brown, *The Gospel according to John, I–XII* (AB, 29; Garden City, NY: Doubleday, 1966), 99-100.

27. 'Points', 147.

28. Rehkopf, *Sonderquelle*, 30.

29. Perry, *Sources*, 108; Léon-Dufour, 'Passion', col. 1445; Neirynck, *Agreements*, 172.

30. 'St John', 69, citing Taylor, *Behind*, 40-41.

31. E.g. Neirynck, *Agreements*, 172. Notice, however, that even here the textual problem is recognized.

32. See Metzger, *Textual Commentary*, 64.

33. The differences between Mark and Luke at this point have led scholars to different conclusions. Finegan (*Überlieferung*, 9) argues that Luke simply edited Mark's account. Perry (*Sources*, 107) calls 22.21 a remote parallel to Mark. Taylor (*Passion*, 59-61) contends that this verse is from Luke's special

source. We will have occasion to consider this verse in more detail at several points below.

34. A recent reminder of the vitality and powerful influence of oral tradition comes from W.H. Kelber, *The Oral and Written Gospel: The Hermeneutics of Speaking and Writing in the Synoptic Tradition, Mark, Paul, and Q* (Philadelphia: Fortress, 1983), esp. 1-43. A careful earlier study that showed the continuation of oral tradition alongside the written is H. Köster, *Synoptische Überlieferung bei den apostolischen Vätern* (TU, 65; Berlin: Akademie, 1957), *passim*, esp. 257-67.

Farmer's position (see *Problem*, esp. 199-232) that Mark wrote after Matthew and Luke and used both Gospels as sources does not seem to account for the complexity of this 'minor' agreement between Matthew and Luke. Why would Mark, whose text is closer here to that of Matthew than that of Luke, follow Matthew instead of Luke *and* omit the most prominent common element (the hand) between Matthew and Luke?

35. Hawkins, 'Limitations', 82; Perry, *Sources*, 107; Léon-Dufour, 'Passion', col. 1442; Rehkopf, *Sonderquelle*, 83.

36. P. Parker, 'Luke', 326.

37. Perry, *Sources*, 108; Osty, 'Points', 147; Léon-Dufour, 'Passion', col. 1443; Buse, 'St John', 68-69; Rehkopf, *Sonderquelle*, 27; Klein, 'Passionstradition', 168-69.

38. 'Points', 147.

39. See n. 16 above.

40. 'St John', 69.

41. See Brown, *Gospel XIII–XXI*, 548-72; F.F. Segovia, 'John 13,1-20, The Footwashing in the Johannine Tradition', *ZNW* 73 (1982), 31-51. That the one event described in John 13.4-5 finds two distinct interpretations in vv. 6-11 and vv. 12-20, indicates that a historical catalyst more substantive than the Lukan logion (or a similar logion in a source) lies behind John 13.1-20.

42. Finegan (*Überlieferung*, 14) contends that v. 28 is from Q, the original form of which is in Matt 19.28.

43. Parker, 'Luke', 321.

44. Bailey (*Traditions*, 37-46) suggests that Luke's version of the words of Jesus (31a-32d) are a devolution from the original post-resurrection context that is accurately preserved in John 21. Buse ('St John', 70) says that v. 32 causes the reader to think of John 17. He suggests further that 32c-d may be compared to John 21.15-18. Parker ('Luke', 321) offers the most elaborate line of comparison between Luke and John here.

45. See Léon-Dufour, 'Passion', col. 1443.

46. Compare Klein ('Passionstradition', 33-34) who argues that there are three agreements between Luke 22.33-34 and John 13.36-38. He lists (1) the cock crows but once, (2) Peter's readiness to give his life, and (3) the address 'Lord'. The third is dealt with in the next section. Peter's readiness to die is

recorded in all four Gospels (Mark 14.31; Matt 26.35; Luke 22.33b; John 13.37); so there is no special significance to the agreement between Luke and John.

47. See above n. 34.

48. Perry (*Sources*, 107) describes v. 8 as a transposition of Markan order. Yet he suggests elsewhere (40) that while vv. 7-13 seem to agree thoroughly with Mark, vv. 14f. are from Luke's special source. Verse 14, he suggests, was originally preceded by another introduction. He notes that v. 8 names the disciples specifically whereas they are not named in Mark. He also argues that the conversation is recast in Luke. He suggests that v. 8 forms a good introduction to the account of the supper in v. 14 and following. He claims that with the exception of *pascha* v. 8 rests on Luke's special source.

49. See Hawkins, 'Limitations', 81; Perry, *Sources*, 107; Finegan, *Überlieferung*, 12; Schneider, *Verleugnung*, 144-51, esp. 146. Similarly Léon-Dufour ('Mahl', 35) suggests that 18a-c is a parallel to Mark 14.25. Taylor (*Passion*, 122-23) regards this difference in order as the result of the insertion of 19a from Mark (14.22) into Luke's other source.

50. See Hawkins, 'Limitations', 82; Perry, *Sources*, 107; Finegan, *Überlieferung*, 9; Léon-Dufour, 'Passion', col. 1447; Schneider, *Verleugnung*, 144-51, esp. 146 and *Evangelium*, II, 446; Schweizer, *Evangelium*, 235. Taylor (*Passion*, 122-23) argues that Luke is following his special source.

51. See Hawkins, 'Limitations', 82; Perry, *Sources*, 107; Léon-Dufour, 'Passion', col. 1447; Schneider, *Verleugnung*, 146. Rehkopf (*Sonderquelle*, 83) maintains that the variation in order in general (the announcement occurring after the meal) and the internal difference (woe before the disciples' questioning) shows the entirely non-Markan origin of this material.

52. Perry (*Sources*, 107) describes 24a-27d as a transposition of Markan material. Others who judge 24a-27d to be based upon Mark 10.41-45 include: Finegan (*Überlieferung*, 13-14); Schmid (*Evangelium*, 264-66); and Schneider (*Evangelium*, II, 450). Still others find the differences in wording and thought to indicate that Luke is using a special non-Markan source: See J.M. Creed, *The Gospel according to St. Luke* (London: Macmillan, 1930), 267; Schürmann (*Abschiedsrede*, 63-99), who concludes that vv. 24-26 are a pre-Lukan insertion into a basic pre-Lukan *Vorlage*: vv. 15-18, 19-20b, 28-30; Taylor, *Passion*, 61-64; Marshall, *Gospel*, 811; and Grundmann, *Evangelium*, 400-401.

53. A similar conclusion is reached by Bailey (*Traditions*, 35) who argues that vv. 25-26 are Luke's version of Mark 10.42b-44.

54. See Hawkins, 'Limitations', 82; Finegan, *Überlieferung*, 15; Schürmann, *Abschiedsrede*, 21-35; Schneider, *Verleugnung*, 144-51, esp. 146.

55. The mention of Peter's readiness to die before the logion about the cockcrow in Luke and after the similar logion in Mark is judged by Schneider (*Verleugnung*, 146) to be a simple transposition of Markan

material by Luke. Taylor (*Passion*, 123) argues, however, that only v. 34 is Markan material; he attributes the change in order to Luke's inserting v. 34 into his other source.

Zahn (*Evangelium*, 667), Plummer (*Gospel*, 503), Rengstorf (*Evangelium*, 240), and Rehkopf (*Sonderquelle*, 84 n. 1) contend that neither v. 33 nor v. 34 comes from Mark but from Luke's special source.

56. Schneider (*Verleugnung*, 146) lists one other 'transposition' not considered in this study. He argues that 'apart from a crowd' appears at Luke 22.6c *after* the conference between Judas and the Jewish leaders, but in Mark 14.1-2, the idea is attributed to the leaders *prior to* the conference with Judas. But the mention of the crowd at 6c is not a transposition of Mark's mention of the crowd at 14.2. Luke 22.2b is the real parallel to Mark's idea, and the mention of the crowd at 6b is a reiteration or reinforcement of what Luke communicated to the reader at 22.2b.

57. *Sources*, 107.

58. Similarly, Neirynck ('Argument', 814-15) warns that attention to any individual phenomenon (his concern is with transpositions) can unduly limit the recognition of the creative activity of the evangelist. F.G. Untergassmair (*Kreuzweg und Kreuzigung Jesu* [Paderborner Theologische Studien, 10; Paderborn: Schöningh, 1980], 5-6) writes, 'H. Schürmann ('Proto-lukanische Spracheigentümlichkeiten? Zu Fr. Rehkopf, Die lukanische Sonderquelle. Ihr Umfang und Sprachgebrauch', *BZ* 5 [1961], 266-86) and, in agreement with him, G. Schneider (*Verleugnung*, 14-15) have pointed to the difficulties and dangers that redaction-critical investigations can encounter if these operate in their methodological process in an overly one-sided manner with linguistic-stylistic arguments of probability (allzu einseitig mit sprachlich-stylistischen "Wahrscheinlichkeits-Argumenten")'.

59. *Passion*, 44.

60. E.g. Hawkins, *Horae*; Easton, 'Evidence'; H.J. Cadbury, *The Style and Literary Method of Luke* (HTS, 6; Cambridge, MA: Harvard University, 1920); Rehkopf, *Sonderquelle*.

61. BDF 267 (2).

62. *Markus-Stoff*, 182-83, 186.

63. 'Matière', 169-70.

64. Finegan (*Überlieferung*, 6), citing 22.31, describes the involvement of Satan in the Passion as a Lukan concern.

65. Finegan, *Überlieferung*, 6.

66. Compare Easton, 'Evidence', 151, 165.

67. Compare Easton, 'Evidence', 145.

68. *Überlieferung*, 9. See also Fitzmyer, *Gospel*, 617-18. Compare Easton, 'Evidence', 145; Rehkopf, *Sonderquelle*, 92.

For a thorough discussion of *the apostles*, see K. Lake, 'The Twelve and the Apostles' in *The Acts of the Apostles*, V (London: Macmillan, 1933), 37-59; compare the position of G. Klein, *Die zwölf Apostel: Ursprung und Gestalt* einer Idee (FRLANT, 77; Göttingen: Vandenhoeck & Ruprecht, 1961).

69. Mark and John do not use the verb *epithymein*. Matthew uses it twice (5.28; 13.17).

70. Pesch (*Abendmahl*, 28) describes *epithymia epethymēsa* as a 'Septuagintalism'. He compares the phrase to Gen 31.30 and 1QapGen XX.10-11 and claims by comparison to Matthew that *epithymein* is preferred Lukan vocabulary—Luke has the word five times, Matthew twice.

71. Both Mark and Matthew use the word absolutely once. Luke uses *paschein* six times, five of which are *pathein*.

72. *Abendmahl*, 28.

73. A. Plummer (*Gospel*, 495) argues that *eucharistein* seems to imply the eucharistic cup. An analysis of Luke's use of this verb does not suggest that it has a 'fixed' meaning in his Gospel. Scholars describing the vocabulary of the putative Lukan source do not list this verb as characteristic of that source. E.g. Easton, 'Evidence'; Rehkopf, *Sonderquelle*.

74. Pesch (*Abendmahl*, 29) judges the phrase to be *Lukan*. Finegan (*Überlieferung*, 12) is in agreement with Pesch; but compare Easton ('Evidence', 145) and Rehkopf (*Sonderquelle*, 92) who claim *apo tou nyn* is typical of Luke's special source.

75. Compare Easton ('Evidence', 165) who suggests that *synzētein* may be characteristic of Luke's non-Markan source.

76. Mark uses *peirasmos* once (14.38) and Matthew twice (6.13; 26.41).

77. Finegan (*Überlieferung*, 15) claims that *deisthai* is characteristic of Luke and is consistent with his interest in prayer throughout Luke-Acts.

Notes to Chapter 3

1. *Markus-Stoff*, 182-83, 186.

2. 'Matière', 169-70.

3. This is the position taken by Bailey, *Traditions*, 29-31.

4. The implausibility of the literary dependence of John on Luke is demonstrated by R.E. Brown, *Gospel I–XII*, xliv-xlvii. See also the work of Parker, 'Luke', *passim*.

5. See Buse, 'St John', 68; Parker, 'Luke', 336; and Brown, *Gospel I–XII*, xlvii.

6. An example of the idea of the involvement of 'Satan' in the death of a righteous man appears in *The Martyrdom and Ascension of Isaiah* 3.11; 5.1. At 3.11, one learns that *Beliar* dwelled in the heart of Manasseh and his compatriots, and then, at 5.1, that Beliar became angry with Isaiah; and so, he brought about the execution of the prophet.

J.H. Charlesworth (*The Pseudepigrapha and Modern Research with a Supplement* [Septuagint and Cognate Studies, 7S; Chico, CA: Scholars, 1981], 125-28) argues that *The Martyrdom and Ascension of Isaiah* is a composite work. The portion containing 3.11 is probably a Jewish writing from around the second century BC. The portion that contains 5.1 is most likely a Christian writing composed around the end of the second century AD. If Charlesworth is correct it is important to notice that the idea of Satan's involvement in the demise of a righteous man is found in a popular work that is perhaps two centuries older than the Gospel of Luke. It is impossible to know whether this particular document influenced Luke and John.

7. Contrary to the well-known opinion of H. Conzelmann (*The Theology of St Luke* [New York: Harper, 1960; German original 1954; 2nd edn 1957], 16 *et passim*) the time of Jesus' ministry is not a Satan-free period. The inadequacy of Conzelmann's position is well demonstrated by S. Brown, *Apostasy and Perseverance in the Theology of Luke* (AnBib, 36; Rome: Biblical Institute, 1969). A summary discussion of this topic appears in Fitzmyer, *Gospel*, 186-87.

8. There is no need to understand the unit 15a-18c as Schürmann does (*Einsetzungsbericht*, 133-50), namely, as the trace of an original simple story of Jesus' last meal with his disciples. At the meal there was a double prophecy of Jesus' imminent death. This simple, original story was later redacted by adding vv. 19-20 to make the Last Supper the scene of the institution of the Eucharist.

Other interpreters understand both cups in Luke's account to have eucharistic significance. These critics suggest parallels to the cup that precedes the bread in *Did.* 9.2 (see K. Lake, *et al.*, *The New Testament in the Apostolic Fathers* [Oxford: Clarendon, 1905], 30) and 1 Cor 10.16 (see P. Benoit, 'Le récit de la cène dans Lc XXII,15-20: Etude de critique textuelle et littéraire', *RB* 48 [1939], 357-93; reprinted in Benoit, *Exégèse et Théologie*, I [Paris: Cerf, 1961], 163-203).

9. Pesch (*Abendmahl*, 26-31) argues persuasively that 22.15-18 is a Lukan product built upon the material from Mark 14.23-25.

10. Finegan, *Überlieferung*, 12; see also Schneider (*Evangelium*, II, 445) who argues that the parallelism accentuates and emphasizes the words of Jesus in these verses.

11. Finegan, *Überlieferung*, 12; Pesch, *Abendmahl*, 31-34.

12. Danker (*Jesus*, 221) claims that *artistically* the narrative moves smoothly from v. 23 to v. 24.

13. Plummer (*Gospel*, 500) argues that while there is an abundant record of such disputes among the disciples, it appears the traditions became confused. He suggests the reader should compare Matt 18.1-5; Mark 9.33-37; Luke 9.46-48; John 13.14; also, Matt 20.24-28; Mark 10.41-45; Luke 22.24-27.

14. Working in different ways, both Bailey (*Traditions*, 35) and C.H. Talbert (*Literary Patterns, Theological Themes, and the Genre of Luke–Acts* [SBLMS, 20; Missoula, MT: Scholars, 1974], 26-29) notice the similarity

between 24b and 9.46.

Finegan (*Überlieferung*, 13) suggests that Luke composed v. 24 by drawing on Mark 9.34. He also suggests that the mention of 'the youngest' at 26b is a reflection of Mark 9.36. It is clear that Luke drew on Mark 9.33-37 for his narrative at 9.46-48. The difference between Finegan's understanding and the interpretation offered above is, therefore, slight. Schweizer (*Evangelium*, 450) also attributes v. 24 to Luke.

15. Büchele, *Der Tod Jesu im Lukasevangelium: Eine redaktionsgeschichtliche Untersuchung zu Lk 23* (Frankfurt: Knecht, 1978), 168-69.

16. See W.G. Kümmel, 'Current Theological Accusations against Luke', *ANQ* 16 (1975; French original 1970), 131-45, esp. 134, 138, 141-43; A. George, 'Le sens de la mort de Jesus pour Luc', *RB* 80 (1973), 166-217; reprinted in *Etudes sur l'œuvre de Luc* (Paris: Gabalda, 1978), 185-212; and Fitzmyer, *Gospel*, 219-21.

17. Compare this interpretation with that of H. Schürmann, 'Das Thomasevangelium und das lukanische Sondergut', *BZ* 7 (1963), 236-60. Schürmann examines *Gos. Thom.* 78 in relation to Luke 22.24-27, arguing that the parallel is not between Luke's special material and *Gos. Thom.* 78. Rather, there is an indirect parallel between *Gos. Thom.* 78 and Luke's *Redequelle*. He contends that this solution is clear from a comparison of Luke and *The Gospel of Thomas* with Matt 23.(8-)11. Schürmann demonstrates that Luke is not dependent upon (a) *Gos. Thom.* 78 or (b) a common source. Moreover, *Gos. Thom.* 78 does not contain material drawn from Luke's special source; rather *Gos. Thom.* 78 depends upon either the Lukan redaction of the *Redequelle* or upon a harmonized Gospel that used Luke as a source.

18. Fitzmyer (*Gospel*, 79) suggests the same parallel.

19. Compare Grundmann (*Evangelium*, 402-403) who claims that vv. 28-30 have a very primitive character. For him v. 28, in its praise of the disciples, stands in tension with vv. 21-24 and vv. 31-38. Luke included these verses here because of the stem agreement between *diatithesthai* (v. 29) and the covenant (*diathēkē*) mentioned in the preceding verses. He also claims that we can understand 30a to be an addition because of the different forms of *basileia* in v. 29 and v. 30.

20. Marshall (*Gospel*, 814-15) holds that the evangelists Matthew and Luke worked with different recensions of the Q document. And so we should understand the form and location of the Q tradition in Luke as the result of his use of a particular version of Q.

21. Danker, *Jesus*, 223.

22. Finegan, *Überlieferung*, 14.

23. Schneider, *Evangelium*, II, 451.

24. See Schneider, *Evangelium*, II, 451; and C.H. Talbert, *Reading Luke: A Literary and Theological Commentary on the Third Gospel* (New York: Crossroad, 1982), 210-11.

25. See Cadbury, *Style*, 95; Fitzmyer, *Gospel*, 91-97, esp. 95-96.

26. Schürmann (*Abschiedsrede*, 99-116) argues that vv. 31-32 are pre-Lukan additions to a basic pre-Lukan *Vorlage* (vv. 15-18, 19-20a, 28-30) that had already been expanded prior to Luke's writing by the insertion of other material (vv. 24-26, 27).

L. Feldkämper (*Der betende Jesus als Heilsmittler nach Lukas* [St. Augustin: Steyler, 1978], 206-207) focuses on the mention of prayer at v. 32, a reference that is one element in the larger dialogue between Jesus and Peter in vv. 31-34. He argues that vv. 31-34 form a self-contained unit that stands apart from the foregoing and following context. Because of the tension he claims exists between the promise and instruction of v. 32 and the announcement of denial in v. 34, Feldkämper concludes that vv. 31-34 is itself made up of materials of distinct origins.

Schneider (*Evangelium*, II, 452-53) contends that vv. 31-32 are from a 'special oral tradition'. Compare Marshall *Gospel*, 819.

27. Other scholars posit a parallel exists between vv. 31- 32 and 2 Sam 15.20-21. See W.K.L. Clarke, 'The Use of the Septuagint in Acts', in F.J.F. Jackson and K. Lake, eds., *The Acts of the Apostles*, II (London: Macmillan, 1920-33), 104; Finegan *Überlieferung*, 15; and Taylor *Passion*, 66.

28. See Feldkämper, *Jesus, passim*, esp. 15-27; and Fitzmyer, *Gospel*, 244-47.

29. *Gospel*, 244.

30. A different interpretation of 22.31-32 appears in R.E. Brown, K.P. Donfried, and J. Reumann, eds., *Peter in the New Testament* (Minneapolis/New York: Augsburg/Paulist, 1973), 120-21.

31. The same conclusion is reached by H.-W. Bartsch, 'Jesu Schwertwort, Lukas xxii.35-38: Überlieferungsgeschichtliche Studie', *NTS* (1974), 190-203. Compare Schürmann (*Abschiedsrede*, 134) who concludes that vv. 35-38 are a pre-Lukan addition to a basic pre-Lukan *Vorlage* that was expanded prior to Luke's writing by the insertion of vv. 24-26, 27. Schürmann suggests that vv. 35-37 (v. 37 only in part) form an older kernel of pre-Lukan material that clearly did not belong in the Passion Narrative. The focus of these verses is not on Jesus but on the fiendish opposition to early Christian missionaries.

32. See 2.49; 4.43; 9.22; 13.33; 17.25; 19.5; 21.9; 24.7, 44.

33. Danker, *Jesus*, 225.

34. See M. Rese (*Motive*, 154-64) who points out that the text here deviates from LXX, not the MT.

35. Finegan (*Überlieferung*, 16) relates the realization of scripture in 37c to 22.49-50; whereas Untergassmair (*Kreuzweg*, 177) and Rese (*Motive*, 162-64) view 37c in relation to 23.32, 39-43.

36. Schneider (*Evangelium*, II, 456) claims that v. 38 goes back to Luke's hand. Compare also J. Gillman ('A Temptation to Violence: The Two Swords in Lk 22.35-38', *Louvain Studies* 9 [1982], 142-53) who argues that

the sword saying should be taken literally, not metaphorically. The statement represents a momentary temptation of Jesus to employ violence. Gillman goes on to argue that the text was preserved in the Lukan and post-Lukan communities as approval of the use of violence. It is difficult to see how Gillman can maintain his position in the light of 22.49-51.

37. Compare Finegan (*Überlieferung*, 16) who argues that the only point of this sword saying is to provide an introduction to the forthcoming sword scene.

38. R. Pesch (*Wie Jesus das Abendmahl hielt: Der Grund der Eucharistie* [Freiburg: Herder, 1977], 33) claims it is typical of Luke that he uses additional pieces of tradition in forming his own redactional compositions. Pesch compares Luke 5.1-11 with Mark 1.16-20; 4.1-2, and John 21.1-14 in order to make this point.

39. See 5.29-39; 7.36-50; 9.12-17; 10.38-42; 11.37-52; 14.1-35; 24.28-31, 41-43(?).

40. At numerous points in the earlier portions of this study, we have seen the agreement in narrative order between Luke and John. In general, there is an agreement between the two evangelists in the inclusion of a farewell address by Jesus at the Last Supper. Specifically, both Luke and John have Jesus announce his betrayal after the meal, and both evangelists have Jesus predict that Peter will deny him before the group leaves the banquet room.

41. See J. Munck, 'Discours d'adieu dans le Nouveau Testament et dans la littérature biblique', in *Aux Sources de la Tradition Chrétienne* (Neuchâtel/Paris: Delachaux & Niestle, 1950), 155-70; E. Stauffer, 'Abschiedsreden', *RAC* 1 (1950), cols. 29-35; Schürmann, *Abschiedsrede*, 1-2; R. Schnackenburg, 'Abschiedsreden Jesu', *LTK* 1 (1957), cols. 68-69; Brown, *Gospel XIII-XXI*, 595-603; G.J. Bahr, 'The Seder of the Passover and the Eucharistic Words', *NovT* 12 (1970), 181-202; Pesch, *Jesus*, 39; Léon-Dufour, 'Mahl'; T. Huser, 'Les récits de l'institution de la Cène. Dissemblances et traditions', *Hokhma* 21 (1982), 28-50.

42. The classical paradigm is the dialogue of Socrates with his students in Plato's *Phaedo*. M. Coffey ('Symposium Literature', *The Oxford Classical Dictionary*, 1028-29) lists works by Xenophon, Aristotle, Epicurus, Maecenas, and Plutarch along with that of Plato. He suggests that 'the genre was used . . . as a vehicle for miscellaneous learning and lore' (1028).

43. See Gen 47.29–50.14; Deuteronomy, esp. chs. 32–33; 1 Sam 12.20-25; 1 Kgs 2; 1 Chron 28–29.

44. See 1 Macc 2.49-70; 2 Macc 6.30; 7.1-42; 4 Macc; Tob 4; 14.

45. See *2 Bar.* 77.1-26; *T. 12 Patriarchs*; *1 Enoch* 91–92; 94-105; *Testament of Job*; *Testament of Moses*; *4 Ezra* 14.18-50; *Testament of Abraham*, *Testament of Isaac*, *Testament of Solomon*, *Testament of Jacob*, *Testament of Adam*.

J.H. Charlesworth (*The Old Testament Pseudepigrapha*, I [Garden City,

NY: Doubleday, 1983], 773) suggests that *Testament of Hezekiah* (in *The Martyrdom and Ascension of Isaiah*, 3.13–4.18), *Testament of Zosimus*, and *Testament of Orpheus* should also be consulted in this connection.

46. See John 13–16; Acts 20.17-38; 1 Tim 4.1; 2 Tim 3.1-4.18; 2 Pet 1.12-15.

47. See *The Epistle of the Apostles*; *The Martyrdom of Peter* 7-10; *Acts of Andrew* 15–18.

48. See E.E. Ellis, *The Gospel of Luke* (New Century Bible; 2nd edn; London: Oliphants, 1974), 251.

49. See Charlesworth, *Old Testament Pseudepigrapha*, 773.

50. See Léon-Dufour ('Mahl') who argues that 22.1-38 generally conforms to the pattern of final testaments in *The Testaments of the Twelve Patriarchs*. He suggests that the general form is (a) past, (b) present, and (c) future. Yet he argues that the most specific parallels can be found between vv. 1-38 and *Testament of Naphtali*. Léon-Dufour develops an elaborate chart of the parallels between these two works (55). Careful study of the parallels does not always support his suggestions. Perhaps the problem is that he tries to match every element of Luke's testament with some information in *Testament of Naphtali*, because he does not allow for sufficient variety in the literary genre. But Léon-Dufour does persuasively show that Luke 22.1-38 belongs to the genre of *testaments*.

See also W.S. Kurz ('Luke 22.14-38 and Greco-Roman and Biblical Farewell Addresses', *JBL* 104 [1985], 251-68) who argues that in having Jesus speak at length after the meal, Luke shows that he 'had enough rhetorical training to recognize and imitate a literary form and genre such as the farewell address'—though he used no 'one farewell speech as his exemplar' (252).

51. This position is different from that taken by Q. Quesnell, 'The Women at Luke's Supper', in R.J. Cassidy and P.J. Scharper, eds., *Political Issues in Luke–Acts* (Maryknoll, NY: Orbis, 1983), 59-79. Quesnell is correct that Luke does number the women followers of Jesus as disciples, but his claim that 'Luke did think in terms of a larger group at the Supper than just the Twelve' (71) flies in the face of the plain sense of the text.

Notes to Chapter 4

1. Three verses of 22.39-71 offer significant problems for textual critics with regard to their authenticity: namely, 43-44 (omitted here) and 62 (included). A quick survey of the problems, the evidence for solving the problems, and the logic of the solutions is available in Metzger, *Textual Commentary*, 177-78; and Marshall, *Commentary*, 831-33, 844-45.

Prominent works that defend the authenticity of 22.43-44 include those of M. Goguel (*The Life of Jesus*, trans. O. Wyon [New York: Macmillan, 1933],

493 n. 1), L. Brun ('Engel und Blutschweiss Lc 22,43-44', *ZNW* 32 [1933], 265-76), G. Schneider ('Engel und Blutschweiss [Lk 22,43-44] "Redaktions-geschichte" im Dienste der Textkritik', *BZ* 20 [1976], 112-16), W.J. Larkin ('The Old Testament Background of Luke XXII.43-44', *NTS* 25 [1979], 250-54), and Marshall (*Commentary*, 831-33). The present study agrees with B.D. Ehrman and M.A. Plunkett ('The Angel and the Agony: The Textual Problem of Luke 22.43-44', *CBQ* 45 [1983], 401-16) that the verses are not a part of the original text of Luke's Gospel.

A similar problem exists with regard to v. 62, where the case for including the verse seems stronger than that for its omission. See Marshall (*Commentary*, 844-45) who argues for the inclusion of v. 62; but compare Schneider (*Verleugnung*, 95-65 and *Evangelium*, II, 465) who does not accept the verse. See below ch. 5 n. 31.

2. There is a sharp disparity between the ways that various scholars understand the material in 22.39-71. For example, on the one hand, Taylor (*Passion*, 124) judges that almost all of this section comes from Luke's 'other' source, to which Luke added 22.46b, 50b, 52b-53a, 54b-61 from Mark. On the other hand, Schneider ('Problem', 326) argues that only 22.43-44, 63-64, 66-68 can certainly be reckoned non-Markan (and pre-Lukan).

3. Taylor (*Passion*, 69-72), J.W. Holleran (*The Synoptic Gethsemane: A Critical Study* [Analecta Gregoria, 191; Rome: Gregorian, 1973], 170-98), and G.S. Sloyan (*Jesus on Trial: The Development of the Passion Narratives and their Historical and Ecumenical Implications* [Philadelphia: Fortress, 1973], 93) contend that v. 39 comes from a source other than Mark's Gospel. Yet B.S. Easton (*The Gospel according to St. Luke* [New York: Scribner, 1926], 330-31), who is persuaded that Luke did have a special source other than Mark, suggests that 22.39 is related to 21.37; and Finegan (*Überlieferung*, 17) argues that there is clear contact between v. 39 and Mark 14.26.

4. We will take up the matter of who makes up the group of the disciples below. It may be helpful at this point to anticipate that discussion in part. In saying, 'just his disciples followed him', Luke seems to make two points. First, this is a larger group than that present at the Last Supper. We saw that Luke refers to the twelve as the Apostles, but he seems to designate a larger body of followers of Jesus with the word *disciples*. Second, the seemingly superfluous *kai* in the line, *ēkolouthēsan de autō kai hoi mathētai*, should be seen as expressly limiting the group (see LSJ 865 [*kai* B.5, 6]). Though he here expands the group beyond the twelve, Luke still limits the group and qualifies it to meet the stipulation expressed at 22.6c—'apart from a crowd'. See further M.L. Soards, 'On Understanding Luke 22.39', *BT* 36 (1985), 336-37.

5. *Überlieferung*, 19.

6. Almost all commentators remark on the relation of 40b and 46c. Usually the lines are described as an *inclusio* or as a framing device. See J.H. Neyrey, 'The Absence of Jesus' Emotions—the Lucan Redaction of Lk

22,39-46', *Bib* 61 (1980), 153-71, esp. 162. See also Talbert, *Reading*, 214; Schweizer, *Evangelium*, 228; LaVerdiere, *Luke*, 263; and Marshall, *Commentary*, 830. Others posit (but diagnose differently) a larger chiastic structure in vv. 40-46. See Ehrman and Plunkett, 'Angel', 413; compare Feldkämper, *Jesus*, 228-29.

7. Taylor, *Passion*, 70.

8. Hawkins (*Horae*, 194) describes the additional material in v. 45 as editorial remarks. His position makes intelligible the different verbs for 'sleep' in Luke (*koimasthai*) and Mark (*katheudein*).

9. This is prepared for by the dialogue about the two swords in 22.38b, but that also has no Markan parallel. See further Feldkämper, *Jesus*, 225.

10. It is difficult to understand why Schneider (*Die Passion Jesu nach den drei älteren Evangelien* [München: Kösel, 1973], 52) brings vv. 49 and 51 into a general comparison of vv. 49-51 with Mark 14.47. Clearly 22.50 alone is the parallel to Mark 14.47.

11. The concern here is not to enter into the discussion of the plausibility of the group that Luke names as being present at the arrest of Jesus. (F.W. Beare, *The Earliest Records of Jesus* [New York: Abingdon, 1962], 231, argues it is unlikely that the chief priests and elders would themselves participate in the arrest. Marshall, *Commentary*, 838, responds that there is nothing improbable about Luke's description of the group.) We are interested here only in the different descriptions of the crowd, which suggest that Luke 22.52b does not have a match in Mark's story.

12. *Überlieferung*, 21.

13. See Schneider (*Passion*, 53) who describes 53c-d as special Lukan material. Schneider contends that Luke has replaced Mark's idea of the fulfillment of scripture with this special material. He observes that one can see the same tendency at Luke 22.22.

14. See Taylor, *Passion*, 77-78; E. Linnemann, 'Die Verleugnung des Petrus', *ZTK* 63 (1966), 1-31, esp. 29-31; Schneider, *Passion*, 81. But compare D.R. Catchpole (*The Trial of Jesus: A Study in the Gospels and Jewish Historiography from 1770 to the Present Day* [Studia Post-Biblica, 18; Leiden: Brill, 1971], 153-203, esp. 161-62) who argues that in this section of the Passion Narrative Luke has added material from Mark to a non-Markan source. Catchpole's work is an excellent example of the minute scrutinizing of Luke in relation to Mark. By focusing on the difference between the two Gospels, especially with regard to structure, he concludes that Luke has a continuous non-Markan source for the Passion Narrative.

15. Bultmann (*History*, 269, 283) contends the line is the product of Lukan editorial work, i.e. a Lukan invention. Catchpole (*Trial*, 168-69) argues that the detail of Jesus' turning is pre-Lukan, a thesis, however, that determines nothing about the historicity of the line.

As for meaning, there are at least three ways to understand how Jesus was in a position to look at Peter: First, he was being moved from one place to another (see Marshall, *Commentary*, 844). This explanation seems unlikely in the Lukan arrangement of the scenes where Jesus is mocked by those in charge of him immediately after Peter goes out and weeps. It does not appear that he is being moved at this point in the story. Second, Jesus looked out from above through an open window at Peter (see Schweizer, *Evangelium*, 231). This understanding stems from the harmonization of Luke and Mark, for in Luke's narrative nothing indicates that Jesus is inside the house. Third, Jesus is being held in the courtyard before he is led before the Assembly. This interpretation seems preferable since (a) it is not in conflict with anything in Luke's account and (b) there is no need to supply information that is not explicit in Luke's story.

16.   Scholars have completely different opinions about the relationship. Finegan (*Überlieferung*, 24) simply equates these portions of Mark and Luke. Perry (*Sources*, 44) admits that the idea portrayed in 22.63-65 is similar to that in Mark 14.65 *but* he maintains that Luke's scene 'contains no materials closely resembling Mark, and its general agreement is but 18 per cent; so it may be ascribed entirely to J [i.e., Perry's symbol for Luke's special non-Markan source]'. In four places, Schneider argues that the 'scoffing' of Jesus in Luke is without Markan parallel. He concludes vv. 63-65 are from a source additional to Mark, although Luke incorporated the Markan command, 'Prophesy', into that source. See *Verleugnung*, 97-104, 137-39; 'Problem', 236; *Passion*, 68-69; and *Evangelium*, II, 437, 464-65.

17.   Perry (*Sources*, 45) observes that 22.66b is secondary and probably Markan. Finegan (*Überlieferung*, 24) claims that 22.66 is Luke's conflation of Mark 14.53b and 15.1. S. Légasse ('Jésus devant le Sanhedrin. Recherche sur les traditions évangéliques', *RTL* 5 [1974], 170-197, esp. 182-89) says it is doubtful that 22.66 depends on anything other than Mark 15.1a; a similar assessment is made by H. Hendrickx, *The Passion Narratives of the Synoptic Gospels* (Manila: East Asian Pastoral Institute, 1977), 65.

18.   Easton (*Gospel*, 338-39) claims that 22.66 cannot be understood as a revision of Mark because of the great differences between the two stories. Bultmann (*History*, 271) contends that the only clear evidence of Luke's special source is seen in 22.66. P. Winter ('Marginal Notes on the Trial of Jesus, II', *ZNW* 50 [1959], 221-51) argues that 22.66 is based on a primitive non-Markan tradition which had the Sanhedrin meeting in the Council hall in the morning—a tradition more historically reliable than Mark's account. Others who argue that 22.66 comes from a source different from Mark include: J.B. Tyson, 'The Lukan Version of the Trial of Jesus', *NovT* 3 (1959), 252-55; in three places, Schneider, *Verleugnung*, 105-118, 137-39; 'Problem', 236; *Evangelium*, II, 437, 467-70; Catchpole, *Trial*, 64-65; Taylor, *Passion*, 124; and Sloyan, *Jesus*, 95. Marshall (*Commentary*, 848) remarks that for 22.66 Luke may either have drawn on Mark 15.1 or a source. Thus, his position is a *tertium quid*.

19.   It is debated what Luke means, i.e. whether the Assembly of the

Elders was composed of *two* groups: the chief priests and the scribes, or the elders are meant to join the chief priests and the scribes as a *third* group. Grundmann (*Evangelium*, 419-20), Hendrickx (*Narratives*, 65), and Ernst (*Evangelium*, 618) favor the latter view because they harmonize Luke 22.66b-c with Mark 15.1 and Luke 20.1 which mentions the three groups as my translation indicates. I disagree. Luke can scarcely have expected the reader to make such a harmonization, and without it, a simple reading of 66b would surely point to the first interpretation. See Schneider, *Evangelium*, II, 469.

20. See Jer 38.15.

21. Finegan (*Überlieferung*, 25) suggests that vv. 66c-68b provide an acceptable clarification of Jesus' silence in Mark 14.61. This is a creative suggestion but it still points to the distinct character of the Lukan lines.

22. *Überlieferung*, 25.

23. See ch. 2, n. 19. *Significant* means agreements that are something other than the presence or absence of particles (e.g. Luke 22.54c and Matt 26.58 have *de* instead of the *kai* at Mark 14.54) or a match that is merely a minor alteration of a Markan word (e.g. Luke 22.46c and Matt 26.41 have *eiselthēte*, whereas Mark 14.38 reads *elthēte*).

24. See Neirynck, *Agreements*, 173.

25. See Buse, 'St John', 70; Temple, 'Traditions', 82; Bailey, *Traditions*, 47-54.

26. See J.W. Doeve, 'Die Gefangennahme Jesu in Gethsemane', in *Studia Evangelica*, K. Aland, *et al.*, eds. (Berlin: Akademie, 1951), 463; Buse, 'St John', 70; Temple, 'Traditions', 82; and Klein, 'Passionstradition', 173.

27. Easton, *Gospel*, 330; Léon-Dufour, 'Passion', col. 1446.

28. Perry, *Sources*, 108; Easton, *Gospel*, 330.

29. Mark uses *plēn* only once.

30. Neirynck, *Agreements*, 173-74.

31. Perry, *Source*, 108; Easton, *Gospel*, 330; Léon-Dufour, 'Passion', col. 1445; and Neirynck, *Agreements*, 174.

32. Finegan, *Überlieferung*, 20; Doeve, 'Gefangennahme', 458; Léon-Dufour, 'Passion', col. 1445; Neirynck, *Agreements*, 175.

33. 'Points', 148.

34. Parker ('Luke', 328) judges correctly that 22.47-48 is less like John 18.2-9 than it is similar to the comparable sections of Mark and Matthew. One should recall that Luke more explicitly gives a prominent role to Judas in Acts 1.16. There he says that Judas was the guide for those who arrested Jesus.

35. Osty, 'Points', 148.

36. Perry (*Sources*, 108) says there is a general narrative agreement between Luke and Matthew. Neirynck ('Argument', 786) remarks that Luke and Matthew agree in placing 'approximately the same' common material at the same place relative to the Markan outline.

37. Hawkins (*Horae*, 210) sees an agreement in fact between Luke and Matthew in Jesus' speaking to Judas, 'though the words recorded are not the same in the two Gospels'. Finegan (*Überlieferung*, 20) observes that Luke and Matthew both knew that Jesus spoke to Judas, but he insists that Luke is entirely different from Matthew here.

38. Easton (*Gospel*, 332) comments that the reproaches in Luke and Matthew are completely different. He claims that the addition of such a reproach 'was inevitable'.

39. Schweizer, *Evangelium*, 229.

40. Compare Bailey, *Traditions*, 47-54.

41. Buse, 'St John', 70; Schweizer, *Evangelium*, 229.

42. Bailey, *Traditions*, 47-54.

43. Neirynck, *Agreements*, 175.

44. See Brown, *John, XIII-XXI*, 812.

45. The mention by both Luke and John of the right ear is the detail most often mentioned by scholars who list agreements between Luke and John. The most creative comment concerning this minor agreement comes from Schneider (*Passion*, 54): He argues that the knowledge of Luke and John that it was the right ear is no proof of a source, but rather, it indicates a common tradition. He contends, therefore, this agreement shows clearly that Luke's redactional activity is not merely freely composed invention.

46. Perry, *Sources*, 108.

47. Osty, 'Points', 148-49.

48. See Brown, *John, XIII-XXI*, 807-808.

49. 'Points', 149; to these references Rehkopf (*Sonderquelle*, 81-83) adds 7.30; 8.20; 12.23, 27, 17.1. Klein ('Passionstradition', 174-76) suggests further 16.2, 4. One should include 2.4 in such lists.

50. Schneider (*Passion*, 53) reasons similarly.

51. Klein ('Passionstradition', 174-76) adds 13.30.

52. R.S. Barbour, 'Gethsemane in the Tradition of the Passion', *NTS* 16 (1969-70), 239.

53. Buse, 'St John', 71.

54. Cadbury, *Style*, 95.

55. Brown, *John, XIII-XXI*, 817.

56. Osty, 'Points', 149; Borgen, 'John', 256; Léon-Dufour, 'Passion', col. 1442; Rehkopf, *Sonderquelle*, 66, 83; Buse, 'St John', 71; Bailey, *Traditions*, 47-54; Schneider, *Verleugnung*, 61-70; Klein, 'Passionstradition', 162-64.

57. Luke uses a participial form of the verb in Acts 1.16 in reference to 'the ones who arrested Jesus'.

58. Schneider (*Verleugnung*, 73) points out that *syllambanein* occurs in Mark 14.48. Moreover, even Taylor (*Passion*, 77-78) argues that while one cannot rule out a non-Markan source for Luke 22.54b-61, the evidence suggests that Mark is Luke's only written source.

59. Léon-Dufour, 'Passion', col. 1443; Ernst, *Evangelium*, 612-13. Taylor

(*Passion*, 78) suggests some knowledge of a common oral tradition by Luke and John may be inferred, but not with certainty.

60. For example, (a) there is another unnamed disciple present who plays a prominent role in the story as John tells it; (b) Peter denies Jesus once before he gets to the fire; (c) a precise identity is given for Peter's final inquisitor; and (d) there is no mention of Peter's going out from the courtyard.

61. A helpful sixteen-point chart comparing the denials by Peter in all four Gospels appears in Brown, *John, XIII–XXI*, 838-39.

62. Perry, *Sources*, 108; Osty, 'Points', 150. Compare the positions of Linnemann, 'Verleugnung', 29-31; Schneider, *Verleugnung*, 73-96 (a summary of *Verleugnung* is in *Passion*, 80-82).

63. See n. 61.

64. Not all interpreters recognize the authenticity of this line. See above, n. 1.

65. *Passion*, 84, citing Buse, 'St John', 71.

66. Léon-Dufour, 'Passion', col. 1442; Schneider, *Verleugnung*, 61-70; Ernst, *Evangelium*, 618.

67. Bailey, *Traditions*, 55-63.

68. Léon-Dufour, 'Passion', col. 1442; Schneider, *Verleugnung*, 61-70; Hendrickx, *Narratives*, 66; Bailey, *Traditions*, 55-63.

69. Léon-Dufour, 'Passion', col. 1443; Schneider, *Verleugnung*, 61-70; Osty, 'Points', 150.

70. Schneider, *Verleugnung*, 61-70.

71. Léon-Dufour, 'Passion', col. 1443; Schneider, *Verleugnung*, 61-70.

72. Schneider, *Verleugnung*, 61-70; Bailey, *Traditions*, 55- 63.

73. Grundmann, *Evangelium*, 418.

74. On the cock-crow, see Brown, *John XIII–XXI*, 828; and on the narrative device portraying simultaneous events, see the same, 827.

75. Léon-Dufour, 'Passion', col. 1442; Neirynck, *Agreements*, 183.

76. On the similarities between Luke and Matthew see Perry, *Sources*, 108; Easton, *Gospel*, 338; Schneider, *Verleugnung*, 46-60; Neirynck, *Agreements*, 178.

On the similarities between Luke and John see P. Winter, 'Luke XXII 66b-71', *ST* 9 (1955), 112-15; Schneider, *Verleugnung*, 61-70; Klein, 'Passionstradition', 165; Schweizer, *Evangelium*, 230-31.

77. Schneider (*Verleugnung*, 46-60) suggests that the omission of the Markan version of Jesus' answer (*egō eimi*) by both Luke and Matthew may imply a literary contact (a common written source?) at a stage prior to the writing of both Gospels.

78. Perry, *Sources*, 108; Osty, 'Points', 150; Léon-Dufour, 'Passion', col. 1443; Schneider, *Verleugnung*, 61-70.

79. 'Passionstradition', 165.

80. Perry, *Sources*, 45; Finegan, *Überlieferung*, 25; Bailey, *Traditions*, 56 n. 3; Rese, *Motive*, 199; in three places, Schneider, *Verleugnung*, 137-39;

Passion, 70; *Evangelium*, 437; D. Catchpole, 'The Problem of the Historicity of the Sanhedrin Trial', in E. Bammel, ed., *The Trial of Jesus* (SBT, 13; London: SCM, 1970), 64-65.

81. Easton, *Gospel*, 338; Léon-Dufour, 'Passion', col. 1445; Schneider, *Verleugnung*, 46-60; Neirynck, *Agreements*, 178.

82. Easton, *Gospel*, 338; Léon-Dufour, 'Passion', col. 1445; Schneider, *Verleugnung*, 46-60; Neirynck, *Agreements*, 178.

83. Perry (*Sources*, 41, 107) argues that 39a is Luke's transposition of Mark 14.32. He avers that 'the transposition of the departure from the upper room to a point after the warning to Peter (cf. Mark 14.26) would indicate . . . that vs. 39 stood in J'. As argued above, it is not clear that Luke transposed v. 39. See also Holleran (*Gethsemane*, 184), who understands v. 39 to be part of a larger transposition (vv. 39-40a, par Mark 14.26).

84. *Überlieferung*, 19.

85. Holleran (*Gethsemane*, 184) argues that 40b is a doublet for 46c. We demonstrated above that the grammar and force of these lines are different. Holleran and Perry (*Sources*, 42) take this so-called doublet to be a sign of Luke's use of a source other than Mark.

86. Rehkopf (*Sonderquelle*, 83) and Schneider (*Verleugnung*, 146-47; *Passion*, 52) pay particular attention to the changed position of the arrest. Other scholars, like Ernst (*Evangelium*, 644), refer to the whole of 22.54-62 as having a narrative sequence different from Mark's. 22.54b-55c does, however, occur in the same order as Mark's parallel lines (14.53a, 54).

87. 61a is not included in the consideration of 56a-62b because there is no parallel to this line in the Markan Passion Narrative.

88. J.R. Donahue (*Are You the Christ? The Trial Narrative in the Gospel of Mark* [SBLDS, 10; Missoula, MT: Society of Biblical Literature, 1973], esp. 53-101) describes the trial of Jesus in Mark 14 as 'intercalated material' and attributes the location of the trial in Mark's Passion Narrative to 'the Marcan insertion technique'. Donahue offers this analysis of the Markan text:

14.54 [55-65] 66-72

It is puzzling that Donahue severs 14.53 from 14.54-72. Had he included v. 53 in the unit that he analyzes, he would have achieved very different results. When we consider 14.53-72 as a complete unit, we see an A/B/A'/B' pattern:

14.53 [54] 55-65 [66-72]

This structure suggests it is the Peter material that has been inserted, not actually intercalated, into the story of the Passion of Jesus. This A/B/A'/B' pattern is not particularly Markan. These findings cause one to wonder whether, as Donahue claims, the creative hand of Mark has been detected in this section of the Markan Passion Narrative.

89. Schneider (*Passion*, 80) suggests that vv. 54b-61 are repositioned in Luke's account. Fitzmyer (*Gospel*, 71) recognizes vv. 54c-62 as those verses

of Luke with a 'varied sequence', from Mark's account. Perry (*Sources*, 44, 107) claims that vv. 56–62 are in a sequence different from Mark's and are to be attributed to source J. In agreement is J. Jeremias, 'Perikopen-Umstellungen', 115-19. The difference is also noticed by Hawkins, 'Limitations', 82; Léon-Dufour, 'Passion', col. 1447; and Schneider, *Verleugnung*, 146–47.

90. Scholars generally recognize that Jesus is mocked at different points in the narratives of Mark and Luke, even if they understand Luke to use a source different from Mark here. See Perry, *Sources*, 44, 107; Hawkins, 'Limitations', 82; Finegan, *Überlieferung*, 24; Jeremias, 'Perikopen-Umstellungen', 115-19; Léon-Dufour, 'Passion', col. 1447; Schneider, *Verleugnung*, 146–48 and *Passion*, 67; Taylor, *Passion*, 79-80; Ernst, *Evangelium*, 644.

91. The usual scholarly practice is to speak of 22.66a-71c as a part of Luke's Passion Narrative different in sequence from Mark's order. See Perry, *Sources*, 44-45, 107; Jeremias, 'Perikopen-Umstellungen', 115-19; Ernst, *Evangelium*, 664; and Fitzmyer, *Gospel*, 71. As we saw above, however, 66a-d is best accounted for as Lukan Passion Narrative material without a Markan parallel.

92. Ernst (*Evangelium*, 619) remarks that Luke's account breaks up the the association of Jesus' Messiahship and Sonship. This difference between Luke and Mark will be examined below. One should note here, however, that this difference provides the basis for different lines of agumentation. Some argue Luke's account is more historically reliable because it does not blend the ideas of Messiah and Son of God (see Marshall, *Commentary*, 849). Others contend the difference is the result of Luke's editing: He divided the one question from Mark in order to position the title 'Son of God' as the climax of the episode (see Rese, *Motive*, 199).

93. Especially helpful are Hawkins, *Horae*; Easton, 'Evidence' and *Gospel*; Cadbury, *Style*; and Rehkopf, *Sonderquelle*. On Rehkopf's work, see, however, Schürmann, 'Spracheigentümlichkeiten'.

94. Easton, *Gospel*, 331; Taylor *Passion*, 70.

95. See Hawkins, *Horae*, 16, 35-36; Easton, *Gospel*, 331; K.G. Kuhn, 'Jesus in Gethsemane', *EvT* 12 (1952-53), 260-85; Taylor, *Passion*, 70; Feldkämper, *Jesus*, 231.

96. Compare Easton, 'Evidence', 163.

97. Compare Easton, 'Evidence', 147.

98. In agreement see Schneider, *Passion*, 54.

99. See Finegan, *Überlieferung*, 23; and Linnemann, 'Verleugnung', 28.

100. Schneider, *Verleugnung*, 81-82.

101. See Finegan, *Überlieferung*, 23; Linnemann, 'Verleugnung', 28.

102. The instances where Luke differs from Mark are 5.25 (par Mark 2.12); 8.44 (par Mark 5.29); 8.55 (par Mark 5.42); 18.43 (par Mark 10.50).

103. On this verb see Schneider, *Verleugnung*, 99-100.

104. Bultmann, *History*, 271.
105. Cadbury, *Style*, 194; Easton, *Gospel*, 336.
106. Taylor, *Passion*, 81.
107. Easton, *Gospel*, 338.
108. Easton, *Gospel*, 338; Taylor, *Passion*, 82.
109. See Finegan, *Überlieferung*, 25; Klostermann, *Lukasevangelium*, 221; Schneider, *Verleugnung*, 123.
110. Schneider, *Verleugnung*, 59.
111. Schneider, *Verleugnung*, 122-23.
112. Taylor (*Passion*, 70) and Klein ('Passionstradition', 173) describe *ethos* as Lukan; compare Easton ('Evidence', 149), who attributes the word to Luke's source.
113. On *the following of Jesus* as a theme of Luke's Gospel, see Fitzmyer, *Gospel*, 241-43.
114. The phrase does occur at Mark 4.10.
115. See Fitzmyer, *Gospel*, 244-47.
116. Feldkämper (*Jesus*, 228-29) argues that the key to this section is the structure formed by the prayer language in 22.40b-46.
117. Kuhn, 'Jesus', 268.
118. Cadbury, *Style*, 95; Finegan, *Überlieferung*, 19.
119. This suggestion is made by T. Lescow, 'Jesus in Gethsemane bei Lukas und im Hebräerbrief', *ZNW* 58 (1967), 215-39, esp. 222-23. Another interpretation that relates Luke's explanation to Hellenistic philosophy appears in Neyrey, 'Absence', 153-71.
120. Schweizer, *Evangelium*, 229.
121. See Fitzmyer, *Gospel*, 208-11, esp. 211.
122. Cadbury (*Style*, 92) cites instances where Luke omits Jesus' use of physical contact in working cures. The evidence above shows, however, there is no consistency in Luke's presentation on this score.
123. See H. van der Loos, *The Miracles of Jesus* (NovTSup, 9; Leiden: Brill, 1968), 558.
124. Hendrickx, *Narratives*, 62.
125. See Fitzmyer, *Gospel*, 200-203. Rehkopf (*Sonderquelle*, 95) lists *kyrios* as proto-Lukan usage. Schneider (*Verleugnung*, 92) argues that Luke knew the title from his sources.
126. The idea of *repentance* is a significant one for Luke. It is closely related to the Lukan understanding of the effect of the Christ event, i.e. the forgiveness of sin. On this subject, see Fitzmyer, *Gospel*, 237-39.
127. See above, ch. 2 n. 74.

Notes to Chapter 5

1. Finegan (*Überlieferung*, 17) claims there is clear contact between 22.39

and Mark 14.26. Feldkämper (*Jesus*, 229) argues that vv. 39-40a are clearly transitional and serve to introduce the material that follows. He includes vv. 39-40a in a group of verses made up of 3.21-22 and 9.28ff. He claims that these three points in Luke's Gospel provide the milestones along the way of Jesus (300).

A further comparison is made by W. Radl, *Paulus und Jesus im lukanischen Doppelwerk: Untersuchungen zu Parallelmotiven im Lukasevangelium und in der Apostelgeschichte* (Europäische Hochschulschriften, 49; Bern/Frankfurt: Lang, 1975), 166-68. Radl compares 22.39-46 with Acts 20.36-38; 21.5-6, 13-14. He claims that Jesus (in Luke) and Paul (in Acts) are alike in that (a) they look toward their deaths, (b) their followers are sorrowful, and (c) they are obedient to the will of God.

2. See Finegan, *Überlieferung*, 17; Easton, *Gospel*, 330-31; Barbour, 'Gethsemane', 235.

3. Luke portrays Jesus in action and then loosely appends his disciples to him at 8.1.

4. Similarly see Hawkins, *Horae*, 194; Finegan, *Überlieferung*, 19; compare Taylor, *Passion*, 124.

5. See Lescow, 'Jesus', 221. Lescow contends that the purpose of Luke's creating v. 40 was to portray a *typical* martyr scene with Jesus as the ideal martyr.

6. Matthew and Mark agree here against Luke in (a) mentioning Gethsemane; (b) having Jesus issue the command, 'Sit here while I pray', to all his disciples; (c) having Jesus separate Peter, James, and John (Matt: the two sons of Zebedee) from the others; (d) mentioning that Jesus was greatly distressed and having him say so; (e) saying that Jesus *fell* to his prayer posture; (f) having Jesus go away from and return to the three disciples three times; (g) having Jesus address Peter separately in an extended statement; and (h) recording a lengthy statement by Jesus that includes a prediction of the betrayal immediately before the event.

7. Marshall (*Commentary*, 831) raises the possibility that one should understand the agreements between Luke and Matthew to be the result of oral tradition. But he also suggests that it is possible that Luke had another source at this point. It is, however, difficult to understand how at the same time Luke and Matthew could be extremely different in their narrative but quite similar in the words of Jesus' prayer if one thinks of Luke possessing another (written) source here.

8. On this point, see R.E. Brown, 'The Pater Noster as an Eschatological Prayer', in *New Testament Essays* (Garden City, NY: Image, 1965-reissued by Paulist, 1982), 276-320, esp. 277, 297-301.

9. On oral tradition see Kelber, *Gospel*, 1-43; H. Koester, *Introduction to the New Testament*, Vol. II, *History and Literature of Early Christianity* (Foundations and Facets Series; Philadelphia/New York: Fortress/W. de Gruyter, 1982), *passim*, esp. 44-49. A.J. Mattill, Jr ('The Jesus-Paul Parallels

and the Purpose of Luke–Acts: H.H. Evans Reconsidered' *NovT* 17 [1975], 32) compares the words of Jesus in this prayer to the words of Paul's friends at Acts 21.14, 'let the will of the Lord come to be'. This statement is made in response to Paul's saying that he is ready to be imprisoned and to die in Jerusalem. The words Paul speaks are similar to the boast by Peter at Luke 22.33 that he is ready to go with Jesus to prison and even to die. But, as one learns in reading Acts, Paul behaves more like Jesus than like Peter.

10. *The Passion Narrative according to Matthew: A Redactional Study* (BETL, 39; Leuven: University, 1975), 125-27.

11. Schneider (*Passion*, 52) compares vv. 49-51 to Mark 14.47. Examination of the passages show, however, that only 22.50 is comparable to Mark 14.47.

12. See Feldkämper (*Jesus*, 225) for a more detailed comparison of 22.49ff. and 22.38.

13. As Fitzmyer (*Gospel*, 82-84, 826) suggests, it is almost impossible to decide whether there is anything pre-Lukan in this passage. It is not necessary for us to make such a decision for the purposes of the present investigation.

14. This verse is the opening line of the so-called Lukan Travel Narrative, which extends from 9.51 through 19.27. See Kümmel, *Introduction*, 125-26; H.L. Egelkraut, *Jesus' Mission to Jerusalem: A redaction critical study of the Travel Narrative in the Gospel of Luke, Lk 9.51-19.48* (Europäische Hochschulschriften, 80; Bern/Frankfurt: Lang, 1976), 1-61; and Fitzmyer, *Gospel*, 823-32.

15. Hawkins (*Horae*, 194) judges v. 49 to be editorial. Finegan (*Überlieferung*, 21) attributes the question, the detail about the 'right' ear, and Jesus' remonstration all to Luke's artistry as a story-teller. Compare Perry, *Sources*, 107; Taylor *Passion*, 124; Rehkopf, *Sonderquelle*, 83; Beare, *Records*, 231; Marshall, *Commentary*, 837.

16. Perry, *Sources*, 42.

17. Finegan, *Überlieferung*, 21. Bultmann (*History*, 269) comments that this detail shows how the legendary elements continued to grow and attach themselves to the basic traditions.

18. Grundmann, *Evangelium*, 414; Schneider, *Passion*, 53; and R.J. Karris, *Invitation to Luke* (Garden City, NY: Image, 1977), 251.

19. Schneider, *Passion*, 52.

20. Ernst, *Evangelium*, 609.

21. Ernst, *Evangelium*, 610.

22. Bultmann, *History*, 269. Similarly, V. Taylor (*The Gospel according to Mark* [2nd edn; London: Macmillan, 1966], 560) observes that Mark 14.48f. 'appears to imply the presence of the priests'. From this observation Taylor speaks of Luke's editorial adjustment of Mark.

23. Beare, *Records*, 231.

24. Compare Marshall (*Commentary*, 838) who maintains there is nothing

improbable about Luke's description of the group that came out to arrest Jesus.

25. See Ernst, *Evangelium*, 611. In conjunction with this interpretation, Ernst contends that Luke has an apologetic interest in these verses. He claims Luke did not cast the Romans in a poor light—but, at this point, neither did Mark.

26. Admitted even by Perry, *Sources*, 43; Easton, *Gospel*, 332; Rehkopf, *Sonderquelle*, 71-82; Taylor, *Passion*, 72-76, 124; and Sloyan, *Jesus*, 93.

27. See Taylor, *Gospel*, 561.

28. See Conzelmann, *Theology*, 182; Beare, *Records*, 231; Schneider, *Evangelium*, 2.463; Ernst, *Evangelium*, 611; Hendrickx, *Narratives*, 21-22.

29. This is the position taken by Bultmann, *History*, 269. For a list of scholars who agree with Bultmann see Marshall, *Commentary*, 844.

30. See Catchpole, *Trial*, 168-69.

31. The verse in Luke is textually uncertain. It is not found in ms. 0171 and various Old Latin texts (a, b, e, ff2, i, l*, r), but there is no obvious reason to omit the lines. Nevertheless, many scholars do not consider v. 62 to be a part of Luke's original text. In favor of omission, see Finegan, *Überlieferung*, 24; Grundmann, *Evangelium*, 417; Schneider, *Evangelium*, II, 465. Compare Talbert, *Reading*, 215.

32. Luke probably found this line particularly to his liking. Except for the word *pikrōs* every word is typical of his vocabulary. Indeed, when viewed in the context of Greek literature contemporary to Luke, there is nothing particularly remarkable about *pikrōs* except that it occurs in this agreement between Luke and Matthew. Moreover, Luke probably used *klaiein* deliberately, indicating that Peter's crying was symbolic of his genuine *repentance*, an idea certainly characteristic of Luke. See LSJ, 1404; BAGD, 657; and esp. J.H. Moulton and G. Milligan, *The Vocabulary of the Greek New Testament: Illustrated from the Papyri and other Non-Literary Sources* (Grand Rapids: Eerdmans, 1930), 513.

33. Above all, see Schneider, *Verleugnung*, *passim*, esp. 96-104.

34. Compare Schweizer (*Evangelium*, 232) who argues that the exact verbal agreement between Luke 22.62, 64 and Matt 26.75, 68 cannot be accounted for in terms of oral tradition. Recent studies suggest that Schweizer underestimates the power of memory and the vitality of oral tradition in pre-Guttenberg cultures. See Kelber, *Gospel*, 13.

35. See Marshall, *Commentary*, 846. Marshall argues that this explanation would account for other non-Markan elements found in Matthew's version of this story.

36. Compare Bultmann (*History*, 271) who argues that *tis estin ho paisas se* is 'in all probability a wholly secondary conformation to Matthew'.

37. It is possible that what one evangelist knew from oral tradition the other knew from a written source. Since Matthew is closer to Mark here than is Luke, it would seem more reasonable to say that it is possible that what

Matthew knew from oral tradition, Luke knew from a written source. There are good reasons, however, to reject this line of reasoning. First, the introduction of a hypothetical written source adds still another stage to the process of reconstruction. The interpretation given above is a simpler reconstruction. Second, if we are to understand that Luke exercised significant editorial freedom in using Mark's story, is it not equally likely he would have done likewise with 'another' source? In this case the likelihood of agreement between Luke and Matthew would be less than if we understand them to depend upon a common level of oral tradition.

Compare E. Lohse (*History of the Suffering and Death of Jesus Christ* [Philadelphia: Fortress, 1967], 40, 72), who remarks that while Luke may be dependent upon a tradition other than Mark, it is difficult, if not impossible, to determine exactly *if* and *what* that tradition was.

38. Schneider, *Evangelium*, II, 465.

39. Bultmann, *History*, 271; Klostermann, *Lukasevangelium*, 221; Finegan, *Überlieferung*, 25.

40. See, in agreement, Finegan, *Überlieferung*, 24. One of the major objections to the understanding of 22.63-65 articulated here is that in its grammatical context the pronominal object of the mockery (*auton*) refers to Peter, not Jesus (see Marshall, *Commentary*, 846). Two factors overrule this objection: First, Peter is clearly out of the scene. Second, no one has been in charge of Peter. Therefore, it is best to understand that Luke thought the phrase (*hoi andres hoi synechontes*) governing 'him' provided sufficient grammatical context for *auton*.

41. Compare Ernst (*Evangelium*, 616) who claims it was *guards* who had custody of Jesus prior to the Assembly meeting. *Pace* Ernst, from Luke's story, there is no clear change of groups from the arrest to the mockery.

42. See Schneider, *Evangelium*, II, 464-65; Karris, *Invitation*, 254-55.

43. D.L. Miller ('*EMPAIZEIN*: Playing the Mock Game [Luke 22.63-64]', *JBL* 90 [1971], 309-313) treats these verses in relation to references to games in ancient literature. He argues that Jesus is the victim in a game, *chalkē muia*, like 'blindman's buff'. While Miller does argue his case persuasively, see his work for the range of possible ancient games that could have been played on this occasion.

44. This intimidation is related to an 'intimidation motif' often found in martyr literature. See Schneider, *Evangelium*, II, 464-65; Hendrickx, *Narratives*, 64; and n. 58 below.

45. An enormous body of literature exists treating the trial of Jesus. For a thumbnail sketch of the various issues at stake, see P. Parker, 'Trial of Jesus', *IDB* IV (1962), 697-98; and D.R. Catchpole, 'Trial of Jesus', *IDBSup*, 917-19. Especially prominent among the periodical literature on this topic are A. Jaubert, 'Les séances du sanhedrin et les récits de la passion', *RHR* 166 (1964), 143-69 and 167 (1965), 1-33; J. Blinzler, 'The Trial of Jesus in the Light of History', *Judaism* 20 (1971), 49-55. Among the spate of books on the

trial of Jesus, see J. Blinzler, *Der Prozess Jesu* (4th edn; Regensburg: Pustet, 1969); E. Bammel, ed., *The Trial of Jesus* (SBT, 13; London: SCM, 1970); Catchpole, *Trial*; P. Winter, *On the Trial of Jesus* (Studia Judaica, 1; 2nd rev. edn; Berlin/New York: W. de Gruyter, 1974).

46. In agreement, see Finegan, *Überlieferung*, 24. Compare Easton (*Gospel*, 338-39) who argues Luke's account differs from Mark's so significantly that the two are not to be compared.

47. Similarly see Hendrickx, *Narratives*, 68; compare Schweizer, *Evangelium*, 232.

48. For a fuller treatment of 'narrative time', especially as it relates to the Gospels, see Rhoads and Michie, *Mark*, 37; and Culpepper, *Anatomy*, 53-75. If, as it seems, Luke is concerned primarily with the smooth and logical progress of his narrative, it may be unnecessary to make such comparisons as those made by H. Danby ('The Bearing of the Rabbinical Criminal Code on the Jewish Trial Narratives of the Gospels', *JTS* 21 [1920], 54-55) between Luke and the Mishnah.

49. Though it is impossible to determine what, if any, is the relation, one should notice that a similar statement is made by Jeremiah in Jer 38.15.

50. Rese (*Motive*, 199) argues that Luke methodically divided the question in Mark 14.61 into two parts and redacted this section of the Markan Passion Narrative in order to position the title 'Son of God' as the climax of the entire scene.

51. Finegan (*Überlieferung*, 25), who does not understand that Luke employed a source in addition to Mark for his Passion, argues that 71a-c depends on Mark 14.63b-64a. But, Perry (*Sources*, 45), Bultmann (*History*, 271), B.H. Streeter (*The Four Gospels: A Study in Origins* [New York: Macmillan, 1925], 222), and Creed (*Gospel*, 278), who hold that Luke used a source other than Mark for 66a-71c, all describe 71a-c as a Markan interpolation. Nevertheless, Fitzmyer (*Gospel*, 67, 84) and Schweizer (*Evangelium*, 236) allot v. 71 to Luke's special source/material.

52. See above, ch. 3 n. 38.

53. Grundmann (*Evangelium*, 412-13) and Talbert (*Reading*, 212-15) are prominent among those scholars who understand the Passion and death of Jesus in Luke as a *martyrdom*. They argue that Luke portrays the Passion and death of Jesus so that Jesus' sufferings become a *model* or an *example* for the Christian community to follow. Grundmann goes so far as to refer to Jesus as the *Urmärtyrer*. This description seems unduly to limit the Passion and death of Jesus to the genre of martyrology. As Schneider (*Evangelium*, II, 464-65), T. Baumeister (*Die Anfänge der Theologie des Martyriums* [Münsterische Beiträge zur Theologie, 45; Münster: Aschendorff, 1980]), and others have recognized, certain features of Luke's Passion are similar to the established features of martyr accounts. But for Luke Jesus is far more than a mere martyr. The way that Jesus' death fulfills the plan of God sets it apart from the suffering of other righteous humans (see esp. Schneider,

Evangelium, II, 439).

54. There is an early indication of Jesus' deliberateness in Luke's story of the boy Jesus in the Temple in 2.41-51.

55. An understanding of Jesus' activity similar to the one offered here may have led a scribe to introduce the legendary event narrated in Luke 22.43-44.

56. In agreement, see Grundmann, *Evangelium*, 414; and Schweizer, *Evangelium*, 229.

57. An *intimidation motif* is an established feature of martyr accounts in both Jewish and non-Jewish Hellenistic literature of Luke's day. Schneider (*Evangelium*, II, 464-65) lists 2 Macc 7.1-2, 7, 12; 4 Macc 6.3-30; 8.12-14.10 as examples of the intimidation motif in Jewish literature. S.K. Williams (*Jesus' Death as Saving Event: The Background and Origin of a Concept* [HDR, 2; Missoula, MT: Scholars, 1975] attends to these texts and others in Philo, Plato, and Plutarch (see esp. 141-44). Luke employed the motif to reinforce the image of Jesus as being in charge of all that occurs around him.

58. Similarly, Luke focused the readers' attention on the idea of the Son of God in the way he delineated the genealogy of Jesus in 3.23-38.

59. In agreement see Rese, *Motive*, 199; Baumeister, *Anfänge*, 125.

60. This exposition of the function of irony in this portion of Luke's Passion Narrative is indebted to the stimulating treatment of irony in Culpepper, *Anatomy*, 165-80.

61. See Brown, *Birth*, 461-66.

62. The phrase 'inaugurated eschatology' is borrowed from W.S. Kurz, 'Acts 3.19-26 as a Test Case of the Role of Eschatology in Lukan Christology', *SBLASP* 11 (1977), 309-23. This discussion is indebted to Kurz not only for the phrase but also for much of the meaning attached to that phrase in the present study.

63. One of the most common reasons given for the inclusion of 22.35-38, 49-51 is that Luke wanted to show that Jesus in no way was associated with politically revolutionary activity (for example, see Grundmann, *Evangelium*, 414).

Notes to Chapter 6

1. Perry (*Sources*), Taylor (*Passion*), and those who hold that Luke used, and even preferred, a source for his Passion Narrative other than Mark ask this question.

2. See Jeremias, 'Perikopen-Umstellung'.

3. See Marshall (*Commentary*, 381) for a list of those holding this position.

4. Marshall (*Commentary*, 381), who does not posit a special source for

Luke here, offers a summary of the evidence for and against Luke's use of a source other than Mark. See also Fitzmyer (*Gospel*, 791-804), who is in agreement with Marshall's position.

5. Though working toward a different point, Neirynck ('Argument', 784-815, esp. 814) makes a similar observation.

6. See Neirynck, 'Argument', 814.

7. D. Juel (*Luke-Acts: The Promise of History* [Atlanta: Knox, 1983], 4) represents the consensus in saying, 'His [Luke's] history is revisionist, an attempt to improve what had preceded (though the sense in which he intended to improve on his predecessors is yet to be determined)'.

8. The inspiration for much of what follows comes from the stimulating essay by J.L. Martyn, 'Attitudes Ancient and Modern Toward Tradition about Jesus', *USQR* 23 (1968), 129-45.

9. See Martyn, 'Attitudes', 140 and 144.

10. In making this suggestion, I do not wish to take lightly the sound warning of L.T. Johnson ('On Finding the Lukan Community: A Cautious Cautionary Essay', *SBLASP 1979*, I, 87-100) that the exegetical approach usually referred to as the 'mirror method' has 'only limited applicability' and may pay minimal, if not questionable dividends when applied to Luke-Acts (89). It is clear, however, that no biblical author, including Luke, writes in a vacuum. Indeed, Johnson himself argues that a redactional analysis of Luke's work may put us 'only in contact with *Luke's* perception of the community's needs' (91); moreover, he needs to qualify his assertion by adding that in light of the lack of contrary evidence, Luke's perception of community needs may reasonably be presumed to have a basis in fact. At this point, however, I mean to speak not of the shape of Luke's community but of what the modern reader of Luke's text may discern Luke doing in his work.

Notes to Appendix

1. *Kreuzweg*, see above ch. 2 n. 58.

2. 'The Death of Jesus according to Luke: A Question of Sources', an unpublished paper read before the annual assembly of the Catholic Biblical Association of America in August 1983. I am thankful to the author for making a copy of this study available to me prior to its publication in *CBQ* 47 (1985), 469-85.

In comparing Luke 23 and Mark 15 the reader will find helpful Matera's *The Kingship of Jesus: Composition and Theology in Mark 15* (SBLDS, 66; Chico, CA: Scholars, 1982).

3. The work of Finegan (*Überlieferung*, esp. 1-39) in 1934 is the earliest thoroughgoing argument that Luke's Passion Narrative incorporates diverse legendary pieces into the Markan material and is but a 'neue Handlung' of Mark's account.

BIBLIOGRAPHY

Arndt, W.F. *The Gospel according to St. Luke*. St. Louis: Concordia, 1956.

Auneau, J., *et al. Evangiles Synoptiques et Actes des Apôtres*. Paris: Desclée, 1981.

Bachmann, M. *Jerusalem und der Tempel: die geographisch-theologischen Elemente des jüdischen Kultzentrums*. BWANT, 109. Stuttgart: Kohlhammer, 1980.

Bahr, G.J. 'The Seder of Passover and the Eucharistic Words', *NovT* 12 (1970), 181-202.

Bailey, J.A. *The Traditions Common to the Gospels of Luke and John*. NovTSup, 7. Leiden: Brill, 1963.

Balentine, G.L. 'Death of Jesus as a New Exodus', *RevExp* 59 (1962), 27-41.

Barbour, R.S. 'Gethsemane in the Tradition of the Passion', *NTS* 16 (1969-70), 231-51.

Barrett, C.K. *Luke the Historian in Recent Study*. FBBS, 24. Philadelphia: Fortress, 1961.

—'Luke xxii.15: To Eat the Passover', *JTS* (1958), 305-307.

Bartsch, H.-W. 'Die Bedeutung des Sterbens Jesu nach den Synoptikern', *TZ* 20 (1964), 87-102.

—'Jesu Schwertwort, Lukas 22.35-38: Überlieferungsgeschichtliche Studie', *NTS* 20 (1974), 190-203.

Baumeister, T. *Die Anfänge der Theologie des Martyriums*. Münsterische Beiträge zur Theologie, 45. Münster: Aschendorff, 1980.

Beare, F.W. *The Earliest Records of Jesus*. Nashville: Abingdon, 1962.

Beck, B.E. '"Imitatio Christi" and the Lucan Passion Narrative', *Suffering and Martyrdom in the New Testament: Studies Presented to G.M. Styler by the Cambridge New Testament Seminar*. Horbury, W. and McNeil, B., eds. Cambridge: Cambridge University Press, 1981, pp. 28-47.

Beck, D.M. 'The Passion', *IDB* 3, 662-63.

Becq, J. 'Ponce Pilate et la mort de Jésus', *Bible et Terre Saint* 57 (1963), 2-7.

Benoit, P. 'Le récit de la Cène dans Lc XXII,15-20: Etude de critique textuelle et littéraire', *RB* 48 (1939), 357-93.

Berchmans, J. 'Lukan Studies', *Bible Bhashyam* 2 (1976), 81-90.

Berg, P. 'Die Quellen des Lukasevangeliums', *NKZ* 21 (1910), 337-52.

Blaising, C.A. 'Gethsemane: A Prayer of Faith', *Journal of the Evangelical Theological Society* 22 (1979), 333-43.

Blevins, J.L. 'The Passion Narrative. Luke 19.28-24.53', *RevExp* 64 (1967), 513-22.

Bligh, J. 'Matching Passages 2: St. Matthew's Passion Narrative', *Way* 9 (1969), 59-73.

Blinzler, J. 'Passionsgeschehen und Passionsbericht des Lukasevangeliums', *BK* 24 (1969), 1-4.

—*Der Prozess Jesu*. 4th edn. Regensburg: Pustet, 1969.

Borgen, P. 'John and the Synoptics in the Passion Narrative', *NTS* 5 (1958-59), 246-59.

Bornhäuser, D. 'Die Beteiligung des Herodes am Prozesse Jesu', *NKZ* 40 (1929), 714-18.

Bornhäuser, K. *Die Leidens- und Auferstehungsgeschichte Jesu*. Gütersloh: Bertelsmann, 1947.

—*Studien zum Sondergut des Lukas*. Gütersloh: Bertelsmann, 1934.

Bossuyt, P. and Radermakers, J. *Jésus: Parole de la Grâce, selon Saint Luc*, II.

Brussels: Institut d'Etudes Théologiques, 1981.

Bouttier, M. 'L'humanité de Jésus selon Saint Luc', *RSR* 69 (1981), 33-44.

Bovon, F. *Luc le théologien: Vingt-cinq ans de recherches (1950-1975)*. Neuchâtel/ Paris: Delachaux & Niestlé, 1978.

Broadribb, D. 'Proto-Luko', *Biblica Revuo* 4 (1968), 7-26.

Brown, R.E. *The Birth of the Messiah*. Garden City, NY: Doubleday, 1977.

—*The Gospel according to John (i-xii)*. AB, 29. Garden City, NY: Doubleday, 1966.

—*The Gospel according to John (xiii-xxi)*. AB, 29A. Garden City, NY: Doubleday, 1970.

Brown, S. *Apostasy and Perseverance in the Theology of Luke*. AnBib, 36. Rome: Biblical Institute, 1969.

Browning, W.R.F. *Saint Luke*. Torch Bible Commentaries. 3rd edn. London: SCM, 1972.

Bruce, F.F. 'Herod Antipas, Tetrarch of Galilee and Perae', *The Annual of Leeds University Oriental Society* 5 (1963), 6-23.

Büchele, A. *Der Tod Jesu im Lukasevangelium: Eine redaktionsgeschichtliche Untersuchung zu Lk 23*. Frankfurt: Knecht, 1978.

Bultmann, R. *The History of the Synoptic Tradition*. New York: Harper & Row, 1963; German original 1921.

Burkill, T.A. 'The Trial of Jesus', *Vigiliae Christianae* 12 (1958), 1-18.

Burkitt, F.C. *The Gospel History and its Transmission*. Edinburgh: Clarke, 1906.

Buse, I. 'The Cleansing of the Temple in the Synoptics and in John', *ExpTim* 70 (1958), 22-24.

—'St John and the Passion Narratives of St Matthew and St Luke', *NTS* 7 (1960-61), 65-76.

Cadbury, H.J., *The Book of Acts in History*. New York: Harper, 1955.

—*The Making of Luke-Acts*. New York: Macmillan, 1927.

—*The Style and Literary Method of Luke*. HTS, 6. Cambridge, MA: Harvard University, 1920.

Caird, G.B. *The Gospel of St Luke*. London: Penguin, 1963.

Catchpole, D.R. *The Trial of Jesus: A Study in the Gospels and Jewish Historiography from 1770 to the Present Day*. Studia Post-Biblica, 18. Leiden: Brill, 1971.

Chadwick, H. 'The Shorter Text of Luke XXII.15-20', *HTR* 50 (1957), 249-58.

Conzelmann, H. 'History and Theology in the Passion Narratives of the Synoptic Gospels', *Int* 24 (1970), 178-97.

—*The Theology of St Luke*. New York: Harper, 1960; German original 1954; 2nd edn. 1957.

—*et al. Zur Bedeutung des Todes Jesu. Exegetische Beiträge*. Gütersloh: Mohn, 1967.

Cousin, H. 'Dieu a-t-il sacrifié son fils Jésus?', *Lumière et Vie* 29 (1980), 55-67.

Creed, J.M. *The Gospel according to St. Luke*. London: Macmillan, 1930.

Crossan, D.M. 'Anti-Semitism and the Gospel', *TS* 26 (1965), 189-214.

Dahl, N.A. 'Die Passionsgeschichte bei Matthäus', *NTS* 2 (1955), 17-32.

Daly, R. 'The Eucharist and Redemption: The Last Supper and Jesus' Understanding of His Death', *BTB* 11 (1981), 21-27.

Danker, F.W. *Jesus and the New Age: According to St. Luke—A Commentary on the Third Gospel*. St. Louis: Clayton, 1972.

—*Luke*. Proclamation Commentaries. Philadelphia: Fortress, 1976.

Daube, D. '"For they know not what they do": Luke 23,34', *Studia Patristica* 4 (1959-61), 58-70.

Davies, P.E. 'Did Jesus Die as a Martyr-Prophet?', *BR* 2 (1957), 19-30.

—'Did Jesus Die as a Martyr-Prophet?', *BR* 19 (1974), 34-47.

Dechent, H. 'Der "Gerechte"—eine Bezeichnung für den Messias', *TSK* 100 (1927-28), 438-43.

Delorme, J. 'Le Procès de Jésus—ou la parole risquée (Lc 22,54-23,25)', *RSR* 69 (1981), 123-46.

Denker, J. *Die theologiegeschichtliche Stellung des Petrus-evangeliums: Ein Beitrag zur Frühgeschichte des Doketismus.* Europäische Hochschulschriften, 23/36. Bern/ Frankfurt: Lang, 1975.

Derrett, J.D.M. 'Daniel and Salvation-History', *Downside Review* 100 (1982), 62-68.

Dibelius, M. *Botschaft und Geschichte*, I. Bornkamm, G., ed. Tübingen: Mohr, 1953.

—'Gethsemane', *Crozier Quarterly* 12 (1935), 254-65.

—*The Message of Jesus Christ: The Tradition of the Early Christian Communities.* New York: Scribner's, 1939.

Dillon, R.J. *From Eye-Witnesses to Ministers of the Word: Tradition and Composition in Luke 24.* AnBib, 82. Rome: Biblical Institute, 1978.

Doeve, J.W. 'Die Gefangennahme Jesu in Gethsemane', *Studia Evangelica.* Aland, K., *et al.*, eds. Berlin: Akademie, 1951, pp. 458-80.

Donahue. J.R. *Are You the Christ? The Trial Narrative in the Gospel of Mark.* SBLDS, 10. Missoula, MT: Scholars, 1973.

—'Passion Narrative', *IDBSup*, 643-45.

Downing, F.G. 'Common Ground with Paganism in Luke and Josephus', *NTS* 28 (1982), 546-59.

Downing, J. 'Jesus and Martyrdom', *JTS* 14 (1963), 279-93.

Dupont, J. 'La Prière et son efficacité dans l'Evangile de Luc', *RSR* 69 (1981), 45-56.

Durken, D., ed. *Sin, Salvation, and the Spirit.* Collegeville, MN: Liturgical Press, 1979.

Easton, B.S. *The Gospel according to St. Luke.* New York: Scribner's, 1926.

—'Linguistic Evidence for the Lucan Source L', *JBL* 29 (1910), 139-80.

Edwards, O.C., Jr. *Luke's Story of Jesus.* Philadelphia: Fortress, 1981.

Egelkraut, H.L. *Jesus' Mission to Jerusalem: A redaction critical study of the Travel Narrative in the Gospel of Luke, Lk 9.51-19.48.* Europäische Hochschulschriften, 23/80. Bern/Frankfurt: Lang, 1976.

Ehrman, B.D. and Plunkett, M.A. 'The Angel and the Agony: The Textual Problem of Luke 22.43-44', *CBQ* 45 (1983), 401-16.

Ellis, E.E. *The Gospel of Luke.* New Century Bible. 2nd edn. London: Oliphants, 1974.

—'Present and Future Eschatology in Luke', *NTS* 12 (1965), 27-41.

Ernst, J. *Das Evangelium nach Lukas.* Regensburg: Pustet, 1977.

—*Herr der Geschichte: Perspektiven der lukanischen Eschatologie.* SBS, 88. Stuttgart: Katholisches Bibelwerk, 1978.

Farmer, W.R. 'A "Skeleton in the Closet" of Gospel Research', *BR* 9 (1961), 18-42.

—ed. *New Synoptic Studies: The Cambridge Gospel Conference and Beyond.* Macon, GA: Mercer University, 1983.

—'Notes on a Literary and Form-Critical Analysis of Some of the Synoptic Material Peculiar to Luke', *NTS* 8 (1961-62), 301-16.

—*The Synoptic Problem.* New York: Macmillan, 1964.

Feldkämper, L. *Der betende Jesus als Heilsmittler nach Lukas.* St. Augustin: Steyler, 1978.

Feuillet, A. 'Le récit lucanien de l'agonie de Gethsémani (Lc xxii.39-46)', *NTS* 22 (1976), 397-417.

Finegan, J. *Die Überlieferung der Leidens- und Auferstehungsgeschichte Jesu.* BZNW, 15. Giessen: Töpelmann, 1934.

Fitzmyer, J.A. *To Advance the Gospel: New Testament Studies.* New York: Crossroad, 1981.

—'Anti-Semitism and the Cry of "All the People" (Mt 27.25)', *TS* 26 (1965), 667-71.

—*The Gospel according to Luke I–IX.* AB, 28. Garden City, NY: Doubleday, 1981.

—'The Priority of Mark and the "Q" Source in Luke', *Perspectives* 11 (1970), 131-70.

Flender, H. *St Luke: Theologian of Redemptive History.* Philadelphia: Fortress, 1967.

Flusser, D. 'The Crucified One and the Jews', *Immanuel* 7 (1977), 25-37.

—'The Last Supper and the Essenes', *Immanuel* 2 (1973), 23-27.

Foulon-Pignaliol, C.I. 'Le rôle du peuple dans le procès de Jésus. Une hypothèse juridique et théologique', *NRT* 108 (1976), 627-37.

Franklin, E. *Christ the Lord: A Study in the Purpose and Theology of Luke–Acts.* Philadelphia: Westminster, 1975.

Fuller, R.H. 'Die neue Diskussion über das synoptische Problem', *TZ* 34 (1978), 129-48.

Galvin, J.P. 'Jesus' Approach to Death: An Examination of Some Recent Studies', *TS* 41 (1980), 713-44.

Geldenhuys, N. *Commentary on the Gospel of Luke.* London: Marshall, Morgan & Scott, 1950.

George, A. *Etudes sur l'œuvre de Luc.* Paris: Gabalda, 1978.

—'Israël dans l'œuvre de Luc', *RB* 75 (1968), 481-525.

—'Le sens de la mort de Jésus pour Luc', *RB* 80 (1973), 186-217.

Goguel, M. *The Life of Jesus.* New York: Macmillan, 1933.

Goudoever, J. van. 'The Place of Israel in Luke's Gospel', *NovT* 8 (1966), 111-23.

Goulder, M.D. 'Mark xvi.1-8 and Parallels', *NTS* 24 (1978), 235-40.

Grant, F.C. *The Gospels: Their Origin and their Growth.* New York: Harper, 1957.

—*The Earliest Gospel.* Nashville: Abingdon, 1943.

—*The New Testament: The Gospels and the Acts of the Apostles.* Nelson's Bible Commentary, 6. New York: Nelson, 1962.

Gregg, D.W.A. 'Hebraic Antecedents to the Eucharistic *Anamenēsis* Formula', *Tyndale Bulletin* 30 (1979), 165-68.

Grundmann, W. *Das Evangelium nach Lukas.* THKNT, 3. 9th edn. Berlin: Evangelischer Verlag, 1981.

Guillet, J. 'Bulletin d' exégèse lucanienne', *RSR* 69 (1981), 425-42.

—'Luc 22,29: Une formule johannique dans l'évangile de Luc?', *RSR* 69 (1981), 113-22.

Hawkins, J.C. *Horae Synopticae.* 2nd edn. Oxford: Clarendon, 1909.

—'Three Limitations to St Luke's Use of St Mark's Gospel', *Studies in the Synoptic Problem.* Oxford: Clarendon, 1911, pp. 29-94.

Hein, K. 'Judas Iscariot: Key to the Last-Supper Narratives?', *NTS* 17 (1971), 227-32.

Hendrickx, H. *The Passion Narratives of the Synoptic Gospels.* Manila: East Asian Pastoral Institute, 1977.

Héring, J. 'Simples remarques sur la prière à Gethsémané. Matthieu 26.36-46; Marc 14.32-42, Luc 22.40-46', *RHPR* 39 (1959), 97-102.

Holleran, J.W. *The Synoptic Gethsemane: A Critical Study.* Analecta Gregoriana, 191. Rome: Universita Gregoriana, 1973.

Holtzmann, J.H. *Die Synoptiker—Die Apostelgeschichte.* HKNT, 1. Freiburg: Mohr, 1889.

Horbury, W. 'The Passion Narratives and Historical Criticism', *Theology* 75 (1972), 58-71.

Hubbard, B.J. 'Luke, Josephus and Rome: A Comparative Approach to the Lukan *Sitz im Leben*', *SBLASP 1979*, 59-68.

Jaubert, A. 'Les séances du sanhédrin et les récits de la passion', *RHR* 166 (1964), 143-69.

Jeremias, J. *The Eucharistic Words of Jesus*. rev. edn. New York: Scribner's, 1966; based on 3rd German edn. of 1960 with author's revisions to 1964.

—'Perikopen-Umstellung bei Lukas?', *NTS* 4 (1958), 115-19.

Jervell, J. 'Herodes Antipas og hans plass i evangelieoveleveringen', *NorTT* 61 (1960) 28-40.

—*Luke and the People of God: A New Look at Luke-Acts*. Minneapolis: Augsburg, 1972.

Johnson, L.T. 'On Finding the Lukan Community: A Cautious Cautionary Essay', *SBLASP 1979*, 87-100.

Jones, D.L. 'The Background and Character of the Lukan Psalms', *JTS* 19 (1968), 19-50.

—'The Title *Christos* in Luke–Acts', *CBQ* 32 (1970), 69-76.

Jonge, M. de 'De berichten over het scheuren van het voorhangel bij Jezus' dood in de synoptische evangeliën', *NedTTs* 21 (1966), 90-114.

Juel, D. *Luke–Acts: The Promise of History*. Atlanta: Knox, 1983.

—*Messiah and Temple: The Trial of Jesus in the Gospel of Mark*. SBLDS, 31. Missoula, MT: Scholars, 1977.

Karris, R.J. *Invitation to Luke*. Garden City, NY: Image Books, 1977.

—'Windows and Mirrors: Literary Criticism and Luke's Sitz im Leben', *SBLASP 1979*, 47-57.

Keck, L.E. and Martyn, J.L., eds. *Studies in Luke–Acts*. London: SPCK, 1968.

Kee, H.C. 'Scripture Quotations and Allusions in Mark 11-16', *SBLASP 1971*, 475-502.

Kelber, W. *The Oral and the Written Gospel*. Philadelphia: Fortress, 1983.

Kennard, J.S., Jr. 'The Burial of Jesus', *JBL* 74 (1955), 227-38.

Kilpatrick, G.D. 'A Theme of the Lucan Passion Story and Luke xxiii.47', *JTS* 43 (1942), 34-36.

Klein, H. 'Die lukanisch-johanneische Passionstradition', *ZNW* 67 (1976), 155-86.

Klijn, A.F.J. 'Scribes, Pharisees, Highpriests and Elders in the New Testament', *NovT* 3 (1959), 259-67.

Klostermann, E. *Das Lukasevangelium*. HNT, 5. 2nd edn. Tübingen: Mohr, 1929.

Kodell, J. *The Gospel according to Luke*. Collegeville Bible Commentary, 3. Collegeville, MN: Liturgical Press, 1982.

—'Luke's Gospel in a Nutshell (Lk 4.16-30)', *BTB* 13 (1983), 16-18.

—'Luke's Use of *Laos*, "People," Especially in the Jerusalem Narrative (Lk 19,28-24,53)', *CBQ* 31 (1969), 327-43.

—'The Theology of Luke in Recent Study', *BTB* 1 (1971), 115-44.

Koenig, J. *Jews and Christians in Dialogue: New Testament Foundations*. Philadelphia: Westminster, 1979.

Kümmel, W.G. *Introduction to the New Testament*. 17th edn. Nashville: Abingdon, 1975—German original 1973.

—'Luc en accusation dans la théologie contemporaine', *ETL* 46 (1970) 265-81. English translation: 'Current Theological Accusations against Luke', *ANQ* 16 (1975), 131-45.

Kurz, W.S. 'Acts 3.19-26 as a Test Case of the Role of Eschatology in Lukan Christology', *SBLASP* 11 (1977), 309-23.

—'Luke 22.14-38 and Greco-Roman and Biblical Farewell Addresses', *JBL* 104

(1985), 251-68.

Lagrange, M.-J. *Evangile selon Saint Luc*. 4th edn. Paris: Gabalda, 1927.

—'Les Sources du troisième Evangile', *RB* 4 (1895), 5-22; 5 (1896), 5-38.

Larkin, W.J., Jr. 'Luke's Use of the Old Testament as a Key to his Soteriology', *Journal of the Evangelical Theological Society* 20 (1977), 325-35.

—'The Old Testament Background of Luke xxii.43-44', *NTS* 25 (1979), 250-54.

LaVerdiere, E. 'A Discourse at the Last Supper', *Bible Today* 71 (1974), 1540-48.

—'The Gospel of Luke', *TBT* 18 (1980), 226-35.

—*Luke*. New Testament Message, 5. Wilmington, DE: Michael Glazier, 1980.

Leaney, A.R.C. *A Commentary on the Gospel according to St. Luke*. Black's New Testament Commentary. 2nd edn. London: Black, 1966.

Légasse, S. 'Jésus devant le Sanhédrin, recherche sur les traditions évangéliques', *RTL* 5 (1974), 170-97.

Léon-Dufour, X. '"Faites ceci en mémoire de moi", Luc 22,19–I Corinthiens 11,25', *Christus* 24 (1977), 200-208.

—'Jésus à Gethsémani: Essai de lecture synchronique', *ScEs* 31 (1979), 251-68.

—'Das letzte Mahl Jesu und die testamentarische Tradition nach Lk 22', *ZKT* 103 (1981), 33-55.

—'Mt et Mc dans le récit de la Passion', *Bib* 40 (1959), 684-96.

—'Passion (Récits de la)', *DBS* 6 (1960), cols. 1419-92.

Limbeck, M. *Redaktion und Theologie des Passionsberichtes nach den Synoptikern*. Wege der Forschung, 481. Darmstadt: Wissenschaftliche Buchgesellschaft, 1981.

Lindsey, R.L. 'A Modified Two-Document Theory of the Synoptic Dependence and Interdependence', *NovT* 6 (1963), 239-63.

Linnemann, E. 'Die Verleugnung des Petrus', *ZTK* 63 (1966), 1-32.

—*Studien zur Passionsgeschichte*. FRLANT, 102. Göttingen: Vandenhoeck & Ruprecht, 1970.

Lohse, E. *History of the Suffering and Death of Jesus Christ*. Philadelphia: Fortress, 1967.

Loisy, A. *L'Evangile selon Luc*. Paris, 1924.

—*Les Evangiles Synoptiques, I/II*. Haute-Marne: Ceffonds, 1907/1908.

Loos, H. van der *The Miracles of Jesus*. NovTSup, 9. Leiden: Brill, 1968.

Luck, U. 'Kerygma, Tradition und Geschichte Jesu bei Lukas', *ZTK* 57 (1960), 51-66.

McCafferey, U.P. 'Psalm Quotations in the Passion Narratives of the Gospels', *Neot* 14 (1981), 73-89.

Maccoby, H.Z. 'Jesus and Barrabas', *NTS* 16 (1969), 55-60.

Maddox, R. *The Purpose of Luke–Acts*. Edinburgh: Clark, 1982.

Manson, W. *The Gospel of Luke*. MNTC. London: Hodder & Stoughton, 1930.

Marshall, I.H. *The Gospel of Luke: A Commentary on the Greek Text*. New International Greek Testament Commentary. Grand Rapids: Eerdmans, 1978.

—'Recent Study of the Gospel According to St. Luke', *ExpTim* 80 (1968-69), 4-8.

—'The Resurrection of Jesus in Luke', *Tyndale Bulletin* 24 (1973), 55-98.

Martyn, J.L. 'Attitudes Ancient and Modern toward Tradition about Jesus', *USQR* 23 (1968), 129-45.

Matera, F.J. 'The Death of Jesus according to Luke: A Question of Sources', Paper read at the annual meeting of the Catholic Biblical Association of America, August 14, 1983. Published in *CBQ* 47 (1985), 469-85.

—*The Kingship of Jesus: Composition and Theology in Mark 15*. SBLDS, 66. Chico, CA: Scholars, 1982.

Mattill, A.J., Jr. 'The Jesus–Paul Parallels and the Purpose of Luke–Acts: H.H. Evans Reconsidered', *NovT* 17 (1975), 15-46.

Mays, J.L., ed. *Interpreting the Gospels*. Philadelphia: Fortress, 1981.

Merklein, H. 'Erwägungen zur Überlieferungsgeschichte der neutestamentlichen Abendmahlstraditionen', *BZ* 21 (1977), 88-101.

Meyer, H.A.W. *Critical and Exegetical Handbook to the Gospels of Mark and Luke*, I & II. From 5th German edn. Edinburgh: T. & T. Clark, 1880.

—*Die Evangelien des Markus und Lukas*. MeyerK 1/2. 8th edn. Göttingen: Vandenhoeck & Ruprecht, 1892.

Michaelis, W. *'paschō'*, *TDNT* V, 904-24.

Miller, D.L. *Saint Luke*. London: SCM, 1959.

Minear, P.S. 'A Note on Luke xxii 36', *NovT* 7 (1964), 128-34.

Moessner, D.P. 'Jesus and the "Wilderness Generation": The Death of the Prophet like Moses according to Luke', *SBLASP 1982*, 319-40.

Mohr, T.A. *Markus- und Johannespassion: Redaktions- und traditionsgeschichtliche Untersuchung der markanischen und johanneischen Passionstradition*. ATANT, 70. Zürich: Theologischer Verlag, 1982.

Montefiore, H. 'Does "L" Hold Water?', *JTS* 12 (1961), 59-60.

Mosato, M.A. 'Current Theories Regarding the Audience of Luke–Acts', *CurTM* 3 (1976), 355-61.

Moulder, W.J. 'The Old Testament Background and the Interpretation of Mark x.45', *NTS* 24 (1977), 120-27.

Müller, K. 'Jesus vor Herodes. Eine redaktionsgeschichtliche Untersuchung zu Lk 23,6-12', *Zur Geschichte des Urchristentums*. Dautzenberg, G., et al., eds. Quaestiones Disputatae, 87. Freiburg: Herder, 1979, pp. 111-41.

Neirynck, F. 'The Argument from Order and St. Luke's Transpositions', *ETL* 49 (1973), 784-815.

—ed. *L'Evangile de Luc: Problèmes littéraires et théologiques*. BETL, 32. Gembloux: Duculot, 1973.

—*The Minor Agreements of Matthew and Luke against Mark with a Cumulative List*. BETL, 37. Leuven: Leuven University Press, 1974.

Nellessen, E. *Zeugnis für Jesus und das Wort: Exegetische Untersuchungen zum lukanischen Zeugnisbegriff*. BBB, 43. Köln/Bonn: Hanstein, 1976.

Neyrey, J.H. 'The Absence of Jesus' Emotions—the Lucan Redaction of Lk 22,39-46', *Bib* 61 (1980), 153-71.

—'Jesus' Address to the Women of Jerusalem (Lk. 23.27-31)', *NTS* 29 (1983) 74-86.

Nickle, K.F. *The Synoptic Gospels*. London: SCM, 1981.

O'Rourke, J.J. 'The Construction with a Verb of Saying as an Indication of Sources in Luke', *NTS* 21 (1975), 421-23.

Osty, E. 'Les points de contact entre les récits de la passion dans Saint Luc et Saint Jean', *RSR* 39 (1951), 146-54.

Parker, P. 'Luke and the Fourth Evangelist', *NTS* 9 (1962-63), 317-36.

Perry, A.M. *The Sources of Luke's Passion-Narrative*. Chicago: Chicago University Press, 1920.

Pesch, R. *Das Abendmahl und Jesu Todesverständnis*. Quaestiones Disputatae, 80. Freiburg: Herder, 1978.

—'The Last Supper and Jesus' Understanding of His Death', *Bible Bhashyam* 3 (1977), 58-75.

—and Kratz, R. *So liest man synoptisch: Anleitung und Kommentar zum Studium der synoptischen Evangelien, VI & VII. Passionsgeschichte: Erster Teil & zweiter Teil*. Frankfurt: Knecht, 1979/1980.

—*Wie Jesus das Abendmahl hielt: der Grund der Eucharistie*. Freiburg: Herder, 1977.

Plummer, A. *The Gospel according to S. Luke*. ICC. 5th edn. Edinburgh: Clark, 1922.

Price, J.L. 'The Servant Motif in the Synoptic Gospels', *Int* 12 (1958), 28-38.

Potterie, I. de la 'Les Deux Noms de Jérusalem dans l'Evangile de Luc', *RSR* 69 (1981), 57-70.

Radl, W. *Paulus und Jesus im lukanischen Doppelwerk: Untersuchungen zu Parallel-motiven im Lukasevangelium und in der Apostelgeschichte*. Europäische Hochschulschriften, 23/49. Bern/Frankfurt: Lang, 1975.

Ramsey, M. *The Narratives of the Passion*. London: Mowbray, 1962.

Rau, G. 'Das Volk in der lukanischen Passionsgeschichte, eine Konjektur zu Lk 23.13', *ZNW* 56 (1965), 41-51.

Reese, T. 'The Political Theology of Luke–Acts', *Biblical Theology* 22 (1972), 62-65.

Rehkopf, F. *Die lukanische Sonderquelle: ihr Umfang und Sprachgebrauch*. WUNT, 5. Tübingen: Mohr, 1959.

Reiling, J. and Swellengrebel, J.L. *A Translator's Handbook on the Gospel of Luke*. Helps for Translators, 10. Leiden: Brill, 1971.

Rengstorf, K.H. *Das Evangelium nach Lukas*. NTD, 3. 13th edn. Göttingen: Vandenhoeck & Ruprecht, 1968.

Rese, M. *Alttestamentliche Motive in der Christologie des Lukas*. SNT, 1. Gütersloh: Mohn, 1969.

—'Neuere Lukas-Arbeiten: Bemerkungen zur gegenwärtigen Forschungslage', *TLZ* 106 (1981), 225-37.

Richard, E. 'Luke—Writer, Theologian, Historian: Research and Orientation of the 1970's', *BTB* 13 (1983), 3-15.

Rickards, R.R. 'Luke 22.25—They are Called "Friends of the People"', *BT* 28 (1977), 445-46.

Riedl, J. 'Die evangelische Leidensgeschichte und ihre theologische Aussage', *Bibel und Liturgie* 41 (1968), 70-111.

Sabourin, L. 'The Eschatology of Luke', *BTB* 12 (1982), 73-76.

Salazar, A.M. 'Questions about St. Luke's Sources', *NovT* 2 (1958), 316-17.

Sanday, W., ed. *Studies in the Synoptic Problem by Members of the University of Oxford*. Oxford: Clarendon, 1911.

Sanders, E.P. 'The Argument from Order and the Relationship between Matthew and Luke', *NTS* 15 (1968), 249-61.

Sanders, J.T. 'The Parable of the Pounds and Lucan Anti-Semitism', *TS* 42 (1981), 660-68.

—'The Salvation of the Jews in Luke–Acts', *SBLASP 1982*, 465-83.

Sandmel, S. *Anti-Semitism in the New Testament?* Philadelphia: Fortress, 1978.

Schille, G. 'Das Leiden des Herrn', *ZTK* 50 (1955), 161-205.

Schlatter, A. *Das Evangelium des Lukas: Aus seinen Quellen erklärt*. Stuttgart: Calwer, 1931.

—*Das Evangelium nach Markus und Lukas*. Schlatters Erläuterungen zum Neuen Testament, 2. Stuttgart: Calwer, 1947.

Schmid, J. *Das Evangelium nach Lukas*. Regensburg: Pustet, 1951.

Schmidt, D. 'Luke's "Innocent" Jesus: A Scriptural Apologetic', *Political Issues in Luke–Acts*. Cassidy, R.J. and Scharper, P.J., eds. Maryknoll, NY: Orbis, 1983, pp. 111-21.

Schneider, G. 'Engel und Blutschweiss (Lk 22,43-44). "Redaktionsgeschichte" im Dienste der Textkritik', *BZ* 20 (1976), 112-16.

—*Das Evangelium nach Lukas.* Ökumenischer Taschenbuchkommentar zum Neuen Testament, 3/1 & 2. Gütersloh/Würzburg: Mohn/Echter, 1977.

—'Gab es eine vorsynoptische Szene "Jesus vor dem Synedrium"?', *NovT* 12 (1970), 22-39.

—*Die Passion Jesu nach den drei älteren Evangelien.* München: Kösel, 1973.

—'Das Problem einer vorkanonischen Passionserzählung', *BZ* 16 (1972), 222-44.

—'Schrift und Tradition in der theologischen Neuinterpretation der lukanischen Schriften', *BK* 34 (1979), 112-15.

—'"Stärke deine Brüder!" (Lk 22,32). Die Aufgabe des Petrus nach Lukas', *Catholica* 30 (1976), 200-206.

—'Die theologische Sicht des Todes Jesu in den Kreuzigungsberichten der Evangelien', *Theologisch-Praktische Quartalschrift* 126 (1978), 14-22.

—'Die Verhaftung Jesu', *ZNW* 63 (1972), 188-209.

—*Verleugnung, Verspottung und Verhör Jesu nach Lukas 22,54-71. Studien zur lukanischen Darstellung der Passion.* SANT, 22. München: Kösel, 1969.

—'Der Zweck des lukanischen Doppelwerks', *BZ* 21 (1977), 45-66.

Schramm, T. *Der Markus-Stoff bei Lukas: Eine literarkritische und redaktionsgeschichtliche Untersuchung.* SNTSMS, 14. Cambridge: Cambridge University Press, 1971.

Schreiber, J. 'Die Bestattung Jesu. Redaktionsgeschichtliche Beobachtungen zu Mk 15.42-47 par', *ZNW* 72 (1981), 141-77.

Schubert, P. 'The Structure and Significance of Luke 24', *Neutestamentliche Studien für Rudolf Bultmann.* BZNW, 21. Berlin: Töpelmann, 1954, pp. 165-86.

Schürmann, H. *Der Einsetzungsbericht Lk 22.19-20. II. Teil einer quellenkritischen Untersuchung des lukanischen Abendmahlsberichtes Lk 22,7-38.* NTAbh, 20/4. Münster: Aschendorff, 1955.

—*Jesu Abschiedsrede Lk 22,21-38. III. Teil einer quellenkritischen Untersuchung des lukanischen Abendmahlsberichtes Lk 22,7-38.* NTAbh, 20/5. Münster: Aschendorff, 1956.

—'Jesu Todesverständnis im Verstehenshorizont seiner Umwelt', *TGl* 70 (1980), 141-60.

—*Das Lukasevangelium.* HTKNT, 3/1. Freiburg: Herder, 1969.

—*Der Paschamahlbericht Lk 22,(7-14) 15-18. I. Teil einer quellenkritischen Untersuchung des lukanischen Abendmahlsberichtes Lk 22,7-38.* NTAbh, 19/5. Münster: Aschendorff, 1953.

—'Protolukanische Spracheigentümlichkeiten? Zu Fr. Rehkopf, Die lukanische Sonderquelle. Ihr Umfang und Sprachgebrauch', *BZ* 5 (1961), 266-86.

—'Das Thomasevangelium und das lukanische Sondergut', *BZ* 7 (1963), 236-60.

—*Traditionsgeschichtliche Untersuchungen zu den synoptischen Evangelien.* Düsseldorf: Patmos, 1968.

Schütz, F. *Der leidende Christus: Die angefochtene Gemeinde und das Christuskerygma der lukanischen Schriften.* BWANT, 89. Stuttgart: Kohlhammer, 1969.

Schweitzer, A. *The Mysticism of Paul the Apostle.* London: Black, 1931.

Schweizer, E. *Das Evangelium nach Lukas.* NTD, 3. Göttingen: Vandenhoeck & Ruprecht, 1982.

—'Eine hebraisierende Sonderquelle des Lukas?', *TZ* 6 (1950), 161-85.

—*Luke: A Challenge to Present Theology.* Atlanta: Knox, 1982.

Scroggs, R., *et al.* 'Reflections on the Question: Was there a pre-Markan Passion Narrative?', *SBLASP 1971*, 503-85.

Senior, D.P. *The Passion Narrative according to Matthew: A Redactional Study.* Leuven: Leuven University Press, 1975.

Sherwin-White, A.N. *Roman Society and Roman Law in the New Testament*. Oxford: Oxford University Press, 1963.

Simpson, R.T. 'The Major Agreements of Matthew and Luke against Mark', *NTS* 12 (1965-66), 273-83.

Sloan, R.B., Jr. *The Favorable Year of the Lord: A Study of Jubilar Theology in the Gospel of Luke*. Austin, TX: Schola, 1977.

Sloyan, G.S. *Jesus on Trial: The Development of the Passion Narratives and Their Historical and Ecumenical Implications*. Philadelphia: Fortress, 1973.

Smith, R.H. 'Paradise Today: Luke's Passion Narrative', *CurTM* 3 (1976), 323-36.

Sneen, D.J. 'An Exegesis of Luke 1.1-4 with Special Regard to Luke's Purpose as a Historian', *ExpTim* 83 (1971), 40-43.

Soards, M.L. 'Herod Antipas' Hearing in Luke 23.8', *BT* 37 (1986), 146-47.

—'A Literary Analysis of the Origin and Purpose of Luke's Account of the Mockery of Jesus', *BZ* 31 (1987), 110-16.

—'On Understanding Luke 22.39', *BT* 36 (1985), 336-37.

—'The Question of a Pre-Markan Passion Narrative', *Bible Bhashyam* 11 (1985), 144-69.

—'The Silence of Jesus before Herod: An Interpretative Suggestion', *AusBR* 33 (1985), 41-45

—'Tradition, Composition, and Theology in Luke's Account of Jesus before Herod Antipas', *Biblica* 66 (1985), 344-64.

Stagg, F. 'Establishing a Text for Luke-Acts', *SBLASP 1977*, 45-58.

—*Studies in Luke's Gospel*. Nashville: Convention, 1967.

—'Textual Criticism for Luke-Acts', *Perspectives in Religious Studies* 5 (1978), 152-65.

Steichele, H.-J. *Der leidende Sohn Gottes: Eine Untersuchung einiger alttestamentlicher Motive in der Christologie des Markusevangeliums*. Regensburg: Pustet, 1980.

Stephenson, T. 'The Overlapping of Sources in Matthew and Luke', *JTS* 21 (1920), 127-45.

Stöger, A. 'Eigenart und Botschaft der lukanischen Passionsgeschichte', *BK* 24 (1969), 4-8.

—*The Gospel according to St. Luke*, I/II. New York: Crossroad, 1981; German original 1964.

Streeter, B.H. *The Four Gospels: A Study of Origins*. New York: Macmillan, 1925.

Taeger, J.-W. *Der Mensch und sein Heil: Studien zum Bild des Menschen und Sicht der Bekehrung bei Lukas*. SNT, 14. Gütersloh: Mohn, 1982.

Talbert, C.H. *Literary Patterns, Theological Themes, and the Genre of Luke-Acts*. SBLMS, 20. Missoula, MT: Scholars, 1974.

—ed. *Perspectives on Luke-Acts*. Special Studies Series, 5. Danville, VA: Association of Baptist Professors of Religion, 1978.

—*Reading Luke: A Literary and Theological Commentary on the Third Gospel*. New York: Crossroad, 1982.

—'Shifting Sands: The Recent Study of the Gospel of Luke', *Int* 30 (1976), 381-95.

Tannehill, R. 'A Study in the Theology of Luke-Acts', *ATR* 43 (1961), 195-203.

Taylor, V. *Behind the Third Gospel: A Study of the Proto-Luke Hypothesis*. Oxford: Clarendon, 1926.

—*The Gospel according to St. Mark*. London: Macmillan, 1952, esp. pp. 664-67.

—'The Narrative of the Crucifixion', *NTS* 8 (1962), 333-34.

—'The New Testament Origins of Holy Communion', *London Quarterly and Holborn Review* 28 (1959), 84-90.

—*The Passion Narrative of St Luke*. Evans, O.E., ed. SNTSMS, 19. Cambridge:

Cambridge University Press, 1972.

—'Rehkopf's List of Words and Phrases Illustrative of Pre-Lukan Speech Usage', *JTS* 15 (1964), 59-62.

—'Theologians of Our Time: Friedrich Rehkopf', *ExpTim* 74 (1963), 262-66.

—'Theologians of Our Time: Heinz Schürmann', *ExpTim* 74 (1962), 77-81.

Temple, S. 'Two Traditions of the Last Supper, Betrayal and Arrest', *NTS* 7 (1960-61), 77-85.

Tiede, D.L. *Prophecy and History in Luke–Acts*. Philadelphia: Fortress, 1980.

Trilling, W. 'Le Christ, roi crucifié, Lc 23,35-43', *AsSeign* 65 (1973), 56-65.

Trites, A.A. 'Some Aspects of Prayer in Luke–Acts', *SBLASP 1977*, 59-77.

Turner, N. 'The Minor Verbal Agreements of Mt. and Lk. against Mk', *Studia Evangelica*. Aland, K., et al., eds. Berlin: Akademie, 1959, pp. 223-34.

Tyson, J.B. 'The Lukan Version of the Trial of Jesus', *NovT* 3 (1959), 249-58.

—'Jesus and Herod Antipas', *JBL* 89 (1960), 237-46.

—'The Opposition to Jesus in the Gospel of Luke', *Perspectives in Religious Studies* 5 (1978), 144-50.

—'Sequential Parallelism in the Synoptic Gospels', *NTS* 22 (1976), 276-308.

—'The Sources of Luke: A Proposal for the Consultation on the Relationships of the Gospels', *SBLASP 1976*, 279-86.

Unnik, W.C. van. 'Once more St. Luke's Prologue', *Neot* 7 (1973), 7-26.

Untergassmair, F.G. 'Thesen zur Sinndeutung des Todes Jesu in der lukanischen Passionsgeschichte', *TGl* 70 (1980), 180-93.

—*Kreuzweg und Kreuzigung Jesu*. Paderborner Theologische Studien, 10. Paderborn: Schöningh, 1980.

Vanhoye, A. 'Structure et théologie des récits de la Passion dans les évangiles synoptiques', *NRT* 89 (1967), 135-63.

Vawter, B. 'Are the Gospels Anti-Semitic?', *JES* 5 (1968), 473-87.

Vööbus, A. 'A New Approach to the Problem of the Shorter and Longer Text in Luke', *NTS* 15 (1969), 457-63.

—*The Prelude to the Lukan Passion Narrative: Tradition-, Redaction-, Cult-, Motif-Historical and Source-Critical Studies*. Papers of the Estonian Theological Society in Exile, 5/17. Stockholm: ETSE, 1968.

Walaskay, P.W. *'And So We Came to Rome': The Political Perspective of St Luke*. SNTSMS, 49. Cambridge: Cambridge University Press, 1983.

—'The Trial and Death of Jesus in the Gospel of Luke', *JBL* 94 (1975), 81-93.

Weiss, B. *Die Quellen des Lukasevangeliums*. Stuttgart/Berlin: Cotta, 1907.

Weiss, J. *Die Schriften des Neuen Testaments*, I. Göttingen: Vandenhoeck & Ruprecht, 1906.

Wilkens W. 'Zur Frage der literarischen Beziehung zwischen Matthäus und Lukas', *NovT* 8 (1966), 48-57.

Williams, C.S.C. 'Commentaries and Books on St Luke's Gospel', *Theology* 62 (1959), 408-14.

Wilson, R.McL. 'Farrer and Streeter on the Minor Agreements of Matthew and Luke against Mark', *Studia Evangelica*. Aland, K., et al., eds. Berlin: Akademie, 1959, pp. 254-57.

Wilson, W.R. *The Execution of Jesus. A Judicial, Literary, and Historical Investigation*. New York: Scribner's, 1970.

Winter, P. 'Lucan Sources', *ExpTim* 68 (1957), 85.

—'Luke xxii 66b-71', *ST* 9 (1955), 112-25.

—'Marginal Notes on the Trial of Jesus', *ZNW* 50 (1959), 14-33.

—*On the Trial of Jesus*. Studia Judaica, Forschungen zur Wissenschaft des Judentums,

1. Berlin: de Gruyter, 1961.

—and Taylor, V. 'Sources of the Lucan Passion Narrative', *ExpTim* 68 (1956), 95.

—'The Trial of Jesus', *Commentary* 38 (1964), 35-41.

—*et al.* 'The Trial of Jesus', *Commentary* 39 (1965), 10-28.

—'The Trial of Jesus', *The Jewish Quarterly* 16 (1968), 31-37.

—'The Trial of Jesus', *Tablet* 215 (1961), 519-20.

Zahn, T. *Das Evangelium des Lucas.* 3rd & 4th edns. Leipzig: Deichertscher Verlag, 1920.

Zehnle, R. 'The Salvific Character of Jesus' Death in Lucan Soteriology', *TS* 30 (1969), 420-44.

Ziesler, J.A. 'Luke and the Pharisees', *NTS* 25 (1979), 146-57.

Zingg, P. *Das Wachsen der Kirche: Beiträge zur Frage der lukanischen Redaktion und Theologie.* Orbis Biblicus et Orientalis, 3. Göttingen: Vandenhoeck & Ruprecht, 1974.

INDEX

INDEX OF BIBLICAL REFERENCES
(Major discussions are indicated by bold page numbers.)

INDEX OF AUTHORS

JOURNAL FOR THE STUDY OF THE NEW TESTAMENT
Supplement Series